CRITICAL THEORY AND QUALITATIVE DATA ANALYSIS IN EDUCATION

Critical Theory and Qualitative Data Analysis in Education offers a path-breaking explanation of how critical theories can be used within the analysis of qualitative data to inform research processes, such as data collection, analysis, and interpretation. This contributed volume offers examples of qualitative data analysis techniques and exemplars of empirical studies that employ critical theory concepts in data analysis. By creating a clear and accessible bridge between data analysis and critical social theories, this book helps scholars and researchers effectively translate their research designs and findings to multiple audiences for more equitable outcomes and disruption of historical and contemporary inequality.

Rachelle Winkle-Wagner is an Associate Professor of Educational Leadership and Policy Analysis at the University of Wisconsin–Madison, USA.

Jamila Lee-Johnson is a doctoral candidate in the Educational Leadership and Policy Analysis program at the University of Wisconsin–Madison, USA.

Ashley N. Gaskew is a doctoral student in the Educational Leadership and Policy Analysis program and the Curriculum and Instruction program at the University of Wisconsin–Madison, USA.

CRITICAL THEORY AND QUALITATIVE DATA ANALYSIS IN EDUCATION

Edited by Rachelle Winkle-Wagner,
Jamila Lee-Johnson, and Ashley N. Gaskew

Routledge
Taylor & Francis Group

NEW YORK AND LONDON

First published 2019
by Routledge
711 Third Avenue, New York, NY 10017

and by Routledge
2 Park Square, Milton Park, Abingdon, Oxon, OX14 4RN

Routledge is an imprint of the Taylor & Francis Group, an informa business

Library of Congress Cataloging-in-Publication Data
A catalog record for this title has been requested

ISBN: 978-1-138-06700-4 (hbk)
ISBN: 978-1-138-06703-5 (pbk)
ISBN: 978-1-315-15886-0 (ebk)

Typeset in Bembo
by Apex CoVantage, LLC

CONTENTS

FOREWORD

Reflections on Research that is Humanizing

Maisha T. Winn

When my colleague, Django Paris, and I embarked on an endeavor to think about how scholars have aimed to decolonize research methods or *humanize* research (Paris & Winn, 2014), we sought to reclaim the elements that were left on the cutting-room floors, as equity-oriented scholars tried to write up their findings for academic journals and presses that did not have space for the nuanced stories of our methods. How are the moments such as a parent stopping an interview to ask that the researcher intervene in an educational problem or legal issue for their child or their family, accounted for in the analysis process? Where is the space to discuss how a researcher's positionality and shared identity/identities with participants is the only reason a community has allowed them to learn from and with them? What does it mean to collect and analyze artifacts whose rightful place is with the people who created them and not the researcher? We imagined our volume would show the labor that is often invisible to graduate students and emerging scholars. I often wondered and worried if "humanizing research" was an oxymoron—can research ever be humanizing or will it always be a project in colonization? Contributors to the *Humanizing Research* edited volume confirmed and affirmed a commitment in the field of education research to address the wrongdoings and harm in the data collections, analysis, and dissemination processes. *Critical Theory and Qualitative Data Analysis in Education*, then, does this and more by extending some of these values and showing how they work in tandem with theoretical and methodological tools.

One of the key aims of all of the contributors is best described in Nathan Beck's work in which he asks, "Why can't there be many centers?" in an effort to essentially "undo method." This raises many questions that equity-oriented scholars in education have grappled with for years: What is knowledge? Who owns knowledge? Who gets to be a so-called expert and who is worthy of being cited?

Beck reminds us that we can have a "loving critique"—to borrow from Paris and Alim (2014)—and still want to engage in programs of research that are socially responsible, bold, and seeking to do some of the heavy lifting of problem solving for issues that are pervasive in education.

"Transitions on Traditions"[1]

As we imagine what is it means to "undo" method or even reimagine a human-izing paradigm in education research, I want to retell story that I often share with my graduate students. I had the honor of hearing the poet, activist, and institution builder, Sonia Sanchez, speak to an audience at the National Council of Teachers of English (NCTE) in Atlanta, Georgia several years ago. Ms. Sanchez, who was teaching at Temple University at the time, talked about her poetry classes. Her students were surprised, if not dismayed, that she began her poetry by teaching poetic form. When she asked her students what they thought they would be doing in her class, many expressed they thought they would be freestyling. Ms. Sanchez posed a question to her students—and I am paraphrasing here—if one does not learn form, how would they learn how to deviate from it? Ms. Sanchez's response was met with laughter from this audience of mostly Language Arts teachers and lit-eracy scholars. Her story remained with me as I continued to develop my program of research drawing from the tools of ethno-history and critical participant eth-nography. One would argue that these "forms" or "methods" at some point "devi-ated" from more established protocols. We have to reimagine methods—especially data analysis—in ways that speak to the communities in which we work, learn from and with, and who depend on us to be responsible with the stories, artifacts, and experiences they have shared with us—their guests—in communities both in and in out of school contexts.

When I think about how to do the work of extending research methods to match the messiness of real lives, I think about the radio program "Transitions on Traditions" hosted by Greg Bridges. The very notion of having a transition on a tradition, that is, taking something that is part of a so-called canon or reified by the academy and troubling it by considering the human lives and experiences in front of you is what the contributors in this volume are doing. To challenge colo-nizing methodologies is not to sacrifice intellectual rigor or integrity—actually it means to do just the opposite. Methods do matter. However, our relationships with communities matter even more. To be sure, Reavis demonstrates her use of Social Reproduction Theory in Memo Analysis by taking us step by step through her process for coding transcripts of interviews with stakeholders in schools to learn more about how both families and schools influence the col-lege aspirations of young people. Here, Reavis uses her memo analysis tools to accurately portray the values communicated to her from her participants. In a reimagining of Black Queer Theory, Blockett argues that "putting queer color analysis to work requires an analytical framework where data can be studied through a theoretical lens that critiques racialized heteronormativity and contests the limits of status-quo ideologies." This reimagining, or what Blockett refers to as Black Queen Theory, suggests that research methods often take up expired vocabularies that do not accurately portray the nuances of fluid human lives that are in the process of becoming.

A Closer Look

In addition to offering ways for scholars to build on existing methodologies, contributors to this volume also offer new paradigms while inviting all scholars to consider their tools. To be sure, Dennis' work on diffractive analysis using photography offers an analytic process in which the subject and the process are "performative events." As Dennis takes us through the process of analyzing photos, she asserts that the photo is more than a representation of an event but an opportunity to "open a transformative space for material reconfiguration and dialogue through that which one could call realistic." We cannot lose sight of this idea. Data we collect, whether in the form of interviews, memos, artifacts and so many others, coupled with the analysis process, create new possibilities and a space for dialogue. Here, I also call on Blackburn Cohen's use of "Imagination (What is ideal)," "Manifestation (What it has become)," and "Contradiction (What we are still waiting to happen)" in critical geography analysis work. I am encouraged by education researchers' desire to transcend contrived borders and employ the methods, forms of methods, analysis, and strategic reconstruction of these forms in order to ask an entirely new set of questions.

Blackburn Cohen further argues that analyzing data sources such as news articles and meeting minutes and "especially those that are considered alongside a historical approach that traces development over time" cannot be underestimated in the education research process. To be sure, Lee-Johnson and Henderson historicize Black Twitter and the hashtag #BlackWomenAtWork in particular, using critical discourse analysis (CDA) alongside Du Bois' double consciousness theory that Black people in the contexts of the United States must be mindful of how they view themselves as well as how others view them. In order to understand the phenomenon of #BlackWomenAtWork, one must understand the historical trajectory of Black women being viewed as chattel during the enslavement of Africans in the Americas and how Black women were rendered invisible while others benefitted from their labor. When Du Bois' historical framing is partnered with CDA, scholars are able to offer an analysis that is more honest, rigorous, and useful to the field. Similarly, Gaskew's analysis of a for-profit higher education institution's television advertisement must be historicized in the analysis process. The codification of race, gender, and socio-economic levels in these advertisements attempt to access raced and gendered stereotypes while targeting Black people who, in turn, get saddled with debt. Blackburn Cohen, then, would ask of all of these chapters, how does history factor into these analyses and what do we already know that informs what is in front of us?

Analyzing for the Future

In closing, I think it is important to consider how contributors in this volume are preparing education research to analyze data for the future. Here I wish to take on my colleague's, Anna Stetsenko's, challenge to education researchers to imagine what "ought" to be as opposed to what "is" the case (Stetsenko, 2017). As I think about this, I am compelled by Winkle-Wagner, Sulé, and Maramba's use of critical race theory (CRT) to analyze so-called race-neutral college admissions processes. Beginning with low-level coding techniques that often preserve the language of participants, Winkle-Wagner, Sulé, and Maramba created a protocol using CRT questions that coincide with the tenets of CRT. As they examine what has been said about race-neutral admissions—especially in the case of Texas—they try to understand what is being said from the perspectives of "permanence of racism," "experiential knowledge," "Whiteness as property," "critique of liberalism," "interest convergence," and "intersectionality." This kind of in-depth analysis is useful as education research maintains relevance in responding to policies that often harm students from non-dominant communities.

As you engage these chapters, it is useful to ask how the data analysis process can generate change and partake in this powerful toolbox to begin the work.

Note

1 Radio programmer, Greg Bridges, created a show entitled "Transitions on Traditions" on listener-sponsored radio, KPFA in Berkeley, California. Bridges' show explored the many branches on the Black music family tree. This title served as a reminder that the music may have been different but the roots were the same.

References

Paris, D., & Alim, H. S. (Spring 2014). What Are We Seeking to Sustain Through Culturally Sustaining Pedagogy? A Loving Critique Forward. *Harvard Educational Review*, 84(1): 85–100.

Paris, D., & Winn, M. T. (2014). *Humanizing Research: Decolonizing Qualitative Inquiry with Youth and Communities*. Thousand Oaks, CA: Sage Publications.

Stetsenko, A. (2017). *Infinite Potential: Disrupting Inequality in Education and Beyond through Pedagogy of Daring*. Presented at the Literacy Research Association Annual Convention, Tampa Bay, Florida.

PREFACE

Ashley N. Gaskew, Jamila Lee-Johnson, and Rachelle Winkle-Wagner

Critical Theory and Qualitative Data Analysis in Education provides explanations of social theories and then applies those social theories to rigorous qualitative data analysis techniques. By creating clearer and accessible bridges between theories and the practice of analyzing qualitative data, research findings are likely to be more connected to the larger concepts within the social theories. In making these connections, within this volume, there is a clearer specification of how critical theory informs research. This book can help researchers to translate their research designs and findings to multiple audiences (i.e., those who already do critical work, and those who do not). The hope of this volume is that in connecting data analysis to critical social theories, the findings of these studies are more likely to be able to connect to social issues and to social change because the process of connecting theory to data analysis will specify how critical theory concepts relate to the data, and ultimately, to the recommendations for action.

Critical social theory goes beyond merely describing and understanding the social world to offer a deeper understanding of the world around us through dialogue and action (Carspecken, 1996). Critical social theory is action; it brings forth action for more equitable outcomes in society. One issue with many of the scholarly usages of critical social theory is that often the way in which the theory or theories informed the research process, such as data collection, analysis, or interpretation, is not well articulated. While there have been numerous texts that explain the role and importance of critical theory in qualitative research (Canella, Pèrez, & Pasque, 2015; Carspecken, 1996; Dennis, Carspecken, & Carspecken, 2013; Paris & Winn, 2013; Winkle-Wagner, Hunter, & Ortloff, 2009), there have been few texts that have described how to apply critical theories directly to data analysis. *Critical Theory and Qualitative Data Analysis in Education* offers a much needed, path-breaking explanation of how critical theories can be used within the analysis and interpretation of qualitative data.

Critical Theory and Qualitative Data Analysis in Education is one of the first books that brings together multiple examples of how critical theories can inform critical qualitative data analyses. This is important because it will deepen the contribution and rigor of qualitative research more generally. We want our book to be used as a guide to create dialogue for and about critical scholarship. The chapters in our book collectively accomplish this task by discussing the many ways that critical scholarship can be applied and used in research. Pushing to extend the borders beyond traditional qualitative analysis in academia, in this book we assert that critical qualitative research can be applied to new forms of data such as news media, advertisements, public speeches, and television shows.

Audiences for the Book

Critical Theory and Qualitative Data Analysis in Education contributes to an expanding field of critical research and applies critical inquiry to a variety of disciplines and fields. The primary audiences of the book are qualitative researchers, be they emerging scholars or those who are renewing their approaches. This book will be beneficial for those who are interested in qualitative research techniques, social theory, or critical theory. Given that we examine critical theory in this volume and critical theory is inherently interdisciplinary (Dennis *et al.*, 2013), this book is meant for scholars across the humanities, social sciences, and applied fields, such as education. This book is geared towards exposing those who read it to different ways to apply critical theory to data analysis. The variety of examples in the book provides numerous ways for students, faculty, and researchers to explore how critical theory can be applied to different social settings and to different populations. The exemplars in the book offer innovative ways to conduct qualitative studies with marginalized populations. The analysis of critical theories is useful for those interested in pursuing theoretical studies. Also, because the last section focuses on institutions and policy applications of critical theories, some policy scholars may have interest in the book. A secondary audience for the book would be student affairs administrators, as well as senior-level administrators who work with marginalized populations. This book can help them connect theory with data and help them analyze their data through different lenses and better understand and work with marginalized and underrepresented groups.

How to Use This Book

Critical Theory and Qualitative Data Analysis in Education can be read in multiple ways, depending on the needs of the reader. Each chapter opens with a text box that summarizes the critical theory that was used, the type of qualitative data that is highlighted, the new data analysis technique that is developed in the chapter, and the substantive topic of education that is considered. These text boxes can be a useful guide in reading the book so that readers can choose chapters based on their methodological, theoretical, or empirical interests.

Connected to these summative text boxes, there are four ways to use this book:

1. As a primer on critical theories;
2. As an entrée into ways to use various forms of qualitative data;
3. As a data analysis technique guide to learn and apply different analytic tools; and/or
4. To understand marginalized populations and topics that are often left under-studied in education.

Each chapter in the book provides a new way of analyzing data that is deeply related to the critical theory that is taken up in that chapter. There are numerous critical theories that are defined, summarized, and critiqued in this volume. Some of these theories are often considered standard critical theories such as Habermas' critical theory (Chapter 13) or critical race theory (Chapter 12). Other theories that are highlighted within these pages are underutilized or theories that few people in education might have explored such as border thinking/indigenous knowledge (Chapter 3), care theory (Chapter 4), critical materialism (Chapter 9), and critical geography (Chapter 4). Still other theories in this book might not be used as "critical theories" and yet, in this volume the authors make compelling cases for their usage. These more innovative critical theories include Bourdieu's social reproduction theory (Chapter 5), hermeneutic phenomenology (Chapter 6), neo-colonial theories (Fanon and Cèsaire) (Chapters 10 and 11), and Du Bois' double consciousness (Chapter 14).

Within the book, more typical forms of qualitative data such as interviews or observations are used to offer examples of data analysis. Additionally, some of the chapter authors used innovative forms of data such as photography, course syllabi, television advertisements, political speeches, state legislative oral hearings, and Twitter. Together, these various forms of data provide compelling ways that researchers could begin to think about what should and can offer insight into the social world.

The book is separated into three sections, allowing for reflection of various ways to contemplate the connection between critical theory and data analysis. Section I provides theoretical reflection on ways that critical theory has been applied to inquiry, and the strengths and limitations of that application. For instance, Carspecken's chapter (Chapter 2) offers insight into the historical and contemporary usages of critical theory and what aspects of critical theory, such as the idea of recognition, have gone largely unconsidered. Beck's analysis (Chapter 3) offers an honest and serious critique of academia more generally and how critical inquiry has and in some ways can never fully reach the ideals of critical theory within academic spaces. Schwarz (Chapter 4) questions the centerpiece of most college courses, the syllabus, and provides insight into ways that care and emotion can be more centrally connected to learning and to critical theorizing and inquiry. Section II begins with an introduction by McGuire and then centers the critical theory and analysis that has been conducted with marginalized populations. Section III is launched with an introduction by Yao and then explores ways to connect critical theory and data analysis relative to social and educational institutions and policies.

Finally, within this volume there are many different ways to consider the topics of marginality, underrepresented and social categories like race, class, gender, nationality, or sexual orientation. We purposefully invited authors such that both the authors in the volume and the populations with whom these authors worked offer insight into the multifaceted ways that marginalization, oppression, and underrepresentation can manifest in educational spaces. An important highlight of the book is that educational spaces sometimes transcend schools and college campuses and are viewed as permeating multiple social settings. For instance, in the chapters of this book, authors consider topics such as Palestinian farmers (Chapter 3), college classrooms (Chapter 4), high school students' experiences in and out of school (Chapter 5), out-of-classroom spaces in college (Chapters 6 and 7), the experiences of academic refugees (Chapter 8), Ugandan community spaces and schools (Chapter 9), students' experiences in charter schools (Chapter 10), political speeches on education (Chapter 11), college access policy (Chapter 12), television advertisements (Chapter 13), and Black women's experiences in the workplace (Chapter 14). The chapters span the globe and consider all levels of education from primary, secondary, and higher education. Additionally, the authors in this volume assert in their writing that the notion of "education" is broader than schools and college campuses; learning and education can occur in communities, in neighborhoods, in the media, and through politicians and government. This view of learning is in itself a novel aspect of the book—education, broadly defined, is part of the critical inquiry and theorizing.

References

Canella, G. S., Pèrez, M. S., & Pasque, P. A. (2015) *Critical qualitative inquiry: Foundations and future.* Walnut Creek, CA: Left Coast Press.

Carspecken, P. F. (1996). Critical ethnography in educational research. New York: Routledge.

Dennis, B., Carspecken, L., & Carspecken, P. F. (Eds.) (2013). *Qualitative research: A reader in philosophy, core concepts, and practice.* New York: Peter Lang Publishers.

Paris, D., & Winn, M. T. (Eds). (2013). *Humanizing research: Decolonizing qualitative inquiry with youth and communities.* Thousand Oaks, CA: Sage.

Winkle-Wagner, R., Hunter, C. A., & Ortloff, D. H. (2009). *Bridging the gap between theory and practice in educational research: Methods at the margins.* New York: Palgrave Macmillan.

ACKNOWLEDGEMENTS

The impetus for this project stemmed from the deep, critical thinking in a graduate-level seminar at the University of Wisconsin–Madison. The class, called Critical Theory and Data Analysis, presented multiple critical theories and then had students develop unique analytic techniques that connected to those theories. The students in the spring 2016 section of this class were so thoughtful and engaged that an edited volume of their work seemed not only possible, but an important way to continue to build on their good thinking. Many of the students in that seminar present their work in this volume. For all of the students in the seminar, both those whose work is presented here and those whose work ultimately did not end up in the pages of this book, we are very grateful. It is very rare for a seminar class to be so intellectually stimulating for the students and the professor alike that the work results in a book. We are very thankful for all involved.

We also want to thank the Educational Leadership and Policy Analysis department faculty and students at the University of Wisconsin–Madison. We feel grateful to be in an intellectual community where students and faculty can work together toward advancing critical theoretical ideas. We are also thankful to be in a department where faculty and students value research, theory, and practice that emphasizes justice, equity, and social change.

Finally, we want to thank our acquisitions editor, Heather Jarrow. Your thoughtful questions, insights, and ideas were invaluable to the development of this manuscript. We would not have been able to finish this task without you—thanks for believing in our idea.

Ashley N. Gaskew: This process of co-editing a book has been very rewarding and has helped me to grow as a scholar. I would like to thank my parents Larry and Johnnie A. Gaskew and my sister Alexis for their love and support. They have listened to me and encouraged me throughout this process; thank you. I would like to thank my community of supporters who have uplifted me throughout this process: my close friends and family, the Writing Warriors, my mentors, my colleagues at the University of Wisconsin–Madison, and my sorority sisters of Zeta Phi Beta Sorority, Inc. I would like to thank my grandmothers, Honey and Daisy, my guardian angels, who paved the way for me to be here now. And finally, I would like to thank my co-editors Rachelle Winkle-Wagner and Jamila Lee-Johnson for their continuous support and mentorship. Thank you for being two strong women in my life uplifting me and pushing me to reach my potential.

Jamila Lee-Johnson: When co-editing a book, you truly learn more about your strengths and weaknesses, however this experience has truly been rewarding and allowed me to grow more as a scholar. I would like to thank my mother, Laverne Pope, for all of your love and support. I would also like to thank my grandparents Gentral and Clothies Pope, for your words of advice and listening and providing support whenever I needed it. To my close friends and family (especially my aunts and cousins), "The Minis," the Writing Warriors, my sorority sisters of Delta Sigma Theta Sorority, Inc., and mentors, I thank you all for words of encouragement and words of wisdom throughout this process. Lastly, I would like to thank my co-editors Rachelle Winkle-Wagner and Ashley N. Gaskew for believing in me, and supporting all the crazy ideas that brought this book to "fruition." I am so thankful and grateful to work with two wonderful scholars. Thank you.

Rachelle Winkle-Wagner: I am very thankful to have had the opportunity to work with two brilliant scholars, Jamila Lee-Johnson and Ashley N. Gaskew, on this edited volume. It was a joy to create this with you. To my teachers, mentors, and colleagues who either taught me and/or continued to foster my understanding of critical theory and critical inquiry, thank you: Phil Carspecken, Barbara Dennis, Dorian McCoy, Thandi Sulé, and Dina Maramba. Finally, thanks for my writing group of friends here at UW–Madison, all of whom heard about this initial idea before my class started and who supported it the entire time: Linn Posey-Maddox, Christy Clark-Pujara, Erica Turner, Bianca Baldridge, Cherene Sherrard, Ethelene Whitemire, Maxine McKinney de Royston, Ericka Bullock, and Sami Schalk. As always, even down to the day we submitted the manuscript, I was reminded that as a mama-scholar, all of my work is ultimately unable to be untangled from my family. I am thankful to my two children, Eleanor and Abigail, for their patience with their mama in the days when this project took over the house for writing retreats and in the times when I was intellectually distracted because of this work. To Mike Wagner, I am well aware that most of the time when I was working on this book, you were taking the lead with our children and at home—and I am thankful for that. I am persistently grateful to you for your partnership, intellectual compatibility and challenge, and the life we have built together.

The Need for Partnering Critical Theory and Data Analysis in Education

1

THE MISSING LINK IN DATA ANALYSIS

An Introduction to the Use of Critical Theory to Guide Data Analysis

Rachelle Winkle-Wagner, Ashley N. Gaskew, and Jamila Lee-Johnson

Critical theory is a broad category that includes a set of theories that generally critique larger social structures and explore social inequalities. Common to most critical theories is the idea of critiquing social structures, norms, and inequalities. Many critical theories, particularly the ones taken up in this volume, take these social criticisms and then consider ways to move toward social change. Simply put, critical theorists and those scholars who use these theories do not like oppression and they want their work to change it (Carspecken, 1996; Kincheloe & McLaren, 2002). Critical theories, or those theories that have officially been called "critical theories," span the decades from the 1920s through contemporary times. But, many of the ideas that are specified in critical theories can be traced back to Hegelian, Kantian, and later, Marxist, theories as early as the 1800s, as we explain below (Kincheloe & McLaren, 2002).

Critical theories can be modernist, postmodernist, or post-structuralist. While we do not delve deeply into these debates here, it is worth pointing out that there is a longstanding debate between those theories that are considered "modernist", where a sense of being is considered to be more permanent, and postmodernism, which often abandons a sense of permanent being for a state of flux or becoming. Post-structuralism questions most structures but attempts to somehow go between postmodernist and modernist thinking.[1] At the root of the debates between modernism, postmodernism, and post-structuralism is the relationship between the physical and non-physical (i.e., spiritual) realms. The term "transcendental" refers to the thinking that includes metaphysical (a reality or ideas beyond the senses) thinking. That is, some philosophers, often rooted in the thinking of Immanuel Kant (1785/1996), considered both sensory ideas (that which can be seen, heard, touched, etc.) alongside ideas about spirit or non-sensory ways of being as a way to understand how knowledge came into being (epistemology). We could write an entire volume on the differences between these branches of philosophy and about the deep philosophical traditions upon which critical theories were constructed. But suffice it to say here that these terms and distinctions crop up in discussions about critical theories as a way to mark the philosophical roots of the ways of theorizing. Carspecken's analysis in Chapter 2 points out some of these distinctions and some of this philosophical history in more detail too.

Critical theories can be postmodern, meaning those theories and ideas that spanned the late 19th and 20th centuries and attempted to question or depart from earlier ideas. The term postmodern is often paired with the term "post-structuralism" but post-structuralism typically refers more directly to theories by theorists such as Jacques Derrida, Julia Kristeva, or Michel Foucault where the theorists were interested in dismantling structures of language and society, questioning all metaphors, ideas, and norms within society. The idea of post-structuralism is to question all structures, even language, and move beyond them, at least theoretically. We mention this distinction here as a way to place the critical theories in this volume within the larger body of theories that are deemed "critical."

Some critical theories are *not* considered postmodern or post-structuralist and some critical theories that are not connected with postmodernism or post-structuralism can connect to earlier philosophical traditions that are broadly classified as "modernist" theories, such as the critical theory of Jürgen Habermas, which is the root of many of the chapters in this book. Critical theories can elevate and center race, class, gender, sexuality, and inequality or any combination of these categories, especially when these categories are overlooked and neglected.

Perhaps complicating the use of critical theory even more is a debate about terms like "epistemology" and "ontology." Epistemology can be defined as a way of knowing or how one comes to know (Crotty, 1998). Some critical scholars such as Carspecken (1996) have advanced a critical epistemology, or a way of knowing that has inherent critical theoretical ideas embedded within it. Ontology refers broadly to a body of knowledge (Crotty, 1998). One could claim therefore that there could be a critical ontology meaning that there is a body of knowledge that emphasizes critique of oppressive social structures and pathways toward ameliorating that oppression. Carspecken further considers ontologies or bodies of knowledge about the world in his chapter (Chapter 2) and ways that critical epistemology can ultimately create a critical ontology (a body of work that is critical in orientation). Some authors in this volume use the terms epistemology and ontology to refer to both the way that they came to know (or came into knowledge) and the bodies of knowledge upon which they draw. Here we introduce these terms as a way to demonstrate how critical theories have been part and parcel to epistemological (ways of knowing) and ontological (bodies of knowledge) ideas.

It is no wonder that for many people, the entrée into critical theory itself can be confusing or even a bit intimidating. In this introductory chapter, we take a moment to consider the history of critical theory, define critical theory as we are using it in this book, and contemplate some of the many ways that critical theory has been applied to critical inquiry or methodology.

Defining Critical Theory

Critical theory is a branch of social theory that often attempts to understand conflict and oppression in order to bring about social change (Crotty, 1998). Habermas (1989) referred to critical theory as an important element of social change. Typically the change that is intended with critical theory is to dismantle oppressive structures that subordinate or marginalize particular groups of people.

A Brief History of Critical Theory

Much of the philosophical tradition that is categorized as critical theory is in some way connected to the critical theory of Karl Marx and Hegel (Crotty, 1998). While there are obviously more important elements to Hegelian philosophical thought, we provide a very brief primer on some of the elements of Hegel's ideas that were advanced in critical theory. Hegel's (1807/1952/1977) philosophy was centered on the idea of a dialectic, or a process of negation, whereby one could understand the world by understanding what something was not (e.g., not-that, not-that not-that) to understand what something *is*. Ultimately, the notion of dialectic also can be applied to tensions and conflicts within the social world. Embedded in Hegelian theory are class or racial struggles. Hegel (1807/1952/1977) viewed the social world as integrally connected meaning that one part of society could not be oppressed without the entire society being stunted. In other words, the freedom of one person influences the ability for the entire society to be liberated. Inherent in this theory are elements of later critical theory that aim to criticize societal structures and processes that ultimately hamper the liberation of individuals or groups (Hegel, 1807/1952/1977). A less well-developed aspect of Hegelian theory emphasizes the idea of recognition and how one or one's ideas can be either recognized or misrecognized in the social world. Carspecken's chapter (Chapter 2) delves deeper into Hegel's influence on critical theory and particularly the notion of recognition that was highlighted in Hegel's theory.

Marx's (2001) critique of both the social and economic systems in the 19th and 20th centuries was a new way to consider how the capitalist economic system can become embedded in other social systems like education. During his life (1818–1883), his conflict theory considered two classes, the Proletariat and the Bourgeoisie, to be in perpetual conflict, battling for power and social privilege; but the upper class, the Bourgeoisie or ruling class, would have control over all production, social systems, and the larger social ideology. As the middle class eventually is diminished to the point of nonexistence, Marx theorized that the proletariat would unify and their solidarity would lead to revolution and emancipation from their low class status. Marx has been critiqued as overly focused on class status and inequities and much less interested in gender, race, or other categories (Mills, 2003; Solomos, 1986). While some critical theories directly link to Marxist ideas, even those critical theories that no longer name these roots often have some elements of the conflict, critique, and examination of pathways to revolution and emancipation.

Arguably, there are other important roots to critical theory that may not always be identified as such. Anna Julia Cooper (1892a/1995, 1892b/1988) and W.E.B. Du Bois (1903) were writing during the same general time period as Marx, but they have not always been recognized because of race. Cooper and Du Bois' emphasis was more on race than class and they both pointed out the perpetual struggle for status, privilege, and power across racial groups, particularly after Reconstruction (the time period after slavery in the United States). Both Cooper and Du Bois were concerned with how to uplift formerly enslaved people in the United States. Cooper (1892a/1995, 1892b/1988) is considered by some to be one of the first feminist writers because of her emphasis on the empowerment and education of women, and particularly women of color. She was also one of the early theorists to identify overlaps between categories of race, class, and gender. Du Bois was interested in how to educate and train Black people after the long history of enslavement and he wrote extensively on the way that Black people are made to feel, think or act differently in different social settings. It is important to note that neither Cooper nor Du Bois were given proper credit for their critical theories until generations later, and some would argue that they never have received appropriate credit for their important contributions to later critical theory (Cooper, 2000; Morris, 2015). We do so here, as a way to offer a critical analysis of the line of theorizing that aims to point out inequalities, oppression, and ways to ameliorate these societal ills.

Two Generations of Critical Theory

There are two generations of critical theory[2] and the theories were shaped by the social histories in the countries in which they were initiated (Crotty, 1998). In the United States, critical theories initially centered on literary criticism and the critique of language, symbols, and signs; while in Europe, critical theory was centered on social thought (Adams, 1986). But throughout the early history of critical theory, the Marxist roots and the fear of revolution or toppling power structures meant that those who affiliated with critical theory were often targeted by national governments, both in the U.S. and in Europe.

In 1924, the Institute for Social Research in Frankfurt, Germany launched what became known as the "Frankfurt School," which later became known as the first generation of critical theory (Crotty, 1998). The Institute's first members were Jews or affiliated with Jewish people. When Hitler took power in Germany in 1933, the Institute was forced to close and many of the members fled to either the U.S. or to Geneva, Switzerland. Max Horkheimer, one of the Frankfurt School members, went to the U.S. and set up a branch Institute in New York at Columbia University, and another better-known critical theorist, Theordor Adorno, joined soon after. In 1940, the Institute was raided and many of the materials were confiscated amidst McCarthy-era politics and fear of communism in the U.S. Many Institute members moved to Los Angeles.

In the 1950s, much of the Frankfurt School moved back to Germany and launched the second generation of critical theory (Crotty, 1998). Jürgen Habermas joined the Institute as Adorno's assistant in the 1950s and his theorizing became central to the second-generation critical theories that are primarily taken up in this volume. He eventually left the Institute because of his views that critical theory should take a more normative stance than it had taken in the past (Crotty, 1998). In other words, rather than simply pointing out critiques of society, Habermas suggested that critical theories should move toward understanding and toward social change. Habermas (1989) became concerned with the way that critical theory remained only critique without any effort toward social change. Habermas (1984, 1987) ultimately offered a normative version of critical theory that considered praxis (action) as central to the theory. That is, a concern with inequality in the social world should envision social change and actions that could be taken to change that inequality. Additionally, Habermas criticized some postmodern theorists who he argued were only posing questions without a moral or normative suggestion about what should be done next to move society toward liberation and emancipation. Different from many postmodernists and earlier critical theorist, Habermas (1984, 1987) considered theory as a process of human action and an effort toward freedom and liberation. Paulo Freire (1972), a Brazilian critical theorist, also took up the mantle of normative critical theory, combining critique of social inequalities, action, and the idea of what it means to be human.

A Brief Overview of the Chapters in This Volume

Many of the chapters in this volume have an implicit or obvious root in Habermas' or Freire's emancipatory, normatively focused critical theory. For instance, the chapters by Carspecken (Chapter 2), Dennis (Chapter 9), and Gaskew (Chapter 13) are all rooted in Haberamasian critical theory. A number of the chapters in this book use Carspecken's (1996) critical epistemological ideas of applying Habermas to critical methodology. For example, Schwarz (Chapter 4) advances a data analysis technique for care theory that is grounded in Carspecken's initial ideas for data analysis. Forbes (Chapter 10), Gaskew (Chapter 13), and Agyepong (Chapter 11) began with Carspecken's (1996) adaptation of Habermasian critical theory to create their own unique data analysis techniques. Mobley (Chapter 6) employs hermeneutic phenomenology, which may seem disassociated from critical theory, but the theorists he considers were formative in Habermas' critical theory and are therefore in the same general family of theories. Mobley's call for more actionable hermeneutic phenomenology is also aligned with the normative critical theoretical ideas of Freire and Habermas. Lee-Johnson and Henderson (Chapter 14) offer a way to use Du Bois' theory, and that theory also had roots in Hegelian and Marxist ideas but prompted action in ways that were unusual for this time period.

While other theories may not be explicitly related to these earlier second-generation critical theories (Adams, 1986), we attempt in this book to elevate theories that have elements of critique plus action embedded in them. In some ways, we infer a third generation of critical theory here. While there is not a single theoretical root for all of the theories used in the book, the main commonality is the connection between theory and action, which we consider to pay homage to the normative critical theories offered by Habermas (1984, 1987) and Freire (1972). These theories, which we consider second- or third-generation (still needing to be further developed) critical theories, include: indigenous knowledge and border thinking (Beck, Chapter 3), critical geography, (Blackburn Cohen, Chapter 8), critical race theory (Sulé, Maramba, and Winkle-Wagner, Chapter 12), Bourdieu's social reproduction theory (Reavis, Chapter 5), Du Bois' double consciousness (Lee-Johnson and Henderson, Chapter 14), and the neo-colonial theories of Fanon (Forbes, Chapter 10) and Cesaire (Agyepong, Chapter 11).

Critical Theory and the Missing Link in Critical Inquiry

Critical theory has been applied to methodology in ways that have allowed research to become more action and social justice oriented. While the application of critical theoretical ideas could certainly apply to any research methodology (see, for example, Zuberi & Bonilla-Silva, 2008), qualitative researchers took up the challenge from second-generation critical theorists in particular and attempted to think about how methodology can be tied to normative social theory. Some research methodologists have even referred to qualitative researchers as the primary leaders in applying critical theory to research methodologies (Denzin & Lincoln, 2008). Part of the application of critical theory to research methodology has been critiqued and challenged to mainstream or historical research processes that have decentered people, experience, and histories (Carspecken, 1996; Paris & Winn, 2013).

Critical qualitative inquiry is rooted in critical theories such that the research process becomes more "humanizing" and possibly "decolonizing" for the participants and the researchers (Paris & Winn, 2013). Many critical qualitative researchers insist that people and their lives and histories are put at the center of the study and of the care of the research process. As critical theories are applied to methodologies, researchers have become more invested in examining their own positioning in the research process and have promoted ways that research can be empowering or beneficial to participants and communities (Dennis, Carspecken, & Carspecken, 2013; Paris & Winn, 2013). Critical research takes up the normative aspect of second-generation critical theory and attempts to think about research as part of the possibility of liberation and emancipation (Canella, Perèz, & Pasque, 2015; Dennis *et al.*, 2013). There are a few ways that the ideas of liberation and emancipation have manifested in critical inquiry, in terms of: the roles that researchers and participants play in the research process, the practices that are used in the data collection process, the form of reporting or representation of the data, and the self-reflection or reflexivity of the researcher. Most of these ways that critical theories are embedded in critical inquiry are highlighted in the data collection process rather than the process of data analysis. That is, while there seem to be clear distinctions of what makes research "critical" relative to data collection, there is less of a clear delineation as to how to connect critical theory to the data analysis process.

The most important consideration in research that takes on a "critical" orientation is the humanizing and care of participants (Paris & Winn, 2013). Many of the methodological claims and ideas about critical research are centered on the treatment of participants, the roles of researchers/participants, and the ways that the research might influence or impact communities (Canella *et al.*, 2015). Within critical inquiry, researchers' roles have shifted and changed, as have the roles of participants (Dennis *et al.*, 2013). There are various ways that these shifting roles can be demonstrated in research. Sometimes participants may offer feedback on analysis, findings, interpretation, or all three. While member checking is a hallmark of many qualitative data validation techniques, in critical inquiry participants often play a larger role in offering constructive feedback on multiple parts of the research process. For instance, in Behar's (1993/2014) oft-cited narrative life history study, *Translated Woman*, the participant, Esperanza, played a continual role in offering feedback of the data collection, writing, and analysis process. Behar positioned herself alongside Esperanza as a "storyteller." Sometimes participants might even co-author with researchers.

Researchers might be facilitators of experiences, mentors, teachers, friends, or acquaintances. Critical theories are often deeply influential in the choices that are made throughout the data collection process. For example, in Winkle-Wagner's (2009) critical ethnographic study of Black women's college experiences on a predominantly White research university campus, she played the role of researcher, mentor, study guide, friend, acquaintance, and student during the course of the study and these roles changed depending on the relationship that was built with each participant and over the time of the study as the relationships were built. This further shows that in critical research sometimes participants are co-researchers (Irizarry & Brown, 2013). Additionally, in Posey-Maddox's (2014) ethnographic case study methodology with middle-class families in urban schools, she spent many months as a volunteer in a school classroom before she began to develop her research questions and before she contacted possible participants for her study.

A third way that critical inquiry incorporates critical theory is in the blurring of traditional boundaries on the reporting of the data. For instance, Lather and Smithies (1997) book on women in a support group for those living with HIV/ AIDS offers a unique and creative experience for the reader where one half of the page profiles the participants' dialogue without analysis from the researchers, and the other half of the page illustrates the researchers' experiences of doing the research (field notes). Interspersed across the text are "fact boxes" that provide various forms of empirical evidence on HIV and AIDS. Behar's (1993/2014) book is written partly as a testimonial novel and partly as a form of oral storytelling as a way to demonstrate the depth and breadth of the oral history in the book. Some authors may even choose to present their data in artistic ways such as through poetry (Clark & Dennis, 2018) as a way to demonstrate the blurring of social sciences and humanities in critical research (Bronner & Kelner, 1989; Canella et al., 2015). Some scholars who conduct critical inquiry refer to the reporting of their data as "counterstorytelling" and this is another way that data can be presented in unique, creative, and culturally responsive ways (Solórzano & Yosso, 2002).

Finally, one of the more important ideas in the application of critical theory to critical inquiry is in the reflexivity of the research (Carspecken, 1996; Dennis et al., 2013; Shacklock & Smyth, 1998). Carspecken's (2018) volume, *Love in the Time of Ethnography* provides multiple chapters that offer research reflexivity on how they employed or reflected upon love in their critical research. Some critical scholars have offered researchers opportunities to dialogue and reflect on their research processes as the topic of study itself such as the book, *Unlikely Allies in the Academy: Women of Color and White women in conversation* (Dace, 2012). Or, some critical inquiry will provide the participants' narratives and then a reflective accounting of the researcher's relationship or experience with participants, as Boylorn (2013) did in her book *Sweetwater* which was about Black women in the town where Boylorn was raised.

While there are noteworthy exemplars of critical inquiry, there often remains a missing link between critical theories and qualitative data analysis (but see Carspecken, 1996; Dennis et al., 2013). This missing link is prevalent in many qualitative methods texts more generally, both those that are not critical and those that are. For example, many well-known qualitative methods texts describe the analysis process as a process of reading, coding, and clustering codes into themes (Creswell & Poth, 2017; Merriam, 1988, 2002). There are a few qualitative analysis texts that are necessary to consider, particularly for researchers who want to do research toward emergent themes that come from the participants. One of the more well-known analysis texts by Miles and Huberman (1994), *Qualitative Data Analysis*, does offer multiple ideas for qualitative data analysis but these data analysis techniques are not explicitly connected to particular theoretical traditions. A more recent text that was focused on analysis by Saldaña (2017) offered coding techniques. But similar to the Miles and Huberman (1994) text, the analysis techniques that are offered by Saldaña are very useful and applicable to researchers, but not connected to social theories in an obvious way.

Emergent forms of data analysis that are recommended by texts like Miles and Huberman (1994) or Saldaña (2017) are important to allow the data to lead the researchers' interpretations. We recommend using some type of emergent forms of analysis at some point during the data analysis process. But the lack of connection to social theory makes it more difficult to connect qualitative data to larger social structural issues. The reason for this is that qualitative studies typically offer a deeper analysis of a small number of participants as compared to quantitative studies, for instance, that attempt to generalize to larger populations. One of the primary ways that qualitative scholars can connect to larger social issues is through theory or conceptual transfer. That is, qualitative research does not intend to generalize to larger populations, and it is simply not the purpose of most qualitative research. Rather, qualitative research aims to delve deeply into everyday lived experiences, the meaning that people make from their lived experiences, and how processes or events might unfold in real time (Carspecken, 1996; Dennis et al., 2013).

One way that qualitative research can connect to larger social issues such as inequalities by race, class, or gender, is to use social theory (Carspecken, 1996; Dennis et al., 2013). Social theories allow for critical researchers to see how the lived experiences of people are portrayed and embedded in academia as well as society (Gildersleeve, Kuntz, Pasque, & Carducci, 2010). Moreover, critical theory allows researchers and participants to challenge norms that oppress marginalized communities in order to bring about change. Lastly, using social theory in qualitative data analysis adds to the rigorous and thoughtful work done by and with people for people.

Notes

1 Kierkegaard offers some distinctions between these three branches of philosophical thinking, see Best & Kellner (1997) for more details.
2 There may be a third generation of critical theory on the horizon but it is not named as such yet.

References

Adams, H. (1986). Introduction. In H. Adams & L. Searle, *Critical theory since 1965*, Tallahassee, FL: Florida State University Press.

Behar, R. (1993/2014). *Translated woman: Crossing the border with Esperanza's story*. Boston, MA: Beacon.

Best, S., & Kellner, D. (1997). *The postmodern turn*. New York: Guilford Press.

Boylorn, R. M. (2013). *Sweetwater: Black women and narratives of resilience*. New York: Peter Lang.

Bronner, S. E., & Kellner, D. (Eds.). (1989). *Critical theory and society: A reader*. New York: Psychology Press.

Canella, G. S., Perèz, M. S., & Pasque, P. A. (2015). *Critical qualitative inquiry: Foundations and future*. Walnut Creek, CA: Left Coast Press.

Carspecken, P. F. (1996). *Critical ethnography in educational research: A theoretical and practical guide*. New York: Peter Lang.

Carspecken, L. (Ed.) (2018). *Love in the time of ethnography: Essay on connection as the focus and basis of research*. New York: Lexington Books.

Clark, J., & Dennis, B. (2018). We are all ships coming home to ourselves: An autoethnographic poem in two parts. In L. E. Carspecken (Ed.), *Love in the time of ethnography: Essay on connection as the focus and basis of research*. New York: Lexington Books, 115–126.

Cooper, A. J. (1892a/1995). The status of women in America. In B. Guy-Sheftal, *Words of fire: An anthology of African American feminist thought*. New York: The New York Press, 44–50.

Cooper, A. J. (1892b/1988). *A voice from the South*. Oxford, UK: Oxford University Press.

Cooper, A. J. (2000). *The voice of Anna Julia Cooper: Including* A voice from the South *and other important essays, papers, and letters*. Lanham, MD: Rowman & Littlefield.

Creswell, J. W., & Poth, C. N. (2017). *Qualitative inquiry and research design: Choosing among five approaches*. Thousand Oaks, CA: Sage.

Crotty, M. (1998). Critical inquiry: The Marxist heritage. In *The foundations of social research: Meaning and perspectives in the research process*. Thousand Oaks, CA: Sage.

Dace, K. L. (Ed.). (2012). *Unlikely allies in the academy: Women of Color and White women in conversation*. New York: Routledge.

Dennis, B., Carspecken, L., & Carspecken, P. (2013). *Qualitative research: A reader in philosophy, core concepts, and practice*. New York: Peter Lang.

Denzin, N. K., & Lincoln, Y. S. (2008). *The landscape of qualitative research* (Vol. 1). Thousand Oaks, CA: Sage.

Du Bois, W.E.B. (1903). *The souls of Black folk*. Oxford, UK: Oxford University Press.

Freire, P. (1972). *Pedagogy of the oppressed*. New York: Herder and Herder.

Gildersleeve, R. E., Kuntz, A. M., Pasque, P. A., & Carducci, R. (2010). The role of critical inquiry in (re) constructing the public agenda for higher education: Confronting the conservative modernization of the academy. *The Review of Higher Education*, *34*(1), 85–121.

Habermas, J. (1984). *The theory of communicative action: Reason and the rationalisation of society*, Volume 1 (Trans: T. McCarthy). Boston, MA: Beacon.

Habermas, J. (1987). *The theory of communicative action: Lifeworld and system: A critique of functionalist reason*, Volume 2 (Trans: T. McCarthy). Boston, MA: Beacon.

Habermas, J. (1989). The tasks of a critical theory of society. In E. Bronner and M. Kellner, *Critical theory and society: A reader*. New York: Routledge, 292–312.

Hegel, G.W.F. (1807/1952/1977). *Hegel's phenomenology of spirit* (Trans: A. V. Miller). New York: Oxford University Press.

Irizarry, J. G. & Brown, T. M. (2013). Humanizing research in dehumanizing spaces: The challenges and opportunities of conducting participatory action research with youth in schools. In D. Paris & M. T. Winn (Eds.), *Humanizing research: Decolonizing qualitative inquiry with youth and communities*. Thousand Oaks, CA: Sage, 63–80.

Kant, I. (1785/1996). *Kant: The metaphysics of morals.* Cambridge, UK: Cambridge University Press.

Kincheloe, J. L., & McLaren, P. (2002). Rethinking critical theory and qualitative research. In Y. Zou & E. T. Trouba, *Ethnography and schools: Qualitative approaches to the study of education,* Oxford, UK: Rowman & Littlefield, 87–138.

Lather, P., & Smithies, C. (1997). *Troubling the angels: Women living with HIV/AIDS.* Oxford, UK: Westview Press.

Marx, K. (2001). Alienation and social classes. In D. B. Grusky (Ed.), *Social stratification: Class, race, and gender.* Oxford, UK: Westview Press, 87–104.

Merriam, S. B. (1988). *Case study research in education: A qualitative approach.* Hoboken, NJ: Jossey-Bass.

Merriam, S. B. (2002). *Qualitative research in practice: Examples for discussion and analysis.* Hoboken, NJ: Jossey-Bass.

Miles, M. B., & Huberman, A. M. (1994). *Qualitative data analysis: An expanded sourcebook.* Thousand Oaks, CA: Sage.

Mills, C. (2003). *From class to race: Essays in white Marxism and black radicalism.* Oxford, UK: Rowman & Littlefield.

Morris, A. (2015). *The scholar denied: WEB Du Bois and the birth of modern sociology.* Oakland, CA: University of California Press.

Paris, D., & Winn, M. T. (Eds.). (2013). *Humanizing research: Decolonizing qualitative inquiry with youth and communities.* Thousand Oaks, CA: Sage.

Posey-Maddox, L. (2014). *When middle-class parents choose urban schools: Class, race & the challenge of equity in public education.* Chicago, IL: University of Chicago Press.

Saldaña, J. (2017). *The coding manual for qualitative researchers.* Thousand Oaks, CA: Sage.

Shacklock, G., & Smyth, J. (Eds.). (1998). *Being reflexive in critical educational and social research* (Vol. 18). New York: Psychology Press.

Solomos, J. (1986). Varieties of Marxist conceptions of 'race', class and the state: A critical analysis. *Theories of Race and Ethnic Relations,* 84–109.

Solórzano, D. G., & Yosso, T. J. (2002). Critical race methodology: Counter-storytelling as an analytical framework for education research. *Qualitative Inquiry, 8*(1), 23–44.

Winkle-Wagner, R., Ortloff, D. H., & Hunter, C. A. (2009). *Bridging the gap between theory and practice in educational research: Methods at the margins.* New York: Palgrave Macmillan.

Winkle-Wagner, R. (2009). *The unchosen me: Race, gender and identity among Black women in college.* Baltimore, MD: Johns Hopkins University Press.

Zuberi, T., & Bonilla-Silva, E. (Eds.). (2008). *White logic, white methods: Racism and methodology.* Oxford, UK: Rowman & Littlefield.

2

THE MISSING INFINITE

A History and Critique of Mainstream and Counter-Mainstream Methodologies

Phil Francis Carspecken

I read the expression "missing infinite" many years ago in a book by Gillian Rose, *Hegel Contra Sociology* (1981/1995). It was a wonderful experience to read that expression in association with sociology and social theory. The title of Rose's book was itself wonderful. I came across it accidently, browsing books in the Liverpool City Library while working on my doctoral dissertation. Gillian Rose published a sequence of books during the 1980s and 1990s that challenge both mainstream social theories of knowledge (Weber, Durkheim, Parsons, Mannheim, etc.) and the post-structuralist counter-mainstream that was enormously popular during those decades. Post-structuralism remains enormously popular today. Rose's work is also opposed to various versions of critical theory (e.g., Horkheimer, Marcuse, Adorno, Habermas) and neo-Marxist theories of knowledge and society (e.g., Althusser).

In the social "sciences" only critical theory draws upon core Hegelian themes and insights. Critical theory enjoyed a relatively brief period of popularity, It was popularized in methodological and theoretical work specializing in education by Henry Giroux (e.g., Giroux, 1989) and Peter McClaren (e.g., McClaren, 1986) during the late 80s. But in educational research and theory, criticalist publications began to draw upon both critical theory and post-structuralism in the 1990s with confusing, not always coherent, results. This remains the case today.

Post-structuralism remains the most popular counter-mainstream orientation today but post-structuralism, in most of its many versions,[1] completely misses the infinite. I never forgot the expression "missing infinite," but only now am I using it as the theme of a publication. This essay is an effort to draw attention to the missing infinite in our mainstream social and psychological sciences, and its half or three-quarter absence in many of the communities of social researchers self-identifying as criticalists. The philosophical meaning of "critical" in the Western tradition has everything to do with the infinite and hopefully this essay will assist in understanding just what that is all about. In my experience, use of the word "critical" at this time, within communities of social researchers and theorists, misses the key insight.

An understanding of the Hegelian infinite amplifies the sense of "critical" in critical communicative pragmatism—the philosophical orientation underlying most of the essays in this book. The concepts of validity claim, validity horizon, identity claim, "I"/"me," intersubjective structure, and communicative reason invoke suspicion in criticalists whose perspective has a post-structuralist shape, and yet these concepts stay true to the Western philosophical tradition's use of "critical."

The infinite within critical communicative pragmatism concerns the final sections of the essay. Before reaching those sections we must put some work into overcoming several ubiquitous barriers to a comprehension of this infinity and its internal connection to the meaning of "critical" in any critical social philosophy, theory or methodology. These barriers include:

- The unconscious and hence non-critical use of picture-thinking;
- A deep-seated, unnoticed, concept of knowing and knowledge based on an unwarranted extension of visual perception;
- The use of a taken-for-granted ontology of presence;
- A misunderstanding of the meaning of "the subject" and failure to differentiate "the subject" from both "subjectivity" and all forms of presence-ontology;
- Use of a hard and fast separation between knowing and being;
- The conflation of "transcendental" with "transcendent."

"Critical"?

What do we mean by "critical"? We have critical ethnography, critical qualitative research, critical discourse analysis, critical participatory action research, critical race theory, critical cultural studies, critical feminist theory, and on and on it goes. So many names and expressions using the word *critical*. Do we all mean roughly the same thing when we use that word?

We do and we don't. I believe that all such uses of "critical" are informed by an understanding that knowledge and power have a complex interrelation with each other. Knowledge is understood in terms of ideology. It is conditioned by social relationships, social institutions, and the economy such that both common-sense and theoretical forms of knowing function to support and reproduce social, cultural, political, and economic forms of oppression and power. There is usually a necessary problematization of the concepts of "research," "researcher," and "method" precisely because those terms are intrinsic to the production of ideologies. Critical "research" projects (or "critical projects") are done for the purpose of bringing about positive changes to society and culture through community empowerment, the development of collective critical consciousness and collective action, rather than social engineering. Injustice and oppression are understood not only in terms of human needs for safety, economic security, material and cultural resources, and socially structured opportunities *but also* in terms of existential identity needs that include needs for dignity, respect, recognition, self-realization. Critical work operates against ideologies, which block and distort the voices of those most oppressed, deny the existence of daily acts of violence structured by race and gender differences, cover over institutionalized forms of racism and sexism. When we read or hear the word "critical" in the contexts of social research and theory, those are some of the things we can expect to be in play.

But we also don't mean the same thing. Where we find the sharpest differences between communities of criticalists is in our methodological and philosophical work. People whose critical projects will resemble each other's rather well, so that they would agree they are doing critical research, can totally disagree when talking about truth, validity, the subject and so on. This is not trivial. Critical research is necessarily opposed to mainstream ideas about knowledge, facts, truth, objectivity, validity, how to articulate "findings" to the public and many other necessary, unavoidable, inescapable basic concepts. These are ideas that cannot be escaped because one unavoidably takes a position on them as soon as one begins to think of a research project. Doing critical *theory* is itself a movement for socio-cultural change, a *practice*, because mainstream social and psychological research practices, based on beliefs about knowledge, bias, truth and many other fundamentals, reproduce and also extend and intensify ideologies. Survey, psychometric, and assessment "instruments" have actually been changing fundamental notions of what a person is, what is important in life, and what is "natural" and "normal." These fundamental notions are related to consumerist values, over-individualized concepts of personhood, what is acceptable in political activity, what is "success" in life. Mainstream psychological and social research practices are major institutions serving functions for complex social systems we want to change as criticalists. So our methodological and philosophical conversations and writings are not simply how we name and group ourselves, they are critical practices oriented towards liberation.

Uses of the Word "Critical" in Contemporary Communities of Social Researchers and Theorists

Members of the original Frankfurt School, diverse as their work and theory actually is, understood the infinite. Adorno's work is an excellent example as it uses Hegelian forms of thought and dialectic extensively, though with vastly different results. During the 1960s the critical orientation was taken up within forms of theory that are really at odds with each other. Post-structuralism, which like the Frankfurt School includes many authors whose works are radically different from each other, is not on the whole compatible with the concept of critique in the sense of critique within Western philosophy. Critique in the Western tradition of philosophy requires an understanding of "the negative;" of the *non-concept* of the subject, the "I." Foucault's famous statement, "the subject is dead," has been widely applied in counter-mainstream methodological discourses. It has been applied inconsistently and with unacknowledged contradictions. There is no critical theory that does not depend upon an understanding of "the subject" which must be understood in terms of "the negative" that in turn depends upon the concept of infinite.

Many who self-identify as post-structuralists also identify as criticalists and the result at the level of philosophical and methodological discourse is incoherent and contradictory. Poststructuralism influenced, and still influences, philosophical talk within social research communities in ways that are not helpful. They are not helpful either because the sources of the post-structuralist figures of thought used are not very well understood and the application is superficial; or because the post-structuralist author whose work is drawn upon falls within thinking and acting that is subject to what Gillian Rose calls "the broken middle." Rose (1992) wrote a book named *The Broken Middle* where she laments the influence of post-structuralism on social theory and action. Here is a passage from her introduction to the book:

> In post-structuralist discourses ". . . 'truth' is revealed to be a value among values; 'rationality', 'justice', and 'freedom' to be types of domination; the faculties of the soul to serve the administration of bodies; while reflexivity and conceptuality are said to be posited by 'discourses', so that meaning is merely the mark of arbitrary, differential signalizations; . . ."
>
> *(Rose, 1992, p. xiii)*

There is much that is valuable in the work of post-structuralists but their work needs to be read *critically.* The broken middle usually refers to an important insight that is significantly lacking in mainstream theory,[2] which is then used in a way that contradicts the insight itself. The results are well summarized in the above quotation from Rose. Hence during the 1960s the critical orientation was practiced and pursued without a grasp of the infinite under the influence of post-structuralism as well as misunderstandings of post-structuralism. This remains the case today.

Jürgen Habermas, meanwhile, directed critical theory, during the 1960s towards critical communicative pragmatism. Habermas's student, Axel Honneth, continued to develop critical theory with a new and extremely important emphasis on recognition. Social ontology has to include the ontological dimensions of recognition and some of the reasons for that come into discussions below. Habermas and Honneth have *not* been used to any significant extent in counter-mainstream researcher communities. Their work, perhaps especially Habermas's, hasn't been popular nor well understood. When we read or hear "critical" in our field(s) it is very unlikely that Habermas's work, or Honneth's work, has much of anything to do with it.

There is a third form in which "critical" is used in theory and methodology today. We also have theories and discourses that use the word "critical" without, seemingly, much influence from original critical theory *or* post-structuralism. "Critical" is understood to mean an oppositional stance to the oppressive features of socio-political and cultural formations and systems. Use of the word "critical" in this case lacks a connection with its original formulation as a theory of knowledge, power, and both social and personal being, but instead because of the *telos* of critical work—its purposes and goals.

Picture-thinking: What is Wrong with the Perception Paradigm for Knowledge and Ontologies of Presence?

Infinite, In-finite, Not-finite

Now it is time to start clarifying what "the infinite" means in the context of critical philosophy and theory. First, here is what you should *not* think when you read the word "infinite" in essays like this one. When we see or hear the word "infinite" most of us think of a process that never ends (time-framed idea of infinite), or an emptiness that extends without boundaries (space-framed idea of infinite). Those understandings are too limited to capture what the infinite means in critical and dialectical discourse as well as in Derrida's various works performing deconstructions.

Think of "infinite" as "in-finite"; as *not*-finite. The finite is anything that has determinations. Determinations give the boundaries of an object, event, concept, or thought.[3] Because there are boundaries, the entity is finite. So whatever infinite is, it has something to do with not having determinations and/or not having *sufficient* determinations.

What are some of the ways we might use "infinite" in this sense of no or too few determinations? For this essay the focus is on two sorts of infinite: that to which the word "transcendental" is applied and that to which the word "transcendent" is applied. In the first case we have the unknowable yet inescapable non-concept and non-entity represented with "I." The word "I" comes up in explorations of experience through the concepts of form, unity, and judgment. It comes up in explorations of human action through the concept of freedom and the traditional concept of "will." In the second case, "transcendent," we are dealing with the idea of entities, substances, forces, energies, etc. that we believe to exist but that we do not actually experience directly.

The infinite is missing when picture-thinking occurs uncritically to provide understandings and explanations for fundamental concepts like knowing and being. Much of the methodological talk and writing in researcher communities self-identifying as "critical" is stuck or perhaps half-struck in picture-thinking.

Picture-thinking is totally taken for granted in mainstream methodologies for social research, but criticisms of mainstream methodologies mostly substitute one picture for another, or take the basic picture underlying empiricism or positivism and merely remove and/or redefine its specific components. Critical theory in the original sense begins consciously with the full transcendence of picture-thought in general, not with a new picture. What, however, do I mean by picture? We need to examine that next.

What is Picture-thinking?

The term "picture-thinking" does not mean only thinking that uses pictures *literally*. People vary in what they say about how they think. Many people I've known say they do think in almost explicit images. Others claim they do not think in images at all, and yet when they talk or write there does seem to be underlying spatial forms from which the talk or writing came. When reading difficult philosophical texts it is possible to intuit an image structure underlying the linguistically articulated arguments and explications. Once such an intuition occurs, the reading becomes much easier. Everyday talk more explicitly uses images and relations between images to convey concepts. Gestures that accompany talk have shapes that convey ideas pictorially such as pointing to the left when talking about the past, making a wave motion when talking about the ups and downs of life or history or convictions or moods. In the analysis of qualitative interviews it is always good to code for every metaphor used in the talk because metaphors usually convey images and shapes underlying concepts: "My life has been a tough climb," "She hides behind a wall," "Being in that class was being in a dark hole with no hope of escape."

A broader characterization of picture-thinking involves the concepts of "form" and "determination." Abstract concepts like "whole," "hierarchy," "field," "cycle," "inner/outer," "rhythm," "immediate," "beyond," "substance," "differentiated/undifferentiated," "network," "process," "relation," "construction," "position," and so on, correspond to basic spatially conceived forms like "horizontal/vertical," "intersection," "circle," "spiral," "rectangle," "structure," "system," etc. Concepts have a determined, finite form in uncritical picture-thinking. Space, not time, is used to represent differences—when time is used to express a difference, like "I am totally different now than I was back then," the temporal difference has a spatial representation—in the cultures I am familiar with, the past is to the left and the future to the right, or the past is behind and the future is ahead. Or, as in diagrams representing the light-cones of general relativity theory, below is past and above is future. Cultures differ in the spatial relations they give in representations, but the picture, spatial representation itself, is everywhere. Everything that in some sense *is*, can be represented as a component within a picture.

Picture-thinking is not a problem per se, and in fact it is probably unavoidable. We have problems when an effort to understand the process of picturing by representing *that process itself* within the picture it creates. Uncritical picture-thinking cannot be used to *reflect* upon itself without inclusion paradoxes.[4] When ideas spanning *fundamental* concepts like knowing, experience, being, and reality are thought together in a picture we will have a contradiction. When thinking in pictures, pre-pictures, or images we need to do so with *critical* awareness. A picture may arise in the mind when hearing the linguistic expression of a concept like "being," but as it does we need to simultaneously understand that the representation is inherently false if reified. What it represents must be a way of or a direction of thinking *next*.

The point seems obvious when articulated and yet it must be non-obvious and hard to acquire prior to its thematization in discourse because it seems that *all* textbooks on mainstream social science research methodology, discussing both quantitative and qualitative research, are in picture-thought without any expressed awareness that this is the case. The sections on qualitative social research I keep finding in introductory books emphasize looking for *patterns*—which means relations that appear from an external, observation position. Knowledge is understood totally in terms of *models* and when knowledge is in the form of a model, we have picture-thought.

Knowing Understood as Perceiving, Being as Presence

Knowing Trapped within the Paradigm of Visual Perception

When picture-thinking occurs uncritically, the root metaphor for the concept of knowing is that of seeing something clearly. Biases are then thought of as distortions to seeing clearly: wearing colored glasses, seeing from a single privileged perspective determined by culture, seeing from one out of many social positions, seeing in ways that are unconsciously pre-structured by language, etc. How many times have we read or heard the metaphor of "colored lenses" or simply "lenses" to represent the idea of knowing something partially, and/or with bias, and/or relativistically? What about the metaphor of a "standpoint"? How about "perspective," "angle of vision"? But of course there is nothing wrong with these metaphors per se and in fact it is very difficult to refrain from using metaphors for knowing and for bias that do not use imagery from visual perception. But using them unconsciously reproduces a deep-seated, usually taken-for-granted, concept of knowing that has visual perception as its paradigm. Using such metaphors critically is okay. Critical use means that we articulate the metaphor and then next problematize it to give some indication of how it is misleading.

Perception is actually a *derivative* way of knowing, not a primary one. And yet I confess I find it hard myself to refrain from using ocularcentric expressions for knowing. This difficulty no doubt has something to do with culture though I don't believe it is culture alone. In our cultures we have a huge number of commonly used ocularcentric expressions for knowing: "I'm in the dark about such and such," "She showed me the light," "The European Enlightenment," "This theory illuminates such and such."

An Ontology of Presence

Uncritical picture-thinking also carries an ontology of presence with it. Here is how we can understand "ontology of presence." If knowing in general is conceptualized through an extension of the metaphor of visual perception then we have, in the metaphor, in the image, both a perceiver and an object perceived. There is an implicit idea of being associated with the object perceived in this picture. We imagine a universe of objects and events and processes, all of which have the conceptual structure of something that could be brought into the presence of an experiencing (perceiving) subject. This ontology of presence is fundamental to the concepts of time and space that frame the notion of being in terms of presence. Things exist when they persist in time. If we perceive an object and then look away for a while we expect the object to remain where we saw it and as we saw it. If we look again and it has changed shape or moved this is because some force, also existing without dependence on being perceived, acted upon it when we were not looking.

Time is distinct from being. The commonsense ways of understanding knowing, being, time, and space are at bottom consistent with scientific realism. Scientific realism includes models of reality that involve more than three or four dimensions, that represent time as "space-time," that make use of fundamentally non-perceivable entities and forces like electrons and neutrons and that handle pictorial (but not mathematical) contradictions like "wave/particle duality," "superposition," and "entanglement." All of that remains within the fundamental framework of an ontology of presence.

Consciousness, awareness, the perceiver, "mind" are concepts pertaining to the non-objective side of the image of a perceiver and an object perceived. They too are structured conceptually by an ontology of presence, but in ways we need to explore next.

What About the Subject? An Infinity Entailed by Picture-thought

It is very hard indeed to transcend picture-thinking because commonsense understandings of being, existence, time, knowledge and so on are picture-dependent, stuck within the ontology of presence and an epistemology that regards *all* knowing with a single metaphor: visual perception. Hence, how do we think of the *being* of the perceiver and the *being* of the perceiving?

When we move from the being of *objects* of experience to the being of the *experience* itself we find ourselves picturing experience as if it had the being of a physical *process* of some kind. A "process" is something on the objective, not subjective, side of visual perception. If we call experience a process, we have left experience itself and brought in a model from the outside. Now, experience is a concept that is subtly immanent and necessary in any exploration of the concept of being. This is because of such events as misrecognition: experiencing an object as a kind of object (e.g., seeing a butterfly) and then discovering that our initial perception was a misperception (e.g., the butterfly was actually a moth). An appearance versus reality distinction is unavoidable. Experience is always experience *of* something *as being* something. We do not experience experience itself. Yet it is a necessary conceptual contrast that brings out the concept of being and of objects and of objectivity. It is a "negative," as we will soon discover.

The concept of the *subject* of experience is also unavoidable but more difficult to raise into understanding. It has to do with several things that become apparent through careful attention. The "I" is entailed with the unity of experience generally—that fact that all experience is "my" experience for each of us. It also is entailed with responsibility. In Kant's terminology, the experience of an object or a relation between objects, e.g., of a butterfly as a butterfly, is the result of a "judgment" that might be wrong and that an "I" is responsible for. A deep sense of the meaning of responsibility is entailed in our understanding of experience.

But within an ontology of presence, experience cannot be represented accurately. People model it as a process of some kind but that is not true to experience itself. Within an ontology of presence, "the subject" cannot be represented accurately. People do represent it with words like "self" and it is implicit to concepts of "person" but unless we use such terms critically we mistakenly think of "the subject" as if it were an object.

It is difficult to do anything other than think of the being of the perceiver, of the subject, of experience as it they were objects but when this is done we have a self-contradiction. Our first glimpse of the infinite occurs when we understand this conceptual difficulty:

> *Neither the happening of an experience nor the subject of experience can be thought,*
> <u>*without contradiction*</u>*, in terms of something structured as if it could be brought into*
> *the presence of an experiencing subject*

Again, experience cannot itself be experienced. The subject of experience cannot itself be experienced. Any concept of an experiencing subject would have to be of something that *cannot* be experienced itself and hence cannot have the form of being we have in an ontology of presence.

Picture-thinking and the Oppressive Features of Mainstream Social Science

Mainstream social and psychological sciences work uncritically within picture-thinking. The concept of knowledge in general comes from a root metaphor of visual perception. Being is understood in the framework of presence. The subject is not understood: the infinity, what we will soon understand as the pure negativity, of *subject-ness*, of what we are concerned with when we use the word "I," is covertly placed in the position of a universal observer. This constructed position is actually, more fundamentally but also more covertly, that of a universal instrumental-actor (the subject side of *measurement*). Infinities are unrecognized. The infinity of the observer is its unknowability and the infinity of the instrumental actor is an unconsciously presupposed notion of freedom that is covertly entailed by the concept of action itself.

Thus, in mainstream social science, persons are studied as objects to the extent that they are taken to be observational units with attributes that distinguish them from each other. Attributes are operationalized and made into variables that display external correlational relations to other variables based on the operationalization of other attributes.

When correlations are found in mainstream social research there is often an effort to demonstrate causality. But the concept of cause is *entirely* external. When we look for causation in social and psychological phenomena we are trying to produce knowledge in this same structure. We want measureable conditions within which humans act and think; measurable attributes distinguishing persons and groups of persons from other persons and groups. We want to be able to correctly predict what will happen in a way we can measure from an external position when a measurable intervention is made to a known set of initial social and/or psychological conditions.

Social and psychological scientists need not employ a strict definition of "cause" and they can also avoid the concept of causation altogether, while using the same observation-based methods. If we know the gender, socio-economic group, race, and age of a person we can predict, through a probabilistic formula, whether they will vote Republican or Democrat. If we are asked to explain the reason for the probabilities we can give them in non-causal terms: such a person is likely to choose the candidate they vote for because they think the person will act on the same values and for the same interests had by the voter. Those things are in principle also "measureable" within the methodological assumptions of mainstream social science: we can use an "instrument" to find out what values our participants endorse and act on. We can use an "instrument" to find out what various beliefs our participants have. When we conduct research on those things, we fix in advance the range of possible values and beliefs. Or we might use a more qualitative approach, still from the position of an external observer, and have open-ended questions on our "instrument" that we then code. We code with emergent determinations that originate from our participants rather than ourselves.

What we cannot do, using any of these methods, is fully question the validity of values and beliefs we "measure" through communicative reasoning with our participants. As will soon become clear, the validity of this sort of research is entirely canon-based. It tacitly makes a distinction between infinity and finitude that has ideological origins and effects.

Picture-thinking and the Failure of Many *Counter*-mainstream Philosophical and Methodological Discourses

Counter-mainstream social research is implicitly aware of the problems, limitations and oppressive features, of mainstream research. But, in my experience and reading at least, there is no awareness of the missing infinite behind limitations and ideological distortions. Hence they counter the mainstream in their methodological and philosophical talk *without* transcending picture-thinking.

The categories used to distinguish persons and groups from each other are understood to be culturally contingent and too often in the service of differentials in social and cultural power. But the solution provided simply adds a concept of "construction" to the same basic picture.

The claim that there is a universal observer and measurer position is not taken-for-granted as it is in mainstream social research. Indeed, those positions claimed to be universal are actually biased and function to serve privileged groups. The universal neutral-observer positions are not really neutral, they are used to impose power in order to maintain or even extend privilege. Hence the knowledge produced is not in any sense "objective." But the counter philosophical position articulated *continues to think of knowledge as perception* but denies that there is any possible position from which unbiased knowledge could be produced. Hence *all* knowledge is a matter of power as are *all* concepts of truth, and standards of validity.

Counter-mainstream researchers realize that norms in social life are not in any sense absolute but rather exist in some relation to power and privilege, which is especially noticeable if we examine what a culture considers to be "normal." They counter this by claiming that *all* norms are impositions from outside, *all* normativity is something to critique or "deconstruct." There is no such thing as a rationally valid norm. The concept of "norm" is pictured as an external force placed upon already existing individuals and communities. They fail to distinguish between "norm," "normative claim," and "normal;" undermining any possibility of bringing out a viable concept of intersubjectivity for understanding social ontology.

The counter-mainstream discourses grasp the fact that rational arguments are always on hand to legitimize forms of normativity, knowledge claims, typologies of person-types as if those things were "objective." They counter this by claiming that *reason itself* is always a form of power only, and "truth" is always a type of "regime" without any basis other than being claimed to be true by powerful groups of people (or in the case of those influenced by Foucault, through the workings of a subject-less, objectified concept of power that fully instantiates an ontology of presence).

The concept of "subject" is taken-for-granted in mainstream social research. When it is examined, however, we find that we have conceptualized it as if it were an object. Different cultures and the different historical periods of traditions have had different ways of conceptualizing and talking about the human self. As an object, these notions of self have supported ideologies. It is contradictory to think of the "I" as an object, and hence contradictory if we think of selves *only* as objects. Hence counter-mainstream discourses have simply declared the "self" to be an illusion that is best done away with altogether. "The subject is dead." The general picture, however, remains. Just remove the components of the picture that represent "selves." Or keep selves in the picture but add objective processes like discourses or the movements of power and believe that selves are entirely constructed by those processes.

The point is, picture-thinking remains. The perception paradigm is still being used for knowing in general. There is still a missing infinite. Articulated epistemological and ontological positions are self-contradictory.

Infinity and the Transcendental Turn: Critique and Critical Philosophy in Transcendental and Quasi-transcendental Form

Any picture or image used for fundamental concepts of knowing and being produces its concepts of being, objects, and objectivity through an absolute contrast with the subject. The subject cannot be included in the image or picture without contradiction.

When this escaping subject feature of picture-thinking is noticed, another picture comes to mind: a picture of a subject outside a picture. That too, when understood, gives us yet another picture of a picture and we realize quickly that an infinite non-ending sequence, a process, results if we try to produce a determinate concept of subject or "I."

Hegel called non-ending sequences like this the "bad infinite." He meant a form of infinity one encounters on the way to grasping a dialectical "good infinite." In contemporary thought, the infinite series produced when trying to capture the "I" as if it were something knowable in the way we seem to know everything else is called an "inclusion paradox." There are many forms of this paradox that result from self-reference: trying to include the *concept* of some whole *in* that whole itself. Graham Priest examines a great many forms of this paradox in *Beyond the Limits of Thought* (Priest, 2002). Hegel and Priest both produce ontologies that understand contradiction in terms of *being*: "real," "actual," "in-the-world" contradictions. We are moving towards Hegel's work with infinity and must move through the concept of "transcendental" on the way.

Kant: The Transcendental Turn

The infinite, not-finite, unknown and unknowable can be initially explicated with the help of the concept of "transcendental." The word "critical" in the sense of critical philosophy and critical theory originates with the "transcendental turn" in Western philosophy.

In the Western philosophical tradition "critical" originates in Kant's conception of critique: his *Critique of Pure Reason*, *Critique of Practical Reason*, and *Critique of Judgment* (Kant, 1965, 1993, 1952). Kant's idea was that we need to examine the nature of reason *before using* reason in our scientific and philosophical work. Doing so will inform us of the legitimate and illegitimate employments of reason. If we know what those are we will not waste time producing transcendent (not transcendental) metaphysical systems that are the product, according to Kant, of the illegitimate use of reason. Examine reason first, use it in legitimate ways for producing knowledge next.

Hegel famously criticized the idea of clarifying the nature of reason before using it. We have to use reason already to try to clarify what reason is. "But to seek to know before we know is as absurd as the wise resolution of Scholasticus, not to venture into the water until he had learned to swim" (Hegel, 1975, p. 14). Yet Kant's work was very important despite this flaw. It enabled many subtle advances in Western philosophies that followed. We will go to Hegel after we have understood just a few key features of Kantian philosophy.

Kant introduced the modern idea of transcendental conditions of possibility. Let's be sure we understand the important difference between transcend*ent* and transcendent*al*. Kant made this distinction but often in various literature, the two terms are used as if they mean the same thing. Something unknowable but thought to be objectively real is transcend*ent*. Kant thought that phenomena, the objects of experience, must be generated in some way by noumena, things as they really are outside of any experience of them. Noumena are transcend*ent*.

By contrast, transcendent*al* refers to necessary conditions for the possibility of all experience that cannot themselves be experienced. Transcendental also refers to conditions necessarily presupposed in human activity.

Kant distinguished between theoretical reason and practical reason. Theoretical reason is cognitive. It is employed in our perceptions of objects as both external (like physical objects, processes, etc.) and internal (subjective states such as moods, feelings, and sensations). Theoretical reason operates in the synthesis of sensations *received* through senses. Practical reason *produces* its objects rather than synthesizes anything received. Practical reason involves both means–ends reasoning associated with instrumental actions and moral reasoning. The object of an instrumental action is a factual state of affairs that the act brings about. The object of a moral action is the conduct of the actor, the nature of the act itself rather than the consequence of the act.

A transcendental condition for practical reason is freedom, or free will. "Practical means everything possible through freedom" (Rose, 1981: 46). We distinguish between human actions that were caused (such as being pushed from behind) and actions that were not caused by anything other than the actor herself. In everyday life that distinction is unavoidable—we hold people responsible, accountable, for their actions to the extent that their actions will not be externally caused. Yet freedom itself, free will, cannot be *known* to exist or not exist. Nor can it be produced as an object through practical activity. It can at most be *demonstrated* but the effort to demonstrate one's freedom produces contradictions that are addressed in Hegelian dialectics and crucial to critical theory.

Critique is the process used to uncover, articulate, transcendental conditions. It is the use of reflection to explicate those conditions linguistically. Kant called his philosophical work "critical;" "critical philosophy." This was a huge contribution to Western philosophy but there are problems with the method of critique that we will consider shortly.

After Kant: Quasi-transcendental Theories of Knowledge in Social Theory

After Kant the insight underlying the notion of philosophical *critique* was developed in a number of directions. Many of these move from a concept of consciousness as the location of transcendental conditions to sociological, linguistic, and/or cultural-historical conditions. A typical way in which this is done is to *first* conduct an immanent critique, from a participant's position within a social class, a culture, a language etc., that explicates previously unnoticed transcendental conditions used in routine interpretations of experience, concepts of person and world, self-understandings, etc. *Second*, an empirical inquiry is made to discover causes, objective determinants, which produced the transcendental conditions. If the conditions discovered through immanent critique are cultural, then we can ask just why this *particular* culture came into being historically and what functions for the social system associated with this culture are served by those transcendental structures. Hence in Marxist theories, a combination of the historically contingent forces and social relations of production determine ideologies that are equivalent to "false consciousness."

Rose calls the process of developing this sort of theory "meta-critique." They are "meta-critical" theories of knowledge in the sense that the second step taken, seeking empirical explanations for the quasi-transcendental categories, relativizes what had emerged as transcendental, and in this way moves the thought process, the philosophical movements used as critique, to another, broader, domain: the transcendental categories of the position from which contingent transcendental conditions were objectivated.

Transcendental conditions that can be objectivated and subjected to empirical study are not really transcendental. They operated transcendentally until critique revealed them. Once explicated and examined they no longer shape experiences in pre-conscious ways. Hence they should be called "quasi-transcendental."

There is a fundamental problem with theories that use a quasi-transcendental framework. In Rose's (1981) words:

> when it is argued that it is society or culture which confers objective valid-
> ity on social facts or values, then the argument acquires a metacritical or
> 'quasi-transcendental' structure. The social or cultural *a priori* is the pre-
> condition of the possibility of actual social facts or values (transcendental).
> The identified, actual, valid facts or values can be treated as the objects
> of a general logic (naturalistic). The status of the precondition becomes
> ambiguous: it is an *a priori*, that is, not empirical, for it is the basic of the
> possibility of experience. But a 'socio-logical' *a priori* is, *ex hypothesi*, exter-
> nal to the mind, and hence appears to acquire the status of a natural object
> or cause. The status of the relation between the sociological precondition
> and the conditioned becomes correspondingly ambiguous in all sociologi-
> cal quasitranscendental arguments.
>
> *(p. 15)*

This is important to understand because there seem to be *plenty* of uses of meta-critique resulting in a theory that includes quasi-transcendental domains. But there is this self-contradicting circularity in such theories. Classical sociologists like Marx, Durkheim, and Weber were at least aware that their theories of knowl-edge had transcendental features. Durkheim and Weber consciously drew upon neo-Kantian philosophies popular in their day. Marx understood that his base-superstructure model meant that the theory of base and superstructure would itself be determined from the base and hence very possibly be ideologically distorted.

Assessing Transcendental Theories of Knowledge: The Knowing and Being Connection; Limitations

It is Kant's concept of the "transcendental I," with infinity understood as the absolute non-object, and his work on moral-practical reason, with infinity in the form of freedom, that is most relevant to the themes of this essay. This is because these infinities have an intimate relation to human ontology and human needs. The being of a person cannot be captured in any finite representation. This is because what we *are* includes our self-knowledge, sometimes called our "self-relation." And our self-knowledge is self-transcending. Hyppolite (1974) wrote about Hegel's concept of human being as follows: "It is human being that never is what it is and always is what it is not" (p. 150).

In our version of critical communicative pragmatism we take over George Herbert Mead's distinction between the "I" and the "me," as it is expanded by Habermas (see especially Chapter 5 of Habermas, 1987). Our form of existence includes a self-understanding that has an object-like form, the "me," the kind of person from a culturally contingent structure of possible persons we claim to be and receive recognition for being, and an infinite, the "I," understood as the source of our existential claims, the judge of such claims. The "I" feature of human ontology "never is what it is and always is what it is not" (Hyppolite, 1974, p. 174). It is not a thing, not finite in any way, but rather the negative of the "me." The notion of a "transcendental I" is enlightening with respect to human-being because self-knowing is an essential feature of our being.

Kant's infinite in practical reason is freedom, autonomy, the unconditioned (not caused, not determined) source of action, and that which has responsibility, accountability for one's actions. The theory of human identity in our version of critical communicative pragmatism is all about the ontology of *claiming* ourselves in our actions. The infinite is an essential structure of identity claims. As we will soon see in more detail, Kant's theory of moral action helps us understand the ontological motivation to both affirm and confirm ourselves as autonomous, responsible, free agents. There is an interesting contradiction between affirmation and confirmation in Kant's moral theory that has a profound resolution in Hegel's dialectic of moral consciousness.

The *limits* of transcendental thought include their own picture-like status. When we hear "transcendental I" and "the transcendental categories" we can easily imagine a domain of objects that is accessible to our experience with a border enclosing it. On the other side of the border there is a sort of space that in some way possesses transcendental categories, a space that narrows, cone-like, to an end, a point at the tip of a cone, that can be named the "transcendental I." Obviously this is not entirely satisfactory. Helpful as it is, the transcendental "I" of Kant's theoretical reason is too easily thought of as a thing that can be represented in a picture. The transcendental component of Kant's moral theory, and more generally his theory of practical reason, does escape picture-thinking. But, as philosophers after Kant sought to do, theoretical and practical reason can be brought together.

The Place of Validity in an Ontology of Self-movement Towards Self-actualization

Expressivism: Validity as Recognition

An alternative to canon-validity and the knowing-as-perceiving paradigm is what Charles Taylor calls "expressivism" (see Chapter 1 in Taylor, 2015). We experience the idea core to expressivism all the time. Our communicative actions begin with an implicit notion of what the act will communicate if we do act it out rather than censor it. Acting expressively clarifies that beginning, implicit notion. It actualizes the impetus that gave rise to it. When our action has completed we either *recognize* in the result what we implicitly understood just prior to the act, or we do not. Usually what we recognize in our expressions is the partial actualization of the impetus. We can think of artists, novelists, actors, and actresses to help us understand what we experience in mundane ways all the time.

Validity in the form of recognition is a structure of expressive acts and expressive projects. Recognition is very different from canon-validity. There are no explicit rules to apply, no external position from which to determine the validity of the expression. We have to first experience the impetus to express and then perform the expression as an actualization of the impetus and this will result in an experience of recognition, partial recognition, or the failure of the act to express what we wished it to. What we wished to express was not explicitly formulated in any way before the action. It had not yet come into being.

Gillian Rose writes of Hegelian dialectic in a way that conveys what I've just written about expressivism. In the dialectics of Hegel's *Phenomenology of Spirit* (Hegel, 1977) there is a learning process that moves through stages. Consciousness, self-consciousness, actualizes itself in forms of being, moving from one stage to the next after experiencing contradictions. Self-actualizations result in contradictions between what was anticipated in the beginning and what is actualized at the end. The experience of contradiction results in a "notion," a deeper understanding oriented toward a possible future actualization. Here is what Rose writes of that "notion" which forms in the experience of contradiction:

> [The notion] is not pre-judged in two senses: no autonomous justification is given of a new object, and no statement is made before it is achieved. The infinite or absolute is present, but not yet known, neither treated methodologically from the outside as an unknowable, nor 'shot from a pistol' as an immediate certainty. This 'whole' can only become known as a result of the process of the contradictory experiences of consciousness which gradually comes to realize it.
>
> *(Rose, 1981, p. 49)*

Self-certainty, Action, and Being

Saying "I am" produces a non-falsifiable proposition, the validity of which is *demonstrated* in the very act of saying it. This is an ontological certainty. We know it just prior to any act, including any effort to know that we know it. Moreover, this is an implicit certainty of our infinity and essentiality that, however, is not actualized. Self-certainty is the "in-itself" of human existence. It is embedded in actions with the telos of actualizing ourselves so as to confirm ourselves. Our being in-itself is the movement to become being for-itself. We are not creatures who *have* a desire to self-actualize, confirm ourselves, we *are* the self-movement towards self-confirmation.

The Form and Content Distinction in Practical Action

Infinity in practical reason is freedom, the freedom of an agent who acts. Our freedom is our self-certainty, our being in-itself. How can this be actualized as a confirmation of our being? What sort of expressive actions could bring this about?

The *form* of an action that demonstrates our freedom is a purely non-caused act. In Kant's philosophy such an act is moral. Kant's moral theory is this: an action is a moral action if it is not influenced by any inclination (desire, fear, etc.) one might have nor by anything external to the actor such as political laws, threats of sanctions, etc. A moral action occurs when the act is one the actor could will for *all* human beings. No matter what feelings, fears, desires one has at the time, no matter what sanctions, good or bad, are expected as consequences to the act, the moral act is the act that is *right* because of its conformity to universality. Hence, truly autonomous action is moral action for Kant. The idea of an act that comes only from pure duty and is totally selfless accompanies this understanding of morality. Therefore, it is *moral* action that has the form demonstrating our infinity; that is, ourselves as autonomous, free.

Can we act morally though? Kant thought the *form* of an act can be universal—the act being an act that comes from a position of universality. Insofar as we can act from an identification with universal interests, we affirm our essence, our infinite, non-determined, fully autonomous being. But we cannot *confirm* our essence, we cannot *actualize* it because the content of every human action is particular, is related to specific contexts, has desires and fears and so on involved.

Kant's moral theory assumes a sharp distinction between the world of nature governed by causes and the "intelligible world" in which people interact with each other under the assumption of free will. This intelligible world is a world in which people can apply reasons to themselves and reasons are radically different than causes. Hence the form of a moral act affirms autonomy and freedom but its empirical actuality is caught in the world of nature more than the intelligible world.

Hegel critiqued Kant's sharp distinction between the domain of nature, where causal forces rule, and the domain of the "intelligible," where people act with and for reasons. He endorsed the form and content distinction Kant brought out for moral action but articulated it as a developmental dialectic. Understanding the gist of Hegel's moral dialectic will help us in our effort to bring out the infinite in critical communicative pragmatism.

To summarize this section, a non-canon form of validity is the core theme of expressivism. Validity is based on recognition. It is internal to content, not external in a set of rules. It is not applied to being but actually a part of being. Being is here understood as self-developing movement. Human ontology is a movement from a deeply implicit, non-actualized, self-certainty towards its actualization. The validity of a self-actualization is in the form of recognition: what is actualized corresponds to the telos of the impetus that gave rise to it. Validity is something experienced in relation to the affirmation and confirmation of the infinity of human-being: freedom, autonomy, and responsibility. Affirmation and confirmation are also realization and actualization.

The ontological needs for recognition core to human-being require recognition from an Other subject. Hegel presents a number of dialectical movements involved in social relationships and modes of recognition. We will examine two of them next.

Recognition Dialectics: Domination, Forgiveness and Love

Lordship and bondage: Contradictions between Subject–object and Subject–subject Framed Self-knowledge

The dialectic of Lordship and Bondage in the second book of Hegel's *Phenomenology of Spirit* is perhaps the most well-known and most influential segment of his philosophical system. What is less well known is a dialectic that comes later, in the section on the dialectics of moral consciousness, which sort of reverses the Lordship and Bondage form (see Disley, 2015 for a discussion of this). The Lordship and Bondage movement begins with a struggle for domination between two developing self-consciousnesses that results in a social relationship in which one dominates, as Lord, and the other is dominated, as Bondsperson. The dialectic in moral consciousness begins with an effort to act in a purely egoless way, act from pure duty alone, and ends with mutual, reciprocal forgiveness and love.

The second book of the *Phenomenology*, 'Self-Consciousness', is not about a cognitive dialectical progression of concepts but rather a dialectical progression of practices; actions in the world that include social interactions. Here we see the deeply implicit self-certainty of self-conscious existence playing a role in a development of actions and social relationships. Practical action has the telos of manifesting, actualizing, bringing into being the self-certainty that self-consciousness is infinite, essential, and free. This section of the *Phenomenology* begins after developing self-consciousness has learned that negating objects in nature fails to fully actualize its freedom and autonomy. A new desire arises as a result of this learning, the desire for recognition.

The desire for recognition emerges in the form of an implicit subject–subject structure. In the Lordship and Bondage dialectic this is a very primitive subject–subject structure whose contradiction involves the distinction between subject–subject and subject–object relations. Two developing self-consciousnesses, each having implicit self-certainty, attempt to demonstrate, prove, actualize their autonomy, freedom, and independence, forcing the other to recognize it. Each self-consciousness encounters the other and finds what she desires to confirm is external to herself. For each it is like seeing one's self as external to one's self. The struggle has the goal of proving the being of the other self-consciousness to have the form of being-for-me. Coercing recognition from the other should result in the other acting to deny its own essentiality, autonomy, and freedom by acknowledging essentiality and infinity to the other in the struggle. The end of the fight is a form of self-consciousness that is divided between a Lord and a Bondsperson. It is a relationship, a relationship of domination. The Bondsperson now mediates the relation the Lord has with nature by transforming objects of nature into the form of being-for the Lord (producing artifacts for the Lord, cooking food, etc.). The Bondsperson's essence, infinity, is alienated, experienced by the Bondsperson as external to itself in the being of the Lord.

A new learning process commences in the Bondsperson that leads to finding her essence within herself rather than alienated as the Lord. The Bondsperson changes forms in nature, for the Lord, according to her own non-caused plans. The Bondsperson does experience nature as independent in many ways. The Bondsperson changes forms by producing artifacts but cannot change matter, the content of nature's many entities. Some things in nature cannot be changed in their form and what working on nature can produce is constrained by natural "laws." But there is yet some self-affirmation in uncaused actions that change features of the physical world.

Dialectics of Moral Consciousness as Conviction

Does the human subject have to be the product of a life-and-death struggle, ending with domination? Or does it simply have to involve forms of domination which can be very subtle, based on such culturally contingent conditions as social statuses, positions of economic or political power, hierarchies in the evaluation of class cultures and national cultures? Hegel would have regarded this idea very superficial and in fact, wrong. We don't need to dominate other subjects to be a subject ourselves. But this is not a straightforward matter at all, as Hegel's moral dialectics show.

For Kant, moral actions are how we can act freely and autonomously. We act taking the interests of all people into account. We act for universal human interests rather than individual interests. But as we have seen above, the form of a Kantian moral act is self-affirming but its content fails to confirm the actualization of human autonomy and freedom.

Hegel's dialectics involve this contradiction between the form and the content of moral acts. In the final sections of a very long portion on morality in *The Phenomenology of Spirit* we find moral consciousness actualized as conscience in the form of conviction. The moral self-consciousness finds its implicit self-certainty in "conscience," "conviction." It implicitly knows that it will act only from pure duty. This is what it wants to do. This is what leads towards confirmation through further actualization. But in the efforts to act in purely moral ways consciousness learns that it is unable to manage it. This is due to the form and content problem that appears in Kant as an irreconcilable problem. An act may come from conscience, conviction, and thus be an act whose intention is only pure duty but as an empirical act it is within the domain of nature and causal relations. The act is particular, always possible to interpret as selfish and ego-claiming.

To make a detailed dialectic simplified, concentrating only on some of the key moments, I will describe the movements as follows. Self-consciousness is divided between two subjects who play two distinct roles. There is the subject who acts from pure duty and the subject who judges this act. Conviction that one is identified with pure universality is associated with being-for-itself: independence and autonomy, but in this case due to identification with universality. The act itself is associated with being-for-another. The act is only actualized through the recognition of a different consciousness. We can say that infinity is separated between two individuations: the actor identified with universality and acting from pure duty alone; and the consciousness who judges the act from the position of moral universality. The judge is not to judge for any individual motives but rather purely from the position of universal moral consciousness.

With its moral acts, the actor is conscious only of its pure intention to act selflessly. But the result of the act is recognized by the other as carrying selfish identity claims. The form of the act is self-affirming but the content contradicts it and can be experienced as "besmirching" the actor.

After various moments including that of a "beautiful soul" who does not act at all so as not to sully itself, the actor notices that the judge's acts of judgment *also* involve this form and content contradiction. The judgment given from the role of judge cannot be an act from pure universality—the position of universal human interests from which specific actions are morally assessed. The actor:

> looks at what the action [the act of judgment made by the Other] is in itself, and explains it as resulting from an *intention* different from the action itself, and from selfish *motives*. . . . If the action is accompanied by fame, then it knows this inner aspect to be a *desire* for fame. If it is altogether in keeping with the station of the individual, without going beyond this station, and of such a nature that the individuality does not possess its station as a character externally attached to it, but through its own self gives filling to universality, thereby showing itself capable of a higher station, then the inner aspect of the action is judged to be ambition, and so on. . . . . No action can escape such judgment, for duty for duty's sake, this pure purpose, is an unreality.
>
> *(Hegel, 1977, p. 404)*

The actor, not the judge, now acts in a new way. She has seen that the judge, like herself, cannot act from a position of pure universality. She sees herself in the judge, recognizes herself there.

> Perceiving this identity [with the Other, the judge] and giving utterance to it, he confesses this to the other, and equally expects that the other, having in fact put himself on the same level, will also respond in words in which he will give utterance to this identity with him, and expects that this mutual recognition will now exist in fact.
>
> *(Hegel, 1977, p. 405)*

She confesses in expectation that the other will also confess and a form of mutual recognition will actualize. This is not easy. We are familiar with interactions like this. A confession puts oneself at the mercy of the other, makes one vulnerable.

The next moment, however, is one in which the judge receives the confession of the actor but *does not* also confess. The judge position is now in a moment Hegel calls "the hard heart." As the dialectic continues we come to a moment in which the acting self-consciousness forgives the judging consciousness for her "hard heart." "The forgiveness which it extends to the other is the renunciation of itself" (Hegel, 1977, p. 407). The judge then, in turn, forgives the actor and a form of mutual recognition, constituted by forgiveness and love, has been actualized. With the self-renunciation of forgiveness and the reciprocal response of the other, the infinite, the universal and unconditioned, is found within the *intersubjectivity of a community*. It is no longer believed to be located in a single individual.

Relevance of the Moral Dialectic

Human beings cannot help but claim an identity for themselves with every action. Why is that the case? Hegel articulates this well: every action is particular, empirical, concrete, and involves desires. In addition, every act can be interpreted as an individuating identity claim by others, and human consciousness is structured intersubjectively, so that we internalize the positions of possible others and monitor our actions in this way. Acts carry individuating identity claims whether we want them to or not.

Identity claims are odd in several ways. First of all, there is generally something not true about them, something dishonest at a deep, ontological level. All identity claims have implications for the identities of other persons. Identity claims pull upon culturally contingent identity-structures; structures of difference between possible ways to be a person. To claim to be a certain kind of person is to claim one is *not* other possible kinds of person. Identity claims are actually also *identity-structure claims*. A whole structure is claimed valid, a structure of possible ways to be a person and evaluations of them into good, bad, okay, exemplary, etc. Unfortunately the normal case in most human cultures to date are hierarchical identity structures, inescapable identity-claiming reproduces person-structures in hierarchical form. That generally harms and oppresses groups of people. In interactions with friends, peers, and associates we often experience this moral structure: "for me to be someone has implications for *your* existential validity." We all experience the fact that when people interact, the identities claims made by one of the participants will have implications for the identity of the other participant. Like it or not, our identity claiming is a moral issue because it affects others.

The learning process described in Hegel's moral dialectics brings into being new forms of social relationships in which the principle of the unconditioned, the free and autonomous, the infinite, is discovered within the intersubjective milieu of a community. This is a profound insight that will be of help in unpacking the concept of an "emancipatory interest" in various versions of critical theory.

Communicative Action Theory

Habermas's *Theory of Communicative Action* (1981, 1987) is a critical theory that develops a form of communicative pragmatism as well as much more. Communicative pragmatics seems to escape canon-validity because its point of departure is the pragmatics of everyday communicative practices. Validity is *internal* to meaning. Habermas has produced a theory of meaning that resembles truth-conditional semantics. In truth-conditional semantics to understand a statement, with the sentence taken to be the minimal unit, is to understand the conditions under which its truth claim would be true or false. It is not to know *whether* the statement is true or false but the *conditions* of its truth or falsity. Habermas has taken the full speech act, not the sentence, as the minimum unit of meaning and he has expanded from a single truth claim to three validity claims: the objective, subjective, and normative claims. To understand the meaning of a speech act is to understand the conditions under which its validity claims would hold or not hold.

We have built upon Habermasian communicative pragmatics, filling out various regions within his theory and interpreting some of his work in certain directions. Transcendental-like structures appear in our critical theory as *validity horizons* that are internal to meaning in all communicative actions. Validity claims of all three types are internal to the meaning of the act but conveyed implicitly along a continuum from the foreground of meaning towards backgrounded regions. This serves as the horizon of intelligibility for every act and will differ in its components and their structural relations from act to act.

Thus communicative meanings are constituted not only by validity claims in the foreground but *claimed* horizons of intelligibility that serve the function given to transcendental and quasi-transcendental conditions in other socially based theories of knowledge. The components of validity horizons and the structural relations between them are reconstructable. They can be explicated, thematized, as foregrounds of new communicative actions. In everyday human interactions this occurs all the time. It is difficult, however, to explicate the very remote background regions of validity horizons and there is where the most deep-seated resourcing milieu for ideologies reside. Ideologies, however, involve many different levels on the validity horizons that carry them. It is most definitely possible to reconstruct and critique assumptions upon which various ideologies reside.

Ideology Critique

Ideological distortions in culturally contingent forms of knowing, interpreting, and experiencing are analyzed in critical theories of the quasi-transcendental, meta-critical type through a circular, self-undermining logic. First, using the reflective method of critique a transcendental-like domain is made explicit. This invokes an infinite/finite distinction separating form from content and then relating them to each other externally. Form constitutes canon-validity; externally applied rules to determine valid knowledge claims. Second, the infinite domain is brought into finitude, i.e. *empirical* knowability. The quasi-transcendental structures, which critique reveals as form, are now explained in terms of causal and causal-like determinants that come from social structure, economic relations of production, an objectified concept of power, and other entities or forces depending upon the particular theory. What was form now gains *content*. The components of the quasi-transcendental domain are put into empirical causal relations with other empirically accessible entities, systems, and forces. For example, in many versions of Marxism the "base" of society determines the "superstructure" and produces, in a causal manner, false consciousness. But what happens when form is objectified in this way? We have an unnoticed unity of form and content corresponding to the removal of the appearance/reality distinction. The transcendental-like forms employed in the ideological construction of appearances are now supposed to be real, not apparent, empirical objects. Yet the analysis began completely dependent upon the distinction between transcendentally structured experience (ideology) and what experiences are *of* (being). It is philosophically self-contradictory, self-defeating.

Ideological distortions in *critical communicative pragmatism* have the form of distorted conditions of communication. There are different forms of power that must be distinguished within the full theory but I am here concentrating on how power inter-relates with knowledge. Knowledge claims occur as validity horizons. Similar backgrounded regions in the validity horizons of aggregate routine communicative actions are claimed and reclaimed over and over at levels removed so far from meaning foregrounds as to be barely noticed. But they *can* be reconstructed for criticism and they have been in social movements such as GLBTQ movements, the Black Lives Matter movement, and feminist movements.

How is oppression *experienced* by members of oppressed groups? For the most empirically immediate forms of oppression, such as systemic physical violence exerted on Black people by police, the answer is obvious. Distortions in communicative relations involved with routine violence against some social groups by other social groups pertain to the ways that people can talk about legitimacy issues, the rule of law and rights. Serious constraints on oppressed groups for being heard, for their oppression to be widely visible, are a form of distortion in communicative relations. We don't need a complex philosophical theory of knowledge to understand the worst forms of oppression and to act against them.

There are forms of power, however, that operate as deep-ideologies. Many status differences in society are claimed legitimate over and over at remote levels of validity horizons.

There are ideologically functioning values, beliefs about the purpose of life, about what constitutes a good life, about how to be a valid person, an accomplished and respected person, about what a human self actually *is* and how human selves can and should relate to the world within which they live. Conditions for self-understandings, recognizing others, for choosing a course of life have ideological distortions at diverse levels, some accessible for reconstruction and criticism but others that are very hard to access. These are concepts including those of being, knowing, self, freedom. By what criteria, or through what sorts of experiences can we become aware of these most remote and taken-for-granted conditions for knowing, acting, and being?

Intersubjective Infinities

Now I am departing significantly from Habermas's critical theory although what I argue here I believe to be compatible with it. I will introduce, in this section, an answer to this question: "Does Hegelian dialectic have anything to contribute to critical communicative pragmatism?" My answer is "yes," and the contribution specifically concerns the theory of identity claims and their relation to validity claims.

The identity claim/validity claim distinction has the following significance. In terms of the most general relation of social formations and knowledge, the most basic and fundamental concepts constituting the routine communicative actions of a society entail an infinity/finitude distinction. This can change with the emergence of new cultures and social systems when their role in human-being, in existential identity claims, changes as a development of both knowing and being. Changes in our self-actualizations, our mode of existing, are change-contingent instances of infinity/finitude distinctions. Those distinctions are ontological. The infinite and finite of institutions of social practice are experienced within communicative interactions in a deep relation to human individual and collective self-becoming, self-actualizing, and self-realizing.

Philosophically, the identity claim that is unavoidably a part of every human communicative act is where we can find the "middle term" Gillian Rose writes about, the middle term that is missing in both mainstream social theories of knowledge and the most widely known and popular counter-mainstream theories. A validity canon employed in research is itself valid only in relation to the forms of being-through-acting available to members of the society within which such research takes place. The emancipatory interest, human freedom, autonomy, infinity grounds all other forms of validity claim contingent to a culture and society. Validity escapes canons when its ground is sought. The ground is at the unity of knowing and being, understood in terms of self-movement, self-actualizing, and self-realizing.

Form and Content Distinctions in the Structures of Identity Claims

The differentiation of validity claims from identity claims is our interest. Let's look at something like a developmental sequence of identity-claiming starting with the Lordship and Bondage dialectic and ending with communicative action.

1. *Differentiation of form of action from content as action consequence; the Lordship and Bondage dialectic*: the form of the act in the life-and-death struggle of the Lordship and Bondage dialectic is self-affirming because it is free insofar as it risks biological life. Self-certainty, being as free, infinite, and autonomous, is affirmed through the action. The actor acts in opposition to the causal-like fears and desires associated with the body as a form of life in nature. The form of the action is associated with the non-differentiation of an individual "I" and a universal "I."

   The content of the act is the action consequence. Another consciousness is coerced into denying its own autonomy, freedom, independence, and essentiality by recognizing the former actor as Lord, as the essence of its own being. Recognition must come from a free subject to be true recognition. It must not be forced, not be caused.

2. *Differentiation of form of action from content as conduct; the dialectics of moral consciousness as conviction:* the dialectics of moral consciousness in the state of conviction proceed through many moments. The moral consciousness of conviction begins with a distinction in the being of consciousness between being-for-itself and being-for-another. This distinction is actually related to the "I" and "me" distinction we use in critical communicative pragmatism. The "I" is the infinite in the form of the universality of pure duty. Self-certainty has the actualization of conviction, a form of being-for-itself. Hence the form of the act pertains to the pure intention of the actor, of acting from pure duty alone. The content of the act is its particularity whose actualization depends upon recognition from another.

   The infinite begins with a place within two individuals: one who acts with the intention of acting out of pure duty alone, and one who judges the act of the other, not as an individual but as the universality of moral reason.

   The contradiction occurs between the form and the content of the action, associated with the location of the infinite in two individuals. It is resolved through mutual forgiveness and love, infinity as the essence of self-consciousness actualizes within the *intersubjectivity of a community*.

3. *Differentiation of the form of action unified via the identity claim, and the content of action as the validity horizon; communicative reason*: with language, ontological identity claiming is separated from validity claims. The meaning of a communicative act is constituted by judgments expressed as content. Instead of a judgment of acts we have a judgment of judgments; assessing the validity of validity claims. The one addressed by a communicative action is able to judge, criticize the judgments of the communicator in distinction from the identity of the communicator.

   Those who receive speech acts and thus validity claims evaluate the claims with the *same* standards used by the original communicator. For example, an objective validity claim such as, "Her car is yellow," is a judgment made by the communicator with ground criteria of the procedure of observation. The *reasons* the communicator has on hand to legitimate this claim (such as reporting a direct observation of the car) are the *same reasons* that the addressee would use to assess the claim, to judge the judgment.

A validity claim carries a claim to universality similar to the universality associated with Kant's moral principle: we say "yes" or "no" to a validity claim for reasons we expect other humans to agree with because the basis we have for making a validity claim is the same basis that another person would use to assess the validity of the claim.

The formal first, second, and third person positions in the architecture of communicative actions are juxtaposed in the constitution of meaning. If we understand the meaning of a communicative act we understand reasons that would support its constituting validity claims as any first-person actor would understand them, thus as any second-person addressee understands them and as any third-person observer would understand them.

This universality is *claimed* necessarily as part of communication action. The universality claim is unavoidable but it is usually wrong for reasons that become apparent in time: through learning processes and ideology critique.

Thus the infinity of the "I" is universalized in communicative reason. The communicator, the one addressed, an observer of the communication comprise an identity, a "we." Any possible person could take any one of the three formal positions in relation to a communicative act and understand it by understanding reasons that could be articulated in support of it.

Notice that communicative interactions necessarily presuppose the subject-status, the autonomy, infinity, freedom of those participating. "I" communicate to "you" and in doing so I recognize you as a free and autonomous subject, who relates to herself also as "I" and who relates to me as "you." The third person observer position is one in which meaning is understood by virtually taking the positions of the communicators. It is a "she" that is also "I" and "you." When we understand meaning, and reasons that support the validity claims constituting meaning, we are simultaneously in first-, second-, and third-person positions each universalized.

The implicit structure of communication presupposes this equality of the participants and every communicative act is made assuming the autonomy and freedom of the other participants. But this does not mean *actual* recognition of equality, mutual recognition. Indeed, participants in communication can and too often do regard each other more as objects than as fellow subjects. This means that the implicit structures of communication can be in contradiction with how people treat each other. The implicit structures are sort of the "in-itself" of communicative reason. The in-itself is often not actualized, people claiming identities for others that position them oppressively in hierarchies of culturally contingent person typologies.

At the level of the in-itself, the constitution of the communicative situation, the "I," the infinite, resides within *intersubjectivity*, not individuals, in the milieu of communicative reason. It is the "I" that is also "we." It is not an individuated "I" but it actualizes in the moments of identity claiming embedded within the individualities of "me."

Recognizing Reasons/Recognizing Persons

But what are reasons? Reasons that support a validity claim are potential communicative expressions, expressive actions that are *recognized* as such. Recognizing reasons involves expressive validity, recognition validity as discussed in a section rather far above. Recognition validity is within the first-person position of the actor who actualizes an impetus. But reasons have the intersubjectively universal structure: "I" who is "you," "I" who is "we." Hence we do not have to be the actual actors who produce a result that turns out to be recognizable as an actualization of its impetus. We recognize the result because we can *find* that impetus in intersubjective space and thus understanding it meaning knowing how to express it ourselves.

Recognizing reasons is distinct from the recognition of persons in terms of their "me" claims. We can recognize and then actively consent to an expressed validity claim in any number of ways, some affirming the individuated identity of the other and some negating it.

Freedom and Reasons

Reasons are distinguished from causes fundamentally. To agree or disagree with a validity claim is to act *freely*. If an expression of agreement were caused to happen, it would not *be* an agreement. It would not have actualized the freedom, autonomy, of the actor to agree or not agree.

Why do people respond *rationally* to validity claims as opposed to responding to them according to individuated desires and fears? If someone presents us with convincing reasons to deny ourselves sleep in order to help in an emergency, we *can* say "no" even if we are convinced by the reasons. We want to sleep. We don't want to undergo the sacrifices required to provide this help. So why would we ever say "yes" to a reason in a context like this? Sometimes we do not. If we act *for* reasons we endorse then it is because our infinity, our freedom, our subject-being as opposed to object-being, is actualized by doing so. We act from a universal position rather than an individuated one because this affirms our infinity, our beyond-determinations.

All validity claims have this freedom and universality intrinsic to them. If our friend says to us, "Her car is yellow and I know this is true because such and such," we can be convinced by the reasons because we recognize them—they are also *our* reasons in that we have found their impetus and could act from it as our friend did. But we are *free* to just say "No" to this claim. We are not caused to express agreement with it.

The "I–me"

Actual actions in the world always do have individuated, "selfish" features to them. Here we find the dialectical structure of moral consciousness as conviction. But here it is in a different context or level. In the actions of moral consciousness as conviction the entire *act* as a singularity is judged; the identity claim is the act as judged, evaluated by another. The content is the act itself. By contrast, in communicative actions there is a communicative content, composed of objectivated judgments made by the actor and presented for themselves, as judgments, to be judged by those receiving the act. The judgments making up the content is the validity horizon; the validity horizon is independent of the ontological identity claim.

In communicative actions we still have the contrast between purity and self-claiming that we found in moral dialectics. A "me" is claimed along with the "I." The "me" is the individuating feature of an act, oriented toward recognition from a different subject. Every act can be judged in terms of the "kind of person" that the actor is and/or claims to be as indicated by the act. Cultures vary a great deal in terms of the intersubjective resources they provide for claiming "me" and for positioning others as certain types of "me" through one's communicative actions. These are usually hierarchical: some kinds of person are better than others. And often the hierarchies include domination: for one type of person, one "me" to be of value, worthy of recognition and respect, another type of person, another "me," must be less worthy. There are often identity-sets of interdependent types of possible person.

Human identity can be best thought of as "I–me" relations, and this is why. What do we make of intersubjectively based and understood reasons that justify blocking the use of reasons in communicative negotiations? This happens all the time and systemically. The "I" that is the essence of self-consciousnesses within a community, the "I" that is a "we," is often constrained in its opportunities for self-affirming actions. "Because you are such and such a kind of person, we don't need to listen to you. Your reasoning is not of value." The "me" that is claimed *for* another, confining that other, is oppressive because it curtails the infinity, the freedom, of "I." That is an "I–me" relation.

There are many, many diverse forms and levels of ideology that work through contingent *conditions of possibility for acting in freedom*, for affirming the "I." Notice that the actualization, the truth of the "I," is intersubjective, a "we." Possibilities for individuating "me" claims invoke a community structure of potential "me"s in relations with each other, affecting each other, dependent upon an assumed "we."

Freedom is a mode of being and acting. It is the "I" affirming itself in free actions resulting in "me" claims. The "me" feature of identity can be developed as one brings into being one's potentialities as a distinct individual. This is "self-realization." Self-realization is the development of richer and richer versions of ourselves. It is a confirming, ontological movement. The "I" is the universal, something we actualize through learning processes that develop our autonomy. This is "self-actualization." It is an actualizing, self-confirming, and ontological process too.

Power blocks self-actualizing and self-realizing movements at individual and community levels in many various ways. Ideologically the blockage concerns the intersubjective conditions of possibility for self-affirming interactions and a direction in life oriented toward ontologically confirming self-development. The implicit features of communication, its "in-itself," can become actualized, and have been actualized, in degrees. The "I" that is "we" and "we" that is "I" is false when the "we" is not a true "we."

The standard by which ideological distortions can be detected is human experience as human-being. It is ontological as well as epistemological. It is *existential validity*.

Conclusions

This essay has several purposes. It presents a critique of picture-thinking because picture-thinking seems to be dominant in both mainstream and counter-mainstream methodological discourse. It reviews the historical origins of the concept of "critical" in Western philosophy because while critical social research, critical social projects, are doing great work, methodological discussions are not challenging mainstream assumptions about knowing and being and validity as much as they could. Critical theories of the power–knowledge relation are formulated as practices, as an important form of ideology critique because mainstream notions of knowledge and method are indeed ideological and having significant, undesirable, socio-cultural effects.

I themed this essay with the concept of "infinite" and the role played by finite/infinite distinctions in both popular and institutional cultures. The infinite is missing when we have a way of understanding knowing and being in which everything is positive, everything has determinations, nothing escapes. It is actually difficult to escape from that way of thinking but doing so is at the heart of critical work. The infinite is what escapes. It is missing in most methodological discourses.

Finally, I explored critical communicative pragmatics for the infinite and have argued for its internal location in communicative reason. Reason is structured as freedom, as the milieu within which people form themselves, develop and change their self-understandings, form relationships with other people. From the communicative pragmatist perspective, the infinite is the Other in our daily lives and interactions. No model, no theory, no basic concepts (like "person") can reduce subjects to finitude. Ideologies embedded in culture, "scientific knowledge," institutional practices push the Other subject down towards object-being; the finite. This oppression is the most insidious when it is internalized and our self-understandings push us down toward finitude. The infinite is "the subject" that is all of us individually and collectively. Through it can come unexpectedly new conditions of possibility for the knowing that is our being, the being that is our knowing.

Notes

1 The main exception I have found is Derrida's work. Derrida knew exactly what is meant by "missing infinite." I often think of Derrida, especially in relation to his work with deconstruction, as Hegel's dark twin. It is difficult to bring Derrida to social theory for reasons I explain in later sections of this essay.
2 These insights are rarely missed in Hegel's philosophy. Foucault wrote the following about trying to escape Hegel: "We have to determine the extent to which our anti-Hegelianism is possibly one of his [Hegel's] tricks directed against us, at the end of which he stands, motionless, waiting for us" (Hyppolite, 1977, p. xv).
3 Determinations have been conceptualized in terms of consciousness and sensual determinants of perceived objects, in terms of consciousness and both sensual and conceptual determinations of phenomena—the conceptual exceeding the sensual and yet within immediate experience—and in terms of language, discursively structured concepts.
4 For an extensive discussion of inclusion and related paradoxes see *Beyond the Limits of Thought* by Graham Priest (2002).

References

Disley, L. (2015). *Hegel, Love and Forgiveness*. London: Pickering and Chatto.

Giroux, H. (1989). *Schooling for Democracy: Critical Pedagogy and the Modern Age*. New York: Routledge.

Habermas, J. (1981). *The Theory of Communicative Action; Vol. 1, Reason and the Rationalization of Society*. Boston, MA: Beacon Press.

Habermas, J. (1987). *The Theory of Communicative Action; Vol. 2; Lifeworld and System: A Critique of Functionalist Reason*. Boston, MA: Beacon Press.

Hegel, G.W.F. (1975). *Hegel's Logic; Being Part One of the Encyclopaedia of the Philosophical Sciences* (trans. William Wallace). Oxford, UK: Clarendon Press.

Hegel, G.W.F. (1977). *Phenomenology of Spirit* (trans. A. V. Miller). Oxford: Oxford University Press.

Hyppolite, J. (1974). *Genesis and Structure of Hegel's Phenomenology of Spirit*. Evanston, IL: Northwestern University Press.

Hyppolite, J. (1977). *Logic and Existence* (trans. Leonard Lawlor and Amit Sen). Albany, NY: State University of New York Press.

Kant, I. (1952). *The Critique of Judgment* (trans. James Creed Meredith). Oxford, UK: Clarendon Press.

Kant, I. (1965). *Critique of Pure Reason* (trans. Norman Kemp Smith). New York: Macmillan.

Kant, I. (1993). *Critique of Practical Reason* (trans. Lewis White Beck). Upper Saddle River, NJ: Prentice-Hall, Inc.

McLaren, P. (1986). *Schooling as a Ritual Performance.* London: Routledge.

Priest, G. (2002). *Beyond the Limits of Thought.* Oxford, UK: Oxford University Press.

Rose, G. (1981). *Hegel Contra Sociology*, 1st Edition. London: Athlone Press.

Rose, G. (1995). *Hegel Contra Sociology*, Reprint. London: Verso.

Rose, G. (1992). *The Broken Middle.* Oxford, UK and Cambridge, MA: Blackwell Publishers.

Taylor, C. (2015). *Hegel and Modern Society.* Cambridge, UK: Cambridge University Press.

3

TROUBLE THE TRANSLATING

Border Thinking, Indigenous Knowledges, and Undoing Method

Nathan Beck

Theory: Indigenous Knowledges, Border Thinking
Type of qualitative data: Photos, interviews, experiences
New data analysis technique: Border Thinking model
Substantive topic in education: Epistemology

Many centers, few bridges

My aim in this chapter is to offer an example of how to use Indigenous Knowledges and Border Thinking for analysis of qualitative data, to unearth and problematize the industry that guides writing, research, and "knowledge" production and the borders of who and what is given credibility, and, then, to introduce a way of research/being that attempts to negotiate these tensions as researchers learn from and with others. That is, in this chapter I am seeking to expose research as an institution that is rigid, bound, and exclusive, and then propose a methodology that is a way of being, that has and accounts for contradictions. In this chapter I offer a type of data analysis, rooted in Indigenous Knowledges and Border Thinking, which would claim that coding or other forms of analysis are antithetical to justice-centered research. Instead, I will attempt to offer a type of analysis that resists and disrupts the global design of research to create a way of learning that troubles itself while simultaneously troubling the institution of research and knowing. To do this, I may sometimes write in a way that differs from typical academic writing. I write with vulnerability and contradiction because the theoretical framework(s) I embody influence even the presentation of writing and the act of being in relationship with knowledge. This, to me, is the essence of critical theories, understanding how my body/position/status interacts with power, knowledge, and presentation.

What follows in this chapter is critical, but before I start unearthing the tensions in my body, I want to be clear that these critiques are not leveled at classes, colleagues, professors, other chapters in this book, or any individuals operating within higher education. These critiques aren't even level(ed). They are messy, incomplete, vulnerable reflections – full of doubt –generally aimed at the institution of higher education and the *colonies that it represents*. These reflections come from a place of immense privilege and contradiction and they come from a place of "love and anger" (Freire, 2004, p. xxxi). My white cis-male body affords me the ability to even submit this chapter without risk within an institution (higher education in general) that has forcibly excluded, policed, surveilled, and treated as threats Black and Brown bodies since its inception. This is the contradiction that my body most feels as I write.

Rethinking What it Means to do "Critical" Research

And there are other deep tensions running through my body that stop these sentences from surfacing. It is muddied water and charting academic language onto a page and into a structure feels like violence and separation. The assumption under-girding my experience in higher education is that *research happens, there is a role for researchers, and there is legitimacy bestowed upon it all by our institution and our social positioning.* I've been in an industry about itself, and I was about it too. And what if critical inquiry, through pushing at the margins, simply provides the acceptable boundaries for the institution and discipline of inquiry? Even critical inquiry is understood through – and in relation to – a hegemonic institution; it is "dependent on the center that makes its existence possible" (Winkle-Wagner, Ortloff, & Hunter, 2009, p. 10). But, *why can't there be many centers?*

Why aren't we all (learners, knowledge-seekers, humans) bestowed the title researcher and *who does the bestowing anyway?* Why do we in the academy take the ~~burden, responsibility, privilege,~~ profit-producing-job of representation and production? My discomfort – uneasiness – goes beyond just interrogating myself and my role as a researcher, it stretches to the actual structure and purpose of language. The sentences I have written housed within this institution of higher education are tamed by practicality and rendered meaningful only through the neoliberal, individualistic pressure of the job market that penetrates into our writing and our purpose. My words' purpose, here, is the institution. Their purpose is job security. Their purpose is publishing. Those words might say something critical (look, I cited Gramsci, Said, Foucault, Giroux, Freire,

Brayboy, Anzaldúa, Hall . . .), but their real purpose is to move ideas and individuals through the academic job market and to eventually reproduce the institution that birthed them. Can that, no matter what we're writing, ever be liberatory? Can that construct the alternative that our planet desperately needs?

The sentences I have written in these institutions knew the rules. They were low risk. They didn't make me feel vulnerable. They weren't full of self-doubt and uneasiness (like these sentences). It was writing that was colonized – rigidly bound between borders – and purposed full of self-advancement.

Shouldn't critical inquiry aim to excavate the colonization embedded in each of our sentences and the way in which we purpose them? How do I actually talk about critical inquiry if I don't believe in the industry it is embedded within – if the industry is colonized? Then, what is the decolonizing work? Fanon (2004) says, "for the colonized, life can only materialize from the *rotting cadaver of the colonist*" (p. 50). Let's take that seriously. Not just the implications that it has for our/my body(ies), but what would the rotting cadaver of colonized critical inquiry look like, and what possibilities could emerge from it? What might decolonized ~~research, inquiry~~, learning feel like? What if we were granted the courage to imagine – to dream?

What if, rather than critical inquiry, we aim for an approach to ~~knowing~~ being that seeks to liberate inquiry from *the* academy, from the institutions it is embedded within, from research itself. What about inquiry as a human activity done by everyone? Together. Done through the tensions we feel in our bodies as we struggle with injustice and action. Done in the factory, the farm, and the classroom. I call for an inquiry that "we know with our entire body," and that we do "with feeling, with emotion, with wishes, with fear, *with doubts*, with passion" (Freire, 2005, p. 5).

This way of learning would certainly not be a "tight methodological theory" (Carspecken, 1996, p. 3). It would not try to "meet traditional promotion and tenure expectations" (Pasque, Carducci, Kuntz, & Gildersleeve, 2012, p. 88). It would not attempt to translate the "voices and experiences of those at the margins . . . into the *practice of methodology*" (Dennis, 2009, p. 72). It would not take for granted the legitimacy of the academy. It *would* trouble all claims to legitimacy coming from historically (and predominantly) white institutions of state-sponsored power. The Border Thinking that I emphasize would ask the same questions as critical inquiry: "who can create knowledge? How does power circulate . . . what can be known" (Pasque *et al.*, 2012, p. 57), but no *one* would ask them (meaning: marginalized populations). It would share the values of critical inquiry (Carspecken, 1996, pp. 6–7), but not the structure. It would be "a form of praxis – a search for knowledge" (Crotty, 1998, p. 159), but housed within our bodies rather than *our* institutions.

This approach would be love, and it would be anger; motivated by a critique of the sites and conditions where we imagine alternatives from and a deep yearning to begin the journey there.

(Re-)Orienting our Fragments

> What am I? *A third world lesbian feminist with Marxist and mystic leanings.* They would chop me up into little fragments and tag each piece with a label.
>
> *(Moraga & Anzaldúa, 2002, p. 228)*

Research is translation (quite literally, it uses language). Taking from one border to another, from between borders to the borders of language, pages, disciplines; from a lived experience to a linguistic act. Research makes experiences into products, packaged with labeling that academics can understand, bought and sold on the marketplace. Research is the business of exporting, where the exporters make more profit than the makers – the researchers more than the subjects. Research is the business of separation, and those who do the separating are rewarded with tenure, whereas those who are separated get nothing.

Research also requires trust, yet trust is disproportionally required of the translation. We save our trust for the product of research rather than the origin, as if research is a process of legitimization. But, how can we create methodologies that trouble the translating? That is, how can we trouble the notion of who gets to be considered a "researcher" and what gets considered "research/knowledge/empirical truth?" How can we create a conceptual way of understanding that doesn't disappear difference or impose a global design on understanding and knowing? How can it be flexible enough for other purposes? How is it a way of knowing in which many ways of knowing fit? How can we do the "arduous task of building different epistemologies" (Hurtado, 2003, p. 224)?

First, we must know the borders. Second, we must know from the borders.

The Borders

> I am visible—see this Indian face—yet I am invisible . . . they'd like to think I have melted in the pot. But I haven't, we haven't.
>
> *(Anzaldúa, 1987, p. 108)*

Borders, for border dwellers, are impositions that constrain or structure lives with certain disguised preconditions. These borders come in the form of identities, values, and physical limitations, and although they present themselves as naturalized, Anzaldúa (1987) argues that "a borderland is a vague and undetermined place created by the emotional residue of an unnatural boundary" (p. 3). These unnatural boundaries render those who "don't fit" in a border space. Research is complicit in the creation of borders, forcing a lived/felt experience into a page, an article, a theory, and creating artificial – and heavily guarded – boundaries around the basic process of knowing and legitimacy.

Existing between borders, border-dwellers "occupy a liminal space" (Brayboy, 2006, p. 429), that Moraga and Anzaldúa (2002) describes as "the in-between space of nepantla . . . most of us occupy. We do not inhabit un mundo but many"

(p. xxxvii). In other words, people can inhabit multiple worlds or spaces at once, often contradictory, and these tensions between worlds – between spaces that we occupy – are rich arenas to dwell in. Although border dwellers occupy multiple contradictory points at the same time, borders impose an "absolute despot duality that says we are able to be only one or the other" (Anzaldúa, 1987, p. 19). This dichotomizing separates bodies from themselves, but dwelling in and thinking from the borders also provides agency. Herein, Mignolo (2012) believes that "thinking from dichotomous concepts rather than ordering the world in dichotomies" (p. 85) provides a model of resisting colonization and "becomes, then, the necessary epistemology to delink and decolonize knowledge" (p. x).

By resisting "the rigidity of epistemic and territorial frontiers" (Mignolo, 2012, pp. 12–13), Border Thinking provides a platform with which to imagine different analytic approaches that unearth the borders imposed on us through the research process. Essentially, Mignolo (2012) articulates that some local histories develop ideas that are, then, imposed globally. Take, for example, gender as a binary construct mapped onto our bodies, the structure of "standard" English and grammar constraining our language, or the arbitrary physical divisions imposed upon the body of the earth between countries. Each of these "global designs . . . hide the local history from which they themselves emanate and are presented as if they were a natural unfolding history" (Mignolo, 2012, p. xvi). Border Thinking does not rank local histories, but troubles the universal ascription of practices from one space to another, from one body to another, *from one research project to another*. Essentially, "to the extent that global designs are no longer situated in one territory, local histories are correspondingly affected" (Mignolo, 2012, p. 65).

Global designs built on specific local histories render those who "don't fit" in a border space, but, through dwelling in these borderlands, Border Thinking provides the conceptual space to resist imposing global designs. "Border thinking is the pluriversal . . . epistemology," Mignolo (2012) says, "that interconnects the plurality and diversity of decolonial projects" (p. xxii). In other words, Border Thinking becomes a way of knowing in which many ways of knowing fit – a way of knowing that dwells in the entanglements between different "universals." By thinking from the borders (not about them), we are able to resist impositions and colonization. Similarly, Indigenous Knowledges transcend typical epistemic frontiers by centering the relationships between place, landscape, and spiritual tradition as sites of knowledge production (Brayboy & Maughan, 2009; Garcia & Shirley, 2012).

With this foundation, I draw from across Border Thinking and Indigenous Knowledges that trouble (mental and geographic) borders, are rooted in connection to place, body, memory and a distrust of globalization, and engage in critiques of the status quo while seeking to transform the present to develop a model to help us think from the borders. By blending Border Thinking and Indigenous Knowledges, the aim is not to take local histories and create a global design to be applied elsewhere. In other words, I am applying these theoretical ideas to research and research processes as a way to reconsider how one might conduct data analysis such that space, place, power, legitimacy, and knowledge can be challenged. The idea is to unearth the commonalities in border(ed) and indigenous ways of knowing and understanding the world to produce a model for analysis that helps us know from the borders. In so doing, I am both offering a way of analyzing data alongside a way of knowing and thinking (also called epistemology), and eventually, a way of being in relation to research. The primary concepts of knowing within Border Thinking and Indigenous Knowledges that I draw from are: place/land/memory and Indignation, with the body central to both of these.

Place/Land/Memory (Location/Dislocation)

Indigenous Knowledges "are rooted in the lived experiences of people" (Brayboy & Maughan, 2009, p. 3), contend that "landscapes are the sources of knowledge" (Garcia & Shirley, 2012, p. 80), and "are an integral part of survival" for indigenous communities (Brayboy & Maughan, 2009, p. 13). Therefore, "culture, knowledge, and power take on new meaning when examined through an indigenous lens" (Brayboy, 2006, p. 429) as they are "tied to . . . a physical place" (Brayboy, 2006, p. 434). Mignolo (2012) continues this train of thought by linking knowing, thinking, and acting with physical and mental geography. "I am where I think," Mignolo says, "becomes the starting point, the historical foundation of border thinking and decolonial doing" (p. xiv). Going further, Brayboy (2006) contends that "stories are not separate from theory" (p. 429), they are "moral tools [and the] foundations on which indigenous communities are built" (p. 439). Stories, then, are moral tools of cultural and historical memories that emerge from place and ground people in physical and mental locations.

Similarly, Anzaldúa (1987) connects the images of her body, her body's location, and the body of the earth by speaking to the US/Mexico border as a:

> 1950 mile-long open wound/dividing a pueblo, a culture,/running down the length of my body,/staking fence rods in my flesh,/splits me splits me/me raja me raja/This is my home/this thin edge of/barbwire./But the skin of the earth is seamless./The sea cannot be fenced,/el mar does not stop at borders.
>
> *(p. 3)*

Anzaldúa portrays the earth, her body, her culture, and historical memory as intricately connected and she describes the border wall as a wound that dislocates her from "home," but she also attributes agency to the land as a source of strength and resistance. Within discussions of place in Border Thinking and

Indigenous Knowledges, there is an acute awareness of the forces that dislocate indigenous bodies from place, history, culture, and memory. Place, therefore, assumes a more integral and complicated role, as it is understood as a source of strength and survival at the same time that it is always under threat. Similar to the physical landscape that shapes our experiences and understanding, emotions provide a powerful parallel context to interpret and act through. Emotions are not disconnected from place, but interwoven throughout our physical experience of space, primarily love and anger.

Love/Anger (Indignation)

> If humanity wants to survive and improve, its only hope resides in these pockets made up of the excluded, the left-for-dead, the 'disposable'.
>
> *(Marcos, 2001, p. 570)*

Border Thinking also connects action to an emotional landscape as it engages in "a critique of oppression and a desire for social justice" (quoted in Brayboy, 2005, p. 194). Mignolo (2012) contends that Border Thinking is "an ethic and politics that emerge from the experiences of people taking their destiny in their own hands and not waiting for saviors" (p. xxii). This ethic and politics is connected to a body, place, history, and emotion that encourages acting towards transformation. This concept is paramount, as it reveals the urgency for border-dwellers: the preservation of memory and the fate of the planet.

Border dwelling must, then, drive a sense of morality and justice – an approach towards living and research methodologies that seeks to eradicate oppression and oppressive relationships between and among subject/researchers/learners. As Freire (2004) says, "all truly ethical and genuinely human actions are born from two contradictory feelings, and only from those two: love and anger" (p. xxxi). The joining of love and anger in one's body becomes a sense of indignation. Indignation is more than an emotion; it is an embodied approach towards injustice and towards the world, one that holds and makes sense of the tensions between love and anger, one that is felt and experienced in the body even as it is leveled outward towards injustice. "The struggle has always been inner," Anzaldúa (1987) reminds us, "and is played out in the outer terrains. Awareness of our situation must come before inner changes, which in turn come before changes in society" (p. 109).

Indignation allows us to denounce what is, and still have the necessary hope to announce what is possible. Indignation is born because "you know the present so well, you can imagine a possible future of transformation" (Shor & Freire, 1987, p. 186). This indignation, the capacity to act from emotional dualities – love as a vision for the future and anger as a critique of the present – is at the heart of ethical acts. As Mignolo (2012) says, "border dwellers are becoming border thinkers and decolonial actors" (p. xxi). Dwelling in the borders between love and anger should be at the heart of our thinking and our actions.

Centering Border Thinking, bodies, location/dislocation, and indignation in research creates a structured way of thinking from the borders that simultaneously un-structures the "product" of our thinking. This foundation disappears the traditional roles of researchers, participants, and methods, and forces an embodied approach to learning that renegotiates and interrogates every level of research and analysis and troubles the structure of thinking itself as a constraining imposition. Learning becomes a performance to know from the borders, and it is this everyday lived performance that must become our methodology – our way of being in research. Methods, as a type and way of learning, must come from the borders too.

Knowing from the Borders: Undoing Method

The purpose of this approach to research and data analysis is not to produce data – the idea is to produce understanding. In this moment of knowing, we are not researchers, we are not producers; we are learners. By centering ourselves as learners rather than producers, we resist (to some small degree) the global designs imposed on knowing, data, and legitimacy through research methodologies. This is a call for a whole new way of being in research and a new way of thinking about data, analysis, and our roles as researchers.

This Border Thinking model (below) seeks to center and connect the body to a mental and geographic location, even as the body is mentally and geographically dis-located through borders, impositions, and contradictions. This method acknowledges that there is no knowledge without the body, it brings urgency to the "data," and it grounds experiences in an emotional landscape that is attached to land and bodies. This method seeks to lay the groundwork for new ways of being in research. To chart this model out on the borders of paper and with the borders of language is an act of violence, therefore the rigidity of this categorization demands to be troubled.

- The top hemisphere consists of indignation, the combination of love and anger for transformation.
- The bottom hemisphere consists of physical and mental geography, the sites from which we speak.
- The left hemisphere consists of hope for the future grounded in place, history, and memory.
- The right hemisphere consists of historical condition, structural impositions, tensions.
- The center is the body, holding all of these contradictions, not categorizing them, and acting through them.
- Between and among all of these "categories" are borders that render bodies separate.

This conceptual approach helps us identify and think from the borders, it centers the physical and emotional landscapes through which we experience the

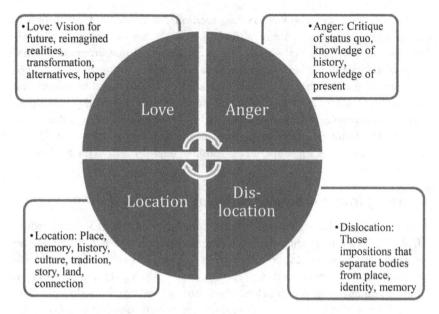

FIGURE 3.1 Border Thinking Model

world. Although portrayed categorically, by centering the body we privilege the interconnections, contradictions, and fluidity of experiences, but that does not mean that this model should be imposed. This model is by nature imperfect, this is simply a tool to help us think from the borders, *if applied with rigidity, it becomes a border itself.*

This model does not seek to impose a method, but seeks to expose the borderlands present in "data" and encourages us to rely on our intuition and experiences, not our translations of them. Logistically and practically, learners could explore "data"/experiences attempting to unearth the visions/desires for the future (love) and critiques of the present (anger), as well as the location (place/memory) and forces of dislocation (impositions/global designs/contradictions), and link all of these to the body. Learners could chunk sections together, completing this model as they go, they could develop a personal coding scheme for love/anger/borders/place/body and use the model as a framework at the end, or they could focus deeply on each hemisphere before seeking to put them together.

To resist imposing a design, I resist offering a detailed explanation of "how" to use this model, although I will show how I have used it in practice. As Subcomandante Marcos (Marcos, Bardacke, López, Ross, & Watsonville, 1995) reminds us, "we neither want, nor are able, to occupy the place . . . from which all opinions will come, *all the answers, all the routes, all the truths*" (p. 248). There is not a singular way to use this model, but multiple; learners should recreate, destroy, reimagine, and discard it as necessary, but thinking in this way should have profound effects on our research and data analysis approach.

Anzaldúa (2002) encourages us to relocate data analysis outside of our minds and our classrooms:

> There is no need for words to fester in our minds. They germinate in the open mouth of the barefoot child in the midst of restive crowds. They wither in ivory towers and in college classrooms. Throw away abstraction and the academic learning, the rules, the map and compass. Feel your way without blinders. To touch more people, the personal realities and the social must be evoked – not through rhetoric but through blood and pus and sweat.
>
> *(Moraga & Anzaldúa, 2002, p. 192)*

So instead of the conventions of the classroom, this model *requires our bodies, emotions, and intuition*, what Anzaldúa (1987) calls "*La facultad* . . . the capacity to see in surface phenomena the meaning of deeper realities, to see the deep structure below the surface . . . images and symbols which are the faces of feelings, that is, behind which feelings reside" (p. 38). This intuition comes from dwelling in the borders and cannot be replaced by a coding scheme. It requires that we engage in "thinking from dichotomous concepts rather than ordering the world in dichotomies" (Mignolo, 2012, p. 85). This model's purpose is to expose those dichotomies even as it simultaneously erodes the borders around them. Engaging in this kind of data analysis forces us to rethink the industry of research that we operate within. In using this model, what is paramount is that learners *must* have the imagination and courage to reinvent this model in different circumstances, and must not have the goal of production or translation.

An Application to Border Thinking

An approach to learning/research that centers Border Thinking can be applied anywhere, and this section will attempt to apply these ideas as an example. Border Thinking compels us to a sense of urgency and renegotiates the terrains upon which learning occurs. The stakes are high for border-dwellers, and to make the stakes visible let's dwell in the borders.

Occupied Palestine

Take, for example, the testimony of a Palestinian farmer whose land Israel confiscated for the construction of the Apartheid Wall. His body, history, and memory are physically and mentally dislocated, under threat, at risk of extinction:

> Since they have taken my land, I feel as if my children and I have no future. I have become poor, and am left with only thirty head of sheep and goats. I began to sell my flock to meet our household needs. In the past, the flock

grazed in wide-open spaces on the land, but now they are confined, and I have to buy them fodder. I feel that I'll end up with not even one sheep, which means that I will have lost my livelihood and my last source of food, having lost my land. I hear the flock moaning, and understand their frustration, just as I understand the frustration of a person who is imprisoned and can't get out. When the time comes for me to feed them, I feel queasy out of sorrow for my flock and the situation they are in.

(B'Tselem, 2005)

Border learning helps us do two things. First "analyze" "the" "data" (all troubling exacting words) by excavating the dichotomies/borders and centering the body in a contradictory space that acts with and through tensions. For example, (in-)completing the model we see that the body is negotiating the following at all times:

Love: Having land that can produce, having family return, having a livelihood, being able to meet our needs, having peace, having sheep be able to graze/roam.

Anger: The occupation has destroyed my livelihood, separated me from family, imprisoned me, caused me fear for my flock and my life, taken my land, put me in danger, I am losing my flock, I can no longer support myself or my family.

FIGURE 3.2 Photo taken by Sol Kelley-Jones in Palestine, July 2015

Location: My land, children, sheep/goats, farming, memories of children on land, wide-open spaces.

Dislocation: Wall built on my land, separation from my land, inability to feed my flock, national borders, diaspora, collective memory of Nakba, freedom/imprisonment, Occupation, property/collectivity, prison.

By unearthing dichotomies and centering the body we disengage from translation and separation in a practice that allows us to learn the "data" in a more embodied way. But, secondly, and more importantly, this model spurs the practice and performance of learning from the borders. Claiming intuition or "the spiritual within the academy," Hurtado (2003) says, "is blasphemous . . . and leaves us bereft of method" (p. 218), but bereft does not mean we are without method, being bereft of method simply makes visible the constraining nature of methodology – allows us to finally see beyond the horizon. This recognition must lead to a rethinking of how we approach research, learning, and thinking. Being bereft of method – bereft of borders – *liberates research from the field-note, the coding scheme, the orientation towards production* and allows the performance of learning with our intuition and our bodies. This performance of methodology involves our souls, our solidarities, and our bodies, it becomes a way of being in relation to research/knowing. The performance of intuition/non-method from the borderlands troubles every aspect of typical research and demands that learning and knowing is a full-bodied experience.

Taking this approach in the setting above learning with/from the Palestinian farmer would renegotiate our methodology. Our methodology would be solidarity, it would be: sitting –unsettled – with the architecture of military Occupation around us and the sound of drones above, it would be stories, it would be witnessing the arch of Israeli bullets aimed at children, it would be sharing olives and friendship, it would be noon prayer on a Friday. It would be صمود (steadfastness), the roots expanding beneath us, and other languages we have yet to tap into. It would be beyond the time-frame of IRB – both un-ending and always starting. It is not a method applied to one research project, but a method applied to our relationship to knowing/research.

It would count as data the scars – and the distance between – our bodies, the freedom of the birds flying above, the story and condition of diaspora, the anguish of being forced from one's home and the keys to homes still held in wrinkled, weary, resilient hands. It would center the stories forced into disappearance – now only in our memories, the distance to the sea – now inaccessible, the consumption of tomatoes and the reliance upon land – now stolen – to produce them. The participants would include stories, ancestors, myth, tradition, culture, Palestinian collective memory, and the earth itself. The earth would talk to us, it would tell us that as it is excavated for the construction of borders, walls, prisons, so too is our humanness, so too is our connection to each other, and to ourselves.

The urgency of knowing from the borderlands would replace the timidity of research. This renegotiates all of the typical terrains of research: what counts as data, what/who is designated as researcher/researched, what are – and how we locate – our methods. It is a way-of-being-in-research, a relationship to knowing that centers our human experience and how our body feels, that does not need an intermediary – a gatekeeper.

In Palestine the stakes are high and visible, but borders and urgency are everywhere. This model could just as easily be used to look at classrooms that are bound by language, time, discipline, hierarchy, race, class, where students are constantly negotiating these tensions with their bodies. Public schools are certainly sites of love, anger, and contestation, and Border Thinking compels us to go beyond singular spaces to see the historical memory that links (or separates) those bodies to place.

Towards a New (Old) Pragmatism, Struggling, and Moving

No doubt, this approach is not "for" the typical committee or research, but many may ask, is this approach even doable? Critiques that come from a platform of practicality, however, are trying to fit this model into the global design of research, they come from thinking within borders, not from the borders. This learning may feel imaginary from the confines of the academy, but those bodies in the borderlands do this knowing every day – it is the condition of their existence. What is more manufactured, a learning that requires experience, solidarity, struggle, and imperfect movement, or a learning that separates and categorizes with codes as an exercise on the route to knowing?

It was in Palestine in 2008 as a 21-year-old, white, cis-male activist that I was first undone by borders – a way of being and knowing was so unsettled and shaken that something new had to emerge. On my first day there, in fact, after navigating check-point. check-point. check-point. I witnessed the arch of bullets aimed at children; and it was from those borderlands, surrounded by the architecture of occupation, having endless cups of tea, staying late into the night having conversations with my hands and a half-dozen words of Arabic that I learned the most about life, that I felt the most rage and love, that place and memory and displacement were always present, that data and actions and methods had consequences. A place where my body had the seemingly magic ability of movement between cities, when others' (slightly browner) bodies didn't, when others risked their lives to pick olives from a tree that has been with their family for centuries. Shouldn't this unsettle us, undo our ways of being and our methods.

These are the borders, and this is what matters.

You can do this learning too; find the borders (wherever you are) find out what matters, and then be and struggle. I do this borderland knowing (imperfectly) in my daily life by setting the notebook down, listening to stories, allowing love and anger, and the tension between, to guide me, by using intuition, by feeling and allowing vulnerability, by marching with, by never knowing, by doubting, by struggling and moving at the same time, and by seeking the borders, the margins, and those who police them. But the academy has separated us from knowing, has translated knowing from a human condition to an academic exercise and we are so deep into the machine – so far from our origin – that we cannot recognize knowing without rigid structure, words like epistemology, and exclusion. We have fallen into the trap of believing in one center and directed our efforts at nudging that center – ever so slightly – towards a more liberatory place at which it will never arrive.

We must move beyond the research–industrial complex – begin the voyage (back or forward) to indigenous ways of knowing and being that have existed for thousands of years but are increasingly under threat. It is from the borderlands that transformation must occur; it is from the borderlands that we must know; it is from the borderlands that a "world in which many worlds fit" (EZLN slogan) is emerging.

As Moraga and Anzaldúa (2002) remind us, "voyager, there are no bridges, one builds them as one walks" (p. 352). I hope this is a small bridge, among many, towards that end.

References

Anzaldúa, G. (1987). *Borderlands/La Frontera: The New Mestiza.* San Francisco: Aunt Lute Books.

B'Tselem. (2005). Under the Guise of Security: Routing the Separation Barrier to Enable the Expansion of Israeli Settlements in the West Bank. Available online at: https://www.btselem.org/download/200512_under_the_guise_of_security_eng.pdf.

Brayboy, B. (2005). Transformational Resistance and Social Justice: American Indians in Ivy League Universities. *Anthropology and Education Quarterly, 36*(3), 193–211.

Brayboy, B. (2006). Toward a Tribal Critical Race Theory in Education. *The Urban Review, 37*(5), 425–446.

Brayboy, B., & Maughan, E. (2009). Indigenous Knowledges and the Story of the Bean. *Harvard Educational Review, 79*(1), 1–20.

Carspecken, P. (1996). *Critical Ethnography in Educational Research: A Theoretical and Practical Guide.* New York: Routledge.

Conversations with colleagues in which these tensions are named, shared, and excavated. And conversations when they're not.

Conversations with my partner.

Crotty, M. (1998). *Critical Inquiry: Contemporary Critics and Contemporary Critique. The Foundations of Social Research: Meaning and Perspectives in the Research Process.* Thousand Oaks, CA: Sage, 138–159.

Dennis, B. (2009). Theory of the Margins: Liberating Research in Education. In R. Winkle-Wagner, C. A. Hunter, & D. H. Ortloff, *Bridging the Gap between Theory and Practice in Educational Research: Methods at the Margins.* New York: Palgrave Macmillan, 63–75.

Fanon, F. (2004). *The Wretched of the Earth.* New York: Grover Press.

Freire, P. (2004). *Pedagogy of Indignation.* Boulder, CO: Paradigm Publishers.

Freire, P. (2005). *Teachers as Cultural Workers: Letters to Those Who Dare Teach*. Cambridge, MA: Westview Press.

Garcia, J., & Shirley, V. (2012). Performing Decolonization: Lessons Learned from Indigenous Youth, Teachers, and Leaders' Engagement with Critical Indigenous Pedagogy. *Journal of Curriculum Theorizing*, 28(2), 76–91.

Hurtado, A. (2003). Theory in the Flesh: Toward an Endarkened Epistemology. *International Journal of Qualitative Studies in Education*, 16(2), 215–225.

Imagination and dreams.

Marcos, S. (2001). The fourth world war has begun. Nepantla: Views from South, 2(3), 559–572.

Marcos, S., Bardacke, F., López, L., Ross, J., & Watsonville (Calif.). (1995). *Shadows of Tender Fury: The Letters and Communiqués of Subcomandante Marcos and the Zapatista Army of National Liberation*. New York: Monthly Review Press.

Memory (mine and others).

Mignolo, W. (2012). *Local Histories/Global Designs: Coloniality, Subaltern Knowledges, and Border Thinking*. Princeton, NJ: Princeton University Press.

Moraga, C., & Anzaldúa, G. (Eds.). (2002). *This Bridge Called My Back: Writings by Radical Women of Color*. Berkeley, CA: Third Woman Press.

Pasque, P., Carducci, R., Kuntz, A., & Gildersleeve, R. (2012). *Qualitative Inquiry for Equity in Higher Education: Methodological Innovations, Implications, and Interventions*. ASHE Higher Education Report: Volume 37, Number 6. Kelly Ward, Lisa E. Wolf-Wendel, Series Editors.

Shor, I., & Freire, P. (1987). *A Pedagogy for Liberation: Dialogues on Transforming Education*. Westport: Bergin and Garvey.

Winkle-Wagner, R., Ortloff, D. H., & Hunter, C. A. (2009). Introduction: The Not-center? The Margins and Educational Research. In R. Winkle-Wagner, C. A. Hunter, & D. H. Ortloff, *Bridging the Gap between Theory and Practice in Educational Research: Methods at the Margins*. New York: Palgrave Macmillan, 1–11.

4

DE-NORMING THE SYLLABUS

An Analysis Situated in Critical and Caring Pedagogies

Virginia M. Schwarz

Theory: Problem-Posing, Critical Pedagogy
Type of qualitative data: Educational Documents, Syllabi
New data analysis technique: Collaborative De-norming
Substantive topic in education: Syllabus design for collaborative, inclusive and socially just classrooms

---

Paulo Freire (1968/2000) argues that "education must begin with the solution of the teacher-student contradiction, by reconciling the poles of the contradiction so that both are simultaneously teachers and students" (p. 72). When this contradiction is made visible and negotiated, teachers and students can become learners capable of co-constructing new, previously unimagined ideas and spaces together. Thus, the purpose of this chapter is to propose "de-norming" as a method of data analysis that calls out the ways language maintains unequitable conditions. Teachers, administrators, and researchers can also employ and build on de-norming processes to better understand and revise common academic statements, policies, and documents.

In this chapter, I apply de-norming to the critical analysis of syllabi to understand the ways a syllabus—as *document* and as an *enactment* of that document—reflect and reproduce ideologies. My intention in selecting this particular text is to illustrate one example where educators might intervene in institutional norms and norming processes that often operate invisibly. The syllabus has become a universal genre in higher education and its purposes and conventions are similar across disciplines. However, there are relatively few studies of syllabi that derive from critical perspectives.[1] Baecker (1998) notes, "for a document that assumes such central importance in the classroom, the syllabus has been largely ignored in the literature. Probably no other contract we will ever encounter is drafted with so little attention paid to language" (p. 61). The language teachers employ matters. For example, syllabi communicate a course's purpose, frame course information, and define participant responsibilities. These decisions are ideological, and they shape what is likely to become possible or perceived as possible. De-norming examines these choice points and explores possible revisions.

I develop de-norming first by briefly describing the theoretical frameworks that inform this method of critical analysis. Specifically, de-norming is rooted in critical pedagogy and includes Paulo Freire's (1968/2000) community inquiry and problem-posing techniques. Additionally, de-norming should also account for affective equality, a social justice principle of interconnectedness and love, care, and solidarity (Lynch, Baker, & Lyons, 2009). After reviewing these critical foundations, I argue that the syllabus is an academic genre with typified features resistant to change. Importantly, there have been teachers who have worked through the student–teacher contradiction Freire (1968/2000) describes and reimagined their classroom documents. They have created what we might call "critical syllabi," and their choices—sometimes made *with* students—make unequitable conditions visible in an attempt to rework them. Finally, I detail de-norming as a method for critical data analysis and provide a collaborative problem-posing heuristic. The chapter ends with possible limitations and a call for future research into the everyday texts that mediate educational spaces.

Freire and Critical Pedagogy

Paulo Freire is one of the central founders of critical pedagogy, the application of critical theory into educational contexts. In Brazil, he developed a practice of teaching literacy for people who were illiterate and living in poverty. As Freire (1968/2000) proposes in *Pedagogy of the Oppressed*, his most well-known work, critical pedagogy, is an approach to learning in which all parties come to know the ways systems of power operate (theory) to expand possible recourse (action). This approach has been adopted into American contexts by several high-profile educators, including bell hooks (1994) and Ira Shor (1992).

Freire (1968/2000) believes that as people come to know one another through dialogue, they will begin to understand that systems of oppression are contextual and change over time. This dialogue is called "problem-posing" and needs to be utilized in a self-reflective, continuous, and ongoing manner. Learning, in this sense, is relational and requires the presence of others (Freire, 1968/2000). Because a majority of academic institutions in the United States privilege Western knowledge production, reasoning, and positivist thinking,[2] this approach to— and understanding of—learning must be intentionally integrated into classroom design. Therefore, the teacher's role is to become a co-learner, proposing generative themes that give students the opportunity to develop a language for understanding their lives and how everyone's lives have been shaped in relation to others. Thus, critical education is not merely a means to an end, but a new way of engaging with the world through inquiry.

Rooted in the everyday lives and experiences of students, Freire's problem-posing techniques provide a framework for interrogating systems, our overlapping complicities in perpetuating them, and our responsibilities in challenging them. For example, if the dominant narrative suggests that education's purpose is for social mobility, then a critical narrative is that education is primarily to learn how to, according to Freire, name the world and participate in its transformation (Freire, 1968/2000). In this way, critical pedagogy offers an alternative understanding of writing classrooms: students are not there because they "don't know how to write well." Students, teachers, classes, and tests are all part of a larger, complex, and interconnected story. When a course labels academic writing conventions as *standard* or *best* or *clearest*, this is a consequence of sexist, racist, classist, and ableist constructions of merit. Without context, analysis often begins with students and their "deficiencies" rather than the systems failing them. Critical educators would argue that all participants should learn the various ways they are implicated in those systems in order to transform them.

Affective Equality

While Freire (1968/2000) does address emotion (hope and an attachment to the future) and love for others (necessary to enter into dialogue), Lynch *et al.* (2009) develop a framework for understanding how affect functions to mediate everyday public interactions and relationships: affective equality. This means, whether we realize it or not, social contexts require love, care, and solidarity for the safety and well-being of participants. Therefore, in addition to the analytical axes of economic, political, and cultural, one must incorporate an affective dimension to any worthy egalitarian vision (Lynch *et al.*, 2009). Affective *in*equality, then, refers to the uneven distribution of and compensation for "nurturing labor" in our society (Lynch *et al.*, 2009). As such, this framework calls attention to the structural barriers that deprive individuals and groups of access to care or perpetuate the uneven distribution of care labor unequally by gender, race, class (Lynch *et al.*, 2009).

The premise here is that *everyone*—to some extent—needs the support of others to survive and grow. People are interdependent and relational. This is relevant in both conceptualizing equitable spaces and developing processes for creating them. Although affect is not considered in rationalist iterations[3] of critical pedagogy, it is an essential part of entering and maintaining social interactions and relationships. Under many circumstances, walking away is easier than coming to terms with the self and the self in relation to another. In this way, giving and receiving *critique* could be understood as an act of love or compassion—a willingness to labor. Conversations *move* people, but the willingness to move and be moved requires logical and emotional learning. When a person takes the position of another and sorts through the ensuing discomfort and pain (Kumashiro, 2000), she must practice openness and self-care at the same time. This difficult process of "crisis"—seeing something in a new way and changing as a result—requires courage, boldness, and an investment in the outcome (Micchiche, 2007).

The intersection of critical theory and affect theory help to elucidate the social, economic, and institutional pressures that make transformative dialogue and care actions virtually impossible in classrooms. For example, oppressive structures work within and between individuals in any given encounter that make the engagement more demanding. In other words, risks inherent in Freire's model overlap with social inequalities (race, gender, class, sexuality, ability) to create uneven positioning and labor demands for participants. The affective needs and well-being of students and teachers often go unacknowledged in discussions about learning. Furthermore, teachers, administrators, scholars, and students practice acts of care mostly on their own time and dollar, even if the institution or select participants benefit from this invisible work. These dynamics constitute a default environment: one that does not account for or value care. The ways people understand learning and prioritize care then becomes embodied in institutional texts with specific, pre-determined features.

Table 4.1 shows key dimensions of a critical classroom that accounts for care. This pedagogy is juxtaposed to a "banking" approach to education. Teachers often employ the language of banking on syllabi, even when attempting to create critical classrooms.

TABLE 4.1 Key Dimensions of a Critical Classroom that Accounts for Care

	Critical/Problem-Posing	Banking
Primary Goal of the Classroom	Critical awareness, inquiry	Adopting and assimilating
Emotion and Care	Emotional awareness; able to practice and have access to care	Considered as additional or optional, or not considered at all
Teacher's Role	Facilitator to co-learner	Holds absolute knowledge maintains control
Student's Role	Problem solvers, conversationalists	Fill up with information (then tested to see what's still there)
Context of the Classroom	Assumes interrelatedness	Removes students from historical, present, and future context (reality is fixed and determined already)
Method of Teaching	Dialogue (most often)	Lectures (most often)
Education and Social Change	Necessary to revolutionary process; social transformation	Maintains systems that serve dominant social groups

Syllabus as an Academic Genre

Critical and affective approaches are not always welcome or valued in relation to teaching and learning. Even in critical spaces, often times language—passed down and reified in routine—may make identifying, critiquing, and changing oppressive systems difficult. In order to better see texts, educators must defamiliarize their features and the way those features are "ideologically active" (Bawarshi & Reiff, 2010, p. 4). Genres are defined as kinds of texts or artifacts that "conceptually frame and mediate how we understand and typically act" (Bawarshi & Reiff, 2010, p. 4). In the case of syllabi, a syllabus exists as a text with normalized genre conventions but also within a classroom typification, or recognizable social routine, with a set of implied rules.[4] Therefore, the syllabus become fixed over time by a number of overlapping factors, including its construction, its delivery, and its positioning within disciplinary and institutional ideologies.

The syllabus genre resists critical adaptation, in part, from the nature of its construction. A syllabus is supposed to be relational or *cause a relation to occur*, but it continues to be written by one party who is writing to an "imagined other" usually well before the term begins. Bailey (2010) argues that "instructors consciously or unconsciously orient their syllabi and their teaching practices to the image of who they think they are teaching (knowledgeable competent students who want to learn? Irresponsible students who party too much?)" (p. 152). In creating a syllabus, a teacher is not only constructing the ideal class but also the ideal student—one who does a, b, c to get to x, y, z. Thus, many students feel alienated on the first day. For example, absence policies, grading procedures, or accessibility statements may be read as barriers and make enthusiasm for the course near impossible (Womack, 2017). Students may also behave in specific ways from deep, internalized ideas of what they imagine the teacher wants (Bailey, 2010). In both cases, a sort of false position taking occurs that lapses to reinforce teacher and student roles.

There is also a traditional delivery for the syllabus. Across disciplines, instructors commonly issue the syllabus on the first day of the course. This routine serves to cement the document's purpose: to communicate the teacher's goals and expectations for the rest of the term. This move may be made covertly through language practices that disguise power and authority. For example, instructors may use the pronoun *we* rather than *you* to make "claims of community" when "the bulk of work falls on the student but the teacher retains the gatekeeper role" (Baecker, 1998, pp. 60–61). The syllabus usually includes specific course and campus information as well as behavioral expectations for students (Afros & Schryer, 2009). These genre expectations are most likely responsible for the syllabus's primary metaphor: a contract (Baecker, 1998; Fornaciari & Dean, 2014). Baecker (1998) notes, "one of the very first impressions we give our students is provided by our syllabus. It is the one piece of evidence our students can hold in their hands at the end of a day filled with a jumble of confusion" (p. 59). By staying in the class, students are—in a sense—agreeing to the terms and conditions the instructor sets forth. This first-day typification exists primarily as a means for teachers to "establish authority" with their students (Baecker, 1998).

As Afros & Schryer (2009) point out, students are not the only audience for a syllabus. Because of its institutional positioning as a policy document, a syllabus has stakeholders beyond the classroom and additional constraints come with each of these readers. For example, the syllabus introduces students into the discourses of the campus community and of specific disciplines (Afros & Schryer, 2009). Therefore, it may need to include a mandated lesson on plagiarism written by institutional personnel or subject-area terminology that students will learn in the class itself. Department colleagues and administrators also hold a set of expectations. In fact, many institutions have common syllabi, templates, or checklists with required language. These documents form a "meta genre" (Bawarshi & Reiff, 2010) that further governs standardization.

Imagining a Critical Syllabus

Bailey (2010) and Womack (2017) argue that if syllabi are capable of reinforcing academic and social norms, then they might also be able to defamiliarize and interrupt those norms. At that point, educators could begin to imagine a "critical syllabus" or ways a syllabus might critically and continuously intervene in the classroom environment and its processes.

In "Teaching is accommodation: Universally designing composition classrooms and syllabi," Womack (2017) re-theorizes "accommodation as the process of teaching itself" and argues that "accessibility is a precondition to all learning" (p. 494). As such, instructors should welcome *all* students and plan for unexpected diversities in the classroom and "the unique immediate needs of students" (p. 521). Because syllabi are usually informational (hierarchical) rather than rhetorical (reciprocal), they tend to be constructed with problematic patterns: text-heavy visual design, negative punishment language, defensive and combative policies, and cold-toned disability statements (p. 501). Through the lens of disability studies, Womack (2017) then details ways writing instructors can make collaborative and inclusive choices in syllabus design and in the everyday acts of teaching.

Bailey (2010), professor of women's studies, also challenges normative assumptions in teacher–student relationships. She does this through the *other syllabus*, a meta-document that accompanies her traditional syllabus. Both of these texts are given to teaching assistants (TAs) in their practicum course. Coming from a feminist perspective, Bailey (2010) pushes back against "certainty" and predetermined notions of the classroom—and the other syllabus is her venue for this work.

> I approached the seminars with two goals in mind: first, to introduce and explore some of the pressing tactical issues facing entering GTAs . . . the second goal . . . was to render visible teaching politics and ambiguities,

the tensions between teaching ideals and practicalities, the contextually-specific forces that shape classroom dynamics—both in the courses GTAs lead and in our own seminar—and the contingent nature of knowledge production in classroom settings.

(p. 140)

Bailey (2010) distributes the other syllabus alongside the traditional syllabus. Both syllabi work in dialogue to create a more complex, nuanced view of teaching and learning. In particular, the other syllabus allows Bailey (2010) to pose problems and model self-reflexive learning practices with students. For example, this document pushes against teaching as a set of finite skills. "From a feminist perspective," she asserts, "pedagogy isn't just something one does, it is knowledge realized in participant interaction" (Bailey, 2010, p. 153). Furthermore, Bailey (2010) encourages her students to look at their own academic socialization in the context of institutional and disciplinary histories, including trends within higher education that have marginalized women's studies. The other syllabus is an intervention to defamiliarize complex, contextual forces that affect TAs and their undergraduate students.

Importantly, the framing of the syllabus—and the work the syllabus does to frame opens some classroom epistemologies while foreclosing others. Developing language that furthers the goals of critical spaces is tricky because all participants bring the habits they have acquired from a stratified and unequal society into the classroom space. This means syllabi are most often instrumental, used to predict and control student behavior. Consequently, the focus remains exclusively on students and student learning and away from systems of knowledge production. Furthermore, the syllabus has become a flattened routine, passed down from instructor to instructor and from year to year. In sum, the possibility of a "critical syllabus" is unlikely because it would be deviating from a set of default genre expectations. However, both Bailey (2010) and Womack (2017) show critical moves in syllabus design that encourage problem-posing and revision through interactions with and evaluations from students. Thus, these syllabi call into question the hierarchies many of us take for granted in educational contexts.

De-Norming: Collaborative Problem-Posing in Critical Data Analysis

In this section, I apply Freire's problem-posing concept to illustrate the data analysis technique of de-norming.[5] The purpose of de-norming is to defamiliarize everyday texts and interactions with those texts. In practice, de-norming works through a collaborative, problem-posing heuristic that enables participants to identify the conventions of an institutional document and intervene in its (re)design. This analysis requires more than close readings and codes to trace language patterns in productive ways; it necessitates continuous problem-posing with others, especially to disrupt and push back against individual interpretations.[6] This technique is adaptable to institutional and classroom documents, statements, and policies that mediate relationships and experiences.

During de-norming analyses, participants attempt to identify ideologies working within a document through the textual and performative moves that have accrued specific, socially-constructed meanings over time.[7] In the case of the syllabus, a de-norming group would pose questions and revisions to encourage critical approaches to teaching and learning. While de-norming would most likely take place among faculty members and/or administrators, critical analyses can also happen with students as part of the class itself. Common iterations of this include collaborative curriculum and syllabus building (Shor, 1992) and collaborative articulations of writing assessment (Inoue, 2015). Additionally, Bawarshi and Reiff (2010) describe similar collaborative problem-posing methods to defamiliarize syllabi with students. However, the emphasis for them is on "genres as maps for gaining access to academic scenes" rather than restructuring the scenes themselves (p. 199).

FIGURE 4.1 De-norming Analysis Components

The specific processes of a de-norming analysis stem from anti-racism methodologies that seek to "identify, challenge, and change the values, structures, and behaviors that perpetuate systemic racism and other forms of societal oppression" (Dei, 2005, p. 3). As such, de-norming constitutes four primary actions that often overlap during collaborative problem posing: identifying, challenging, changing, and reflecting. Figure 4.1 details those actions and a discussion that follows applies the analysis specifically to syllabi (the document) and critical pedagogy (as ideology).

1. Identify: What is included in our definition of social justice? What are the typical features of justice-centered and critical pedagogies? What are the typical features of syllabi? How have those features changed over time?

   • How do we define social justice—in what ways could this document allow for growth or variation? What social norms are left unsaid and/or assumed? In what ways is emotional and/ or affective labor addressed? What resources, histories, and other contextual information is included/ excluded?

2. Challenge: How do we challenge the language/actions in the syllabus that we identify as oppositional to social justice and/or socially just practices? What histories, methods or research will help us better understand courses of action?

   • What is a context-specific process we can develop for challenging these aspects of the syllabi?
   • Can we anticipate resistance from stakeholders and/or outsiders—who? why? What methods, theories, frameworks could support us in our challenge of the syllabus?

3. Change: What alternatives could we imagine for the syllabus? How might we make those actionable?

   • In our context, what changes could we recommend that would center both the cognitive and affective needs of students and instructors?
   • What might the affordances and constraints be in these new language choices and counter structures (Shor, 1992)?
   • How do we center social justice in these changes/how do we work in socially just ways to institute these changes? Who should be present in the discussion before instituting these changes?
   • Who do we imagine these changes serving?

4. Reflect: How does our group define de-norming? Who is present/absent? In what ways do our identities and experiences impact our current understanding of critical pedagogy and syllabus design?

   • How might members' positionality affect participation in this context?

- What biases do we have that constrain our individual and collective analysis?
- What social norms might need to be challenged to work towards justice in our context? How might challenging be complicated by potential hierarchical relationships within the group?

Limitations of a Problem-Posing Approach

The primary limitations to this technique are practical: the conditions of the de-norming activity must be equitable. The institution, organization, or department should compensate participants. Several arguments can be made for the value of this collaborative analysis, including faculty and curriculum development. Additionally, syllabus design in particular may lead to productive inquiries into retention, student learning outcomes, assessment practices, and other programmatic concerns. Emphasizing those tangible gains for purposes of funding is crucial. However, some of the labor of de-norming may not be measurable because the goal is not to arrive at a consensus over any documents and policy; rather, the purpose is to ask new questions, which means embracing disagreement and multiple approaches to decision making. De-norming should resist and problematize answers that appear to be clear, obvious, and easy.

This is a formidable challenge: simultaneously designing *for* equity *through* equitable means. Therefore, in addition to compensation, de-norming is limited by its own in-group dynamics. Participants must trust one another enough to critique and be critiqued. In this situation, the inherent risks are complex, different, and unequal. It is important to remember that faculty of color, women, and individuals from other minoritized groups in higher education receive lower teaching and performance evaluations on average, and their authority is frequently called into question in other academic spaces (Ahmed, 2012). Not everyone is in a safe position to participate in classroom or institutional innovation, and not every classroom or institutional innovation will look the same.

Another limitation stems from the nature of texts and how they actually play out in complex interactions. Although understanding genres and typifications can be extremely productive, the *consequences* of documents are never completely knowable in that moment, and de-norming for social justice requires sustained engagement. In her study of institutional diversity documents, Ahmed (2006) argues that "'texts' are not 'finished' as forms of action, as what they 'do' depends on how they are 'taken up'. To track what texts do, we need to follow them around" (p. 105). When Ahmed (2006) follows institutional commitments to antiracism, she finds that stakeholders often point to documents themselves as evidence of progress. Thus, these written commitments counter an actionable, lived commitment to antiracism. Similarly, problematic readings of Freire's problem-posing play out when teachers and administrators co-opt tactics that appear critical but actually placate or coerce. For example, problem-posing dialogues may be empty and meaningless if participants are not intellectually and emotionally invested, or if the teacher/facilitator is leading students/participants to a predetermined place. This means it is important to (re)evaluate texts and actions in circulation over time, noting how they acquire and accumulate meanings within their specific context(s).

Recommendations for critical syllabi are beyond the scope of this de-norming sample; rather, the analysis illustrates the need for ongoing, continuous self-reflection for expanding our attunements to documents and typifications that work against socially just educational spaces.

Conclusion

The "student–teacher contradiction" Freire hopes to solve is complicated and often functions invisibly as the academic common sense (Apple & Beane, 2007). Often TAs and new faculty act in ways that they were taught when they were students themselves. Consequently, previous educational experiences inform their choices and provide models for what is appropriate/possible/necessary in a classroom. These beliefs work alongside/within logical and emotional attachments to (re)produce our shared environments. As such, the criticalist's mission is to trace how documents are made and made possible and what documents actually *do*. This means investigating how they begin to shape our attachments, identities, and decision-making processes in teaching, research, and administration. In this chapter, I propose that this work of tracing is best accomplished collaboratively through problem-posing and critical revision. Hopefully, de-norming directs educators interested in critical inquiry to texts that circulate within the academy and to the ways their enactments connect people and mediate relationships. Once we learn to (re)see the contradictions and boundaries between people and understand how they are maintained, then we may begin to transgress them (hooks, 1994)—enabling more reciprocal, equitable spaces in higher education.

Notes

1 Here I mean the critical perspectives to research that address power relations and center (in)justice, such as feminisms, poststructuralism, critical pedagogy, postcolonial theory, queer theory, and indigenous studies (Cannella, Pérez, & Pasque, 2015). Notably, Shor (1992) examines collaborative syllabus construction in critical classrooms and Inoue (2015) details collaborative assessment for antiracism.
2 Positivist thinking refers to the view that knowledge is logical, certain, and objective.
3 Rationalist here means that reason is the primary source of knowledge. As critical pedagogy has been taken up, some educators have limited the approach to a finite or formulaic set of beliefs rather than an ongoing process of inquiry.
4 Understanding typification is productive for accounting for context and defamiliarizing routine events. In her study of care-in-action, Barbara Korth (2003) defines typifications as the following: "Various possibilities for action, interpretation, and expectation

comprise typifications. More precisely, typifications are recognized social situations (for example, walking into a coffee shop where you have planned to meet a friend), which are, at first, holistically and intuitively grasped" (p. 493).

5 The name for this technique derives from the term "norming," a common practice in English departments where several instructors meet to discuss and grade student work, usually produced during a common exam. The goal of these norming sessions is to come to consensus about definitions and examples of quality writing.

In contrast, a de-norming session would embrace dissensus as a problem-posing method of consistently re-evaluating the norms students are judged by and the processes by which those norms are decided in the first place. Thus, de-norming embraces dissensus and leverages disagreement to defamiliarize conventions in various texts. For example, participants might look at what the disagreements reveal. They might ask what their judgments say about them, their unspoken assumptions of effectiveness and/or merit, and the ways they construct courses around those judgments and conceptions. From this viewpoint, the value of the conversation is in the in-between, in the dialogue and ongoing revision among participants in the group. The goal is not in affirmation of prior knowledge. This means the important learning would take place not in the evaluation of student writing but in the conversation as an evaluation of the norming participants themselves. Very rarely are workshops or classrooms set up this way, where the surfacing of conflict is desirable.

6 However, a similar approach could also be utilized for critical self-reflection as long as the user is not employing the heuristic as a set of finite considerations.

7 For example, the word "welcome" as expressed in-person at a professional conference carries a different weight than the "welcome" on a syllabus. Each of these scenarios plays out with a specific set of understandings between participants.

References

Ahmed, S. (2006). The nonperformativity of antiracism. *Meridians: feminism, race, transnationalism, 7*(1), 104–126.

Ahmed, S. (2012). *On being included: Racism and diversity in institutional life*. Durham, NC: Duke University Press.

Afros, E., & Schryer, C. F. (2009). The genre of syllabus in higher education. *Journal of English for Academic Purposes, 8*(3), 224–233.

Apple, M. W., & Beane, J. A. (2007). *Democratic schools: Lessons in powerful education*. Portsmouth, NH: Heinemann.

Baecker, D. L. (1998). Uncovering the rhetoric of the syllabus: The case of the missing I. *College Teaching, 46*(2), 58–62.

Bailey, L. E. (2010). The "other" syllabus: Rendering teaching politics visible in the graduate pedagogy seminar. *Feminist Teacher, 20*(2), 139–156.

Bawarshi, A. S., & Reiff, M. J. (2010). *Genre: An Introduction to history, theory, research, and pedagogy*. Washington: Parlor Press.

Cannella, G. S., Pérez, M. S., & Pasque, P. A. (Eds.). (2016). *Critical qualitative inquiry: Foundations and futures*. Walnut Creek, CA: Left Coast Press, Inc.

Dei, G. J. S. (2005). Chapter one: Critical issues in anti-racist research methodologies: an introduction. *Counterpoints, 252*, 1–27.

Fornaciari, C. J., & Lund Dean, K. (2014). The 21st-century syllabus: From pedagogy to andragogy. *Journal of Management Education, 38*(5), 701–723.

Freire, P. (1968/2000). *Pedagogy of the oppressed*. New York: Continuum.

hooks, b. (1994). *Teaching to transgress*. New York: Routledge.

Inoue, A. B. (2015). *Antiracist writing assessment ecologies: Teaching and assessing writing for a socially just future*. Fort Collins, CO: WAC Clearinghouse.

Korth, B. (2003). A critical reconstruction of care in action. *The Qualitative Report*, 8(3), 487–512.

Kumashiro, K. K. (2000). Toward a theory of anti-oppressive education. *Review of Educational Research*, 70(1), 25–53.

Lynch, K., Baker, J., & Lyons, M. (2009). *Affective equality: Love, care, and injustice*. Houndmills, Basingstoke: Palgrave Macmillan.

Micciche, L. R. (2007). *Doing emotion: Rhetoric, writing, teaching*. Portsmouth, NH: Boynton/Cook.

Shor, I. (1992). *Empowering education*. Chicago, IL: University of Chicago Press.

Womack, A. M. (2017). Teaching is accommodation: Universally designing composition classrooms and syllabi. *College Composition and Communication*, 68(3), 494.

Critical Theory and Analysis with Marginalized Populations

INTRODUCTION

Keon M. McGuire

The relationship between research(ers) and the "researched" – particularly when the latter constitutes those whom we may rightfully refer to as marginalized – is one that too often exists as a form of exploitation and violence (Tuck & Yang, 2014). Though the academy is at times hailed as a beacon of E/enlightenment, rational thinking, and liberal-democratic possibilities, academically trained researchers frequently operate as constitutive components of the nation-state's surveillance apparatus. Motivated by a seemingly insatiable quest for knowledge accumulation in order to *know*, *manipulate*, and *dominate* the social-material universe, academic research originating from the global north on a grand scale has advanced and operated within the leitmotif of Manifest Destiny (that settlers were destined to colonize and settle). Writing from/within/on the southwest border, I do not use such language lightly. That is to say, legitimized research as an organized, sustained commitment of human activity aimed at make sensing of the worlds we inherit, make and are made by, has progressed in a manner that has deputized (purposefully used here) imperial agents to engage, interpret, and (re)present the lives of *all* people, places, and things as reality/ies and T/truth/s.

While it has been well documented through the collective analyses of ethnic studies, feminist, postcolonial, decolonial and indigenous scholarship, it is worth indexing a few illustrative examples here. Consider how the heteropatriarchal construction of great men historical narratives celebrates the medical advancements of James Marion Sims, crowning him the father of modern gynecology, yet erasing the brutal experimentations he performed on enslaved Black women without anesthesia that led to such 'advancements' (Roberts, 1997). Too, we may recall the grossly unethical Tuskegee experiment in which roughly 400 Black men who tested positive for syphilis were purposefully untreated over the span of four decades (Washington, 2006). Even the history of the development of the birth control pill belies how Puerto Rican, Haitian, and Mexican women were treated as a beta-testing playground as the pill served as technology of population control for neo-colonized women, while later being marketed to middle-class American women as purchasable means of sexual freedom (López, 2008).

These histories are ever present with any of us who seek to work with marginalized populations – both in ways that we are aware of and unconscious to. That is, our institutions, modes of writing, thinking, studying, interpreting, critiquing and creating representations of life are implicated within colonial projects and white supremacist capitalist heteropatriarchal relations (hooks, 1990). With this realization, many scholars continue to advocate for a way of research that aspires to, at the least, interrogate and problematize these taken-for-granted modes of academic inquiry. Such scholars from a broad array of disciplines are committed to deconstructing hierarchical relations between the researchers and the researched, explicitly pursue social justice agendas, make visible positionalities, and engage in more humanizing methodologies that prioritize ethical considerations and do not attempt to speak for any subject (Paris & Winn, 2014; Smith, 1999/2013). As a placeholder, and to remain responsive to the focus of the section, we may collectively refer to such positions as "critical."

Critical qualitative research signifies a diverse set of, and at times divergent, projects that arguably are unified in a "commitment to expose and critique the forms of inequality and discrimination that operate in daily life" (Denzin, 2017, p. 9). Particularly when engaging with marginalized communities, this is a commitment to study such individuals as fully human beings – or in DuBoisan terms, studying sociological problems that humans experience and not humans as problems unto themselves. This intellectual legacy was threaded throughout Du Bois' body of work and is evident, for instance, in his opening to *Black Reconstruction in America: 1860–1880* where he states, "In fine, I am going to tell this story as though Negroes were ordinary human beings, realizing that this attitude will from the first seriously curtail my audience" (Du Bois, 1935/1998). As Gordon (1999) argued, Du Bois was prompting a critical self-reflexive praxis that would interrogate the prejudicial assumptions brought to bear on the analysis of Black people. As Du Bois proclaimed, "we must study even dehumanized human subjects in a humanistic way in order to recognize the dehumanizing practices that besiege them" (Gordon, 1999, p. 24).

As the chapters in this section demonstrate, a central component of critical qualitative inquiry involves the relationship between critical theory and data analysis. Reavis' chapter, Illuminating Systematic Inequality in Education: Using Bourdieu in Critical Qualitative Data Analysis, proffers Bourdieu's social reproduction theory as a way to understand systemic and systematic educational inequality within American schooling. Employing in tandem Bourdieu's four theoretical concepts – cultural capital, social capital, habitus, and field – Reavis makes sense of select data from a "longitudinal multi-site qualitative case study" that focused on "how families and schools influence students' college aspirations and college choice over a four-year period" (p. 85). Outlining detailed strategies for incorporating and engaging theoretical concepts at the stage of reflective memos, Reavis offers a possibility for thinking through inequality as an outcome of certain forms of capital and habitus being legitimized and valued, while others fail to provide necessary currency. In this way, Reavis encourages a form of criticality that moves beyond rational-choice frameworks – typically grounded in notions of abstract liberalism, meritocracy, and individualism – in order to consider the ways certain individuals work to purposefully accumulate additional resources.

In the next chapter, Answering the Methodological "Call" to Position Complex Blackness in Conversation with Hermeneutic Phenomenology, Mobley brings attention to a critical approach that rejects positivism not science and refuses empiricism, but not empirical evidence. In articulating his own intellectual–methodological lineage through/with philosophers such as Heidegger, Gadamer, Lewis Gordon, Fanon, and Husserl, Mobley demonstrates the incredible importance of conducting "research *with* and not *on* his people . . . with both care *and* humility" (p. 93). As someone who himself embodied the very complicated Blackness he explores in his work – the lived experiences of Black students attending Historically Black Colleges and Universities (HBCUs) at the intersections of race and class – Mobley positions hermeneutic phenomenology as a necessary foil to other traditions of phenomenology that privilege distance over closeness and, in this way, Mobley advocates a form of criticality (through which we understand the ways theories are built into methods) that both answers and raises questions; pays attentions to the margins of the margins; stretches the boundaries of what constitutes context and data; and runs towards reflexivity as an inevitable set of opportunities with which we should unapologetically grapple.

Blockett continues our conversation of critical closeness through his contribution, Thinking with Queer of Color Critique: A Multidimensional Approach to Analyzing and Interpreting Data in which he models a way of employing Black queer/quare theory to "unearth the practices that [Black queer men in college] engage as they labor to establish kinship networks at a [predominantly white institution]" (p. 110). In his work, Blockett promotes a mode of critical ethnography that is participatory in a way that refuses colonizing dispositions that fetishize dispassionate relations. Moreover, drawing on queer of color scholars, quare theory, and Queer Crit, Blockett highlights the importance of troubling racialized heteronormativity, challenging status-quo ideologies, and advancing an intersectional analysis concerned with the discursive and material. Similar to Mobley's discussion, Blockett sees positionality as a strategic resource in critical qualitative inquiry when working with marginalized populations – not something that needs to be quarantined or restrained. In this regard, Blockett raises three very important considerations for any scholar working with marginalized populations: (1) the politics of entering the field; (2) the necessity of using a theoretical framework throughout the entire study; and (3) what it might require to be competent as a researcher.

Offering more explicit attention to spatial-material realities, in the chapter Globalization, Higher Education, and Crisis: A Model for Applying Critical Geography toward Data Analysis, Blackburn Cohen uses critical geography to understand the various ways higher education institutions positioned themselves in pre- and post-World War II eras. Blackburn Cohen argues that the central tenets of critical geography are "an acute attention to material practices of power and power dynamics . . . a social justice orientation . . . and a focus toward emancipation, consciousness and change" (p. 125). More specifically related to globalization, Blackburn Cohen carries out an analysis that pays particular attention to three themes – imagination, manifestation, and contradiction. Through document analysis of several contemporary text excerpts, Blackburn Cohen brings these themes to bear on the two aforementioned globalization eras and makes clear the ways aspirational rhetoric and material realities collide, the various structures and processes that find neoliberal rhetoric wanting, and thinks through these realities within the prisms of space (physical) and place (abstract).

In the final chapter of this section, Context and Materiality: Inclusive Appropriations of New Materialism for Qualitative Analysis, Dennis offers an extension on the ways we may think about what constitutes the critical. Drawing on a "cluster of concepts" found in the writing of Karen Barad, Dennis uses her first day of teaching/entering the classroom and a picture of her exchanging money with a school director as a patron for a Ugandan school as data points and grounds for analysis. Employing concepts emerging from new materialism, Dennis refuses the binary between subject–object and human–nonhuman and attempts to enliven our thinking of what constitutes context – particularly material contexts. In this way, Dennis asks how we might think of material contexts as not simply objects of human manipulation, but active co-constructors of social phenomenon. In this way, Dennis' work is reminiscent of Fanon's principle of sociogeny and Sylvia Wynter's important philosophical work, which serves, in part, as an opportunity to bridge the hard and social sciences. In what could be read as a somewhat divergent approach to the other chapters in this section, like other new materialist scholars (Maclure, 2015), Dennis raises the issue of critique itself. That is, should the purpose of critical scholarship *exclusively* focus on unmasking ideological forces through processes of interpretation? Especially in her analysis of the photo, Dennis imagines what might be possible if we engage in a form of analysis that refuses certain assumptions about power, privilege, and global positioning.

While not always aligned, through mapping out specific traces of their processes of data analysis and purposeful selection of and engagement with critical theoretical frameworks, our authors proffer exciting possibilities for critical qualitative analysis. Moreover, they provide potential roadmaps for those hoping to advance an ethical, responsible and critical approach to working with marginalized populations in ways that are humanizing.

References

Denzin, N. K. (2017). Critical qualitative inquiry. *Qualitative Inquiry, 23*(1), 8–16.

Du Bois, W.E.B. (1935/1998). *Black reconstruction in America: 1860–1880.* New York: The Free Press. Gordon, L. (Spring 1999). A short history of the 'critical' in critical race theory. *The APA Newsletter on Philosophy and the Black Experience, 98*(2), 23–26.

hooks, b. (1990). *Yearning: Race, gender, and cultural politics.* Boston, MA: South End Press.

López, I. O. (2008). *Matters of choice: Puerto Rican women's struggle for reproductive freedom.* New Brunswick, NJ: Rutgers University Press.

Maclure, M. (2015). The 'new materialisms': a thorn in the flesh of critical qualitative inquiry? In G. Cannella, M. S. Perez, & P. Pasque (Eds.), *Critical Qualitative Inquiry: Foundations and Futures.* California: Left Coast Press.

Paris, D., & Winn, M. T. (Eds.). (2014). *Humanizing research: Decolonizing qualitative inquiry with youth and communities.* Thousand Oaks, CA: Sage Publications.

Roberts, D. (1997). *Killing the Black body: Race, reproduction, and the meaning of liberty.* New York: Pantheon Books.

Smith, L. T. (1999/2013). *Decolonizing methodologies: Research and indigenous peoples.* London: Zed Books.

Tuck, E., & Yang, K. W. (2014). R-Words: Refusing Research. In D. Paris & M. T. Winn (Eds.), *Humanizing research: Decolonizing qualitative inquiry with youth and communities.* Thousand Oaks, CA: Sage Publications.

Washington, H. A. (2006). *Medical apartheid: The dark history of medical experimentation on Black Americans from colonial times to the present.* New York: Doubleday Books.

5

ILLUMINATING SYSTEMIC INEQUALITY IN EDUCATION

Using Bourdieu in Critical Qualitative Data Analysis

Tangela Blakely Reavis

Theory: Bourdieu's Social Reproduction Theory
Type of qualitative data: Interviews
New data analysis: Social Reproduction Theory Memo Analysis
Substantive topics in education: Higher education access

Pierre Bourdieu (1979/1984) created a theory that explores social and cultural reproduction. Bourdieu's theory is appropriate for understanding persistent inequality in the American education system. It provides a deeper consideration of the larger social inequalities and potential for reproduction of these inequalities that may influence outcomes, actions, and experiences (McCoy & Winkle-Wagner, 2015). In this chapter, I apply social reproduction theory to an example of educational inequalities and specifically to higher education access.

Although more than 60 years have passed since the U.S. Supreme Court declared segregation in schools to be unconstitutional, segregation remains a part of the educational experience for many American schoolchildren (Orfield & Lee, 2005; Reardon & Owens, 2014). Nearly, two-thirds of Black and Latinx students attend schools that are non–White or have high concentrations of poverty (Darling-Hammond, 2010). One primary reason for the overrepresentation of students of color and families below the poverty level in low-income schools is funding. Public schools are financed through state budgets that come from neighborhood property taxes. Poor communities have lower tax rates, which results in less funding and resources for the neighborhood schools (Ladson-Billings, 2006; Lipman, 2004, 2013; Mullen, 2010; Shapiro, 2004). Throughout the U.S., states are spending an average of 15 percent less per pupil in the poorest school districts (where average spending is $9,270 per child) compared to their more affluent counterparts (where average spending is $10,721 per child) (NCES, 2015). Decreases in state funding further exacerbate inequality in low-income school districts. In Pennsylvania, for example, state budget cuts to education during the past several years have contributed to a funding crisis in Philadelphia, a high-poverty district where many schools do not have full-time counselors and where teachers and parents have contributed to help purchase essential resources such as paper (Brown, 2015).

Inequality in secondary schooling has long-term implications for college attendance and, ultimately, life outcomes, creating divergent pathways for students. Many students who attend elite colleges, for example, are following a similar pathway to their families (McDonough, 1997; Mullen, 2010). Some students receive a type of education from their high-resourced high school that prepares them for admissions into top-tier colleges (Mullen, 2010). After college, many of these individuals will enter the workforce and make high salaries, just as their parents did. For students of color or those who come from low-income families and are disproportionately enrolled in low-resourced high schools, the pathways to college are more perilous. Under-resourced high schools often link to less competitive institutions, such as for-profit, open enrollment, and two-year institutions (Bailey & Morest, 2006; Bragg & Durham, 2012). One way of explaining the divergent pathways for students and their families navigating the education system is the theory of social reproduction (Bourdieu, 1979/1984).

In this chapter, I will describe the theoretical concepts in Bourdieu's social reproduction theory and then I will outline a technique that includes the ways one might apply that theory in qualitative data analysis. In particular, I use interview data from a longitudinal study of college-aspiring high school students in order to consider a way of analyzing data that integrates Bourdieu's social reproduction theory. I do this as a way to better connect the data to larger social issues—in this case, to show inequality between schools.

Background of Pierre Bourdieu

French sociologist Pierre Bourdieu (1930–2002) was a prolific author and one of the more important sociological theorists (Winkle-Wagner, 2010). Bourdieu's work combines both theory and empirical data in an attempt to understand and illuminate some of the most complex issues in theory, research, and practice relative to ways that social inequality is reproduced. His work emphasizes how social classes, especially the dominant classes, reproduce themselves despite the assumption that education fosters upward and social mobility. Bourdieu's work rejects the conventional narrative that schools serve as great equalizers for upward mobility, and instead, illustrates how they do the opposite by exacerbating inequality (MacLeod, 2018).

Influenced by the work of Karl Marx (1963), Bourdieu is classified as a conflict theorist. Conflict theorists claim that society is in a perpetual state of conflict between two classes, the bourgeoisie (capitalist) and the proletariat (worker) due to competition for limited resources (Marx, 1963). The argument from conflict theorists is that social structures are maintained by domination and power. Marxists believe the bourgeoisie hold the power and deliberately maintain it, while continuing to suppress the poor and powerless. For Marxists, capitalism not only generates goods and services for profit, but reproduces the system of class relations. In this system, the worker continues to be poor, the employer remains wealthy, and class relations are replicated and transmitted to future generations.

Bourdieu distinguishes himself from Marx and critiques the way that economics and schooling are positioned to explain the perpetuation of social stratification (Winkle-Wagner, 2010). For Bourdieu, class inequality is more nuanced and extends beyond economic constraints to include two other forms of capital: *social capital* and *cultural capital* (Musoba & Baez, 2009). These concepts are described in more detail in the section that follows. Aside from material and economic forms of reproduction, Bourdieu is concerned with showing how class status could be perpetuated through more subtle ways, such as through one's lifestyle or tastes (Winkle-Wagner, 2010). For Bourdieu, one's tastes, actions, and decisions are often situated in one's lifestyle that operates below the level of consciousness, which often appears "normal" and goes unnoticed. For example, an upper-class family's decision to send their children to an elite boarding school comes with the expectation that the school will prepare them to attend the most selective universities so that they can graduate and move into the highest wage labor market positions. These decisions, which may appear to be normal, end up maintaining the prevalent social order of class structures and domination. Children born into upper-class families will maintain their status and reproduce it. Unlike Marx, Bourdieu believed that oppression functions in a more covert and natural way to privilege those in the dominant group (Musoba & Baez, 2009).

Social Reproduction Theory

Bourdieu is perhaps most notable for his theoretical contributions. Scholars use social reproduction theory in education research as a way to show how social status may influence student outcomes in education (Musoba & Baez, 2009; Winkle-Wagner, 2010). It is also used to show how schools serve distinct populations of students, providing different levels of support for their college preparation and college-going decisions (Mullen, 2010). Bourdieu's theoretical apparatus (1979/1984) of social reproduction has four theoretical concepts: (1) cultural capital; (2) social capital; (3) habitus; and (4) field. All theoretical concepts work together to explain an individual's practice or action (Musoba & Baez, 2009). I explain each concept and then demonstrate how it can be applied to qualitative data analysis.

Cultural capital can be defined as the rewards one receives from knowledge, skills, abilities, or formal educational credentials (Bourdieu, 1979/1984). Cultural capital involves a variety of resources such as verbal competence, cultural awareness, aesthetic preferences and knowledge about school, all of which are typically acquired through family upbringing or through education (Bourdieu, 1979/1984). Children from upper-income families inherit substantially different cultural capital than children from working- and lower-class families (Bourdieu & Passeron, 1977). Children from high-income families typically inherit a type of cultural capital which acts as a "power resource" that is valued in social settings such as schools (Winkle-Wagner, 2010). For example, through a competitive admissions process, many top-tier institutions of higher education reward the cultural capital of the upper classes and systematically devalue that of the lower classes.

Social capital can be defined as a durable network of relationships, trust, obligations, or familial connections that establish the norms and values of a social class and provide power and opportunity over those outside of the network (Bourdieu, 1986). Social capital is never independent of economic or cultural capital; one's social networks can drive cultural capital, which can lead to economic capital (income). Social capital is consciously and unconsciously formed and translated between networks, especially between students and their parents as well as between a student's parents and other adults, including those connected to the school that a student attends (Dika & Singh, 2002). For example, a school's reputation is not only developed through statistics such as test scores or college-going rates, but through parents of existing students. Parents that have children attending higher resourced schools are known to inform other like-minded parents about the reputation of a particular school so their child can gain entry.

While cultural and social capital are used to show the persistence of inequality between classes, these concepts should be viewed from an assets-based perspective. For example, one may assert that low-income students do not go to college because they "lack" cultural and social capital as if they are deficient in some way. Everyone *has* cultural and social capital, it is just that those who are in power value the cultural and social capital that typically come from the upper class (Bourdieu, 1979/1984). This argument is important when applying the work of Bourdieu to critical data analysis. I will revisit this idea in the section that follows.

Habitus is the embodied form of one's dispositions, tastes, and preferences, which come from social structures and, in turn, reinforce the social structure (Bourdieu, 1986). It is a set of predispositions about how one responds to stimuli in certain contexts and describes the ways in which individual actions and societal structures are linked (Musoba & Baez, 2009). With habitus, aspirations reflect an individual's view of his or her own chance of getting ahead and are an internalization of objective possibilities. Habitus generates and constrains thoughts, perceptions, and actions, which formed the basis for it in the first place (Musoba & Baez, 2009). Habitus operates below the level of consciousness. The socialization toward a particular habitus begins very early—some research argues—during childhood (Swartz, 1997).

Field, the final concept in Bourdieu's (1979/1984) theoretical apparatus, refers to a structured environment of social positions and a structure of power relations. Fields are the areas of practice and conflict, the spaces in which the interplays of habitus and capital are enacted (Bourdieu, 1979/1984). The field is typically governed by laws of practice and conditions of entry (e.g. economic capital, social capital, cultural capital) (Musoba & Baez, 2009). People are positioned within the field based on their possession of particular forms of capital (e.g. professional degrees). There are many different fields that are often class based and can be in the form of a school, an entire school district, one's family, one's community, and the broader policies which govern them (e.g. increased cost of college, increased competitiveness in terms of getting into college).

Application of Social Reproduction Theory to Critical Data Analysis

In this section, I show one way to apply Bourdieu's concepts of social reproduction to critical data analysis. I use Bourdieu's complete theoretical apparatus (social capital, cultural capital, habitus, and field) because all four concepts work together to explain one's actions or decisions as well as emphasize the persistence of inequality between classes (Musoba & Baez, 2009). Some of the existing literature citing Bourdieu only use parts of the full theory in their data analysis, which can lead to misinterpretation of his work. Studies that use parts of Bourdieu's theory (Kim & Schneider, 2005; Perna & Titus, 2005) may unintentionally frame one's decisions or actions in a deficit way, suggesting that students need to gain relevant cultural capital that they do not have in order to improve their social status (Winkle-Wagner, 2010).

To demonstrate this technique, I used data from a longitudinal multi-site qualitative case study. The purpose of this study was to understand how families and schools influenced students' college aspirations and college choice over a four-year period (student's freshmen year through their senior year of high school). The following sources were used for data collection: in-depth semi-structured interviews, field notes from school site visits, and documents from the school district websites, which contained special reports and school-specific demographic information. For the purposes of this chapter, I present some of the interview data as a way to demonstrate my analytic technique. The application of this technique is also illustrated in my dissertation (see Reavis, 2017). The analytical approach to data analysis that I will demonstrate includes a four-step process. I describe each process below using excerpts of data collected from the study.

Step One: Thorough Read of Transcript Data

Reading individual transcript data allows for emergent thoughts, ideas, and reflection to take place (Miles & Huberman, 1994). Since the data from this study was longitudinal, and followed students throughout each year of high school, the first step was to read the transcripts for each of the students in chronological order, starting with the students' freshmen year and ending with their senior year. I also used the same process for school staff. I read their transcripts in chronological order, starting with the first year they were interviewed and ending with the last year. While reading each transcript, I wrote detailed notes and memos about the students' college-choice process and made notes about how Bourdieu's concept of social reproduction might apply to this study. I also wrote memos from the counselor interviews and field notes, which helped capture the college-going culture of each high school (Miles & Huberman, 1994). The interview data (below) is an excerpt from a guidance counselor at a college preparatory high school. This high school used a competitive selective enrollment process to recruit its student body. Each year, approximately 1,200 students applied for 400 seats, making it so that only about one-third of the students who hoped to attend were invited to enroll. I provide an example of how I made a memo reference to Bourdieu's concept of social reproduction theory. For example, the quote from a high school counselor was:

> So, usually in January, [students are] picking their courses for the following year . . . we always stress that what the graduation requirements are the bare minimum and that they really need to look . . . at what's needed for college . . . most of our students do take the four years of science, four years of math. We require two years of world languages so they have that covered. So we really do stress the rigor. We limit the amount of study halls kids can take, and we don't allow kids to have like half days or work programs. It's just really been a culture here that it's not allowed.

Memo Note: Social Reproduction Theory Connection

Cultural Capital (knowledge, skills or abilities related to postsecondary education). Students needed to test into this school in order to attend so they already bring with them a set of academic skills that are valued.

Social Capital (informal/formal relationships that students or their families have in their communities or at their high schools). The students seem to have a strong support network and curriculum at school, which encourages them to take well beyond the minimum requirements for college.

Habitus (students' aspirations or possible actions). If the culture of the high school promotes normalcy in taking more than the minimum requirements for college, a student will believe they are prepared for college and will feel like college is available to them.

Field (social setting, such as a high school, where forms of capital are enacted). Since the school practices a competitive enrollment process and many of the students have parents that have been to college (when compared to other schools in the district), the reproduction of inequality where only "dominant" forms of social and cultural capital are recognized is legitimized.

Step Two: Development of Low-Level Codes

The next step involves using an in vivo coding/low-level coding process (Merriam, 2009), where I coded approximately 20–30 percent of the transcripts in each person's words. Utilizing this process elicits approximately 150 codes per transcript. Low-level codes were closely aligned to the transcripts, interview protocols, and the explicit statements made by participants. The codes were short phrases aimed at capturing larger amounts of the data (multiple sentences or a paragraph). Low-level codes were taken directly from the text of the transcript in order to accurately capture the student's feelings and experiences. After identifying the low-level codes, I wrote a brief summary of the coding. For example, the interview text is from a freshman high school student:

> [I don't feel like I'm prepared for college] because, I need to work on studying, because as you can see, I only study for 30 minutes. So I do need to work on studying, and . . . I be hearing my English teacher talk about how she did 15 page papers and stuff [in college] . . . I'm so not the paper type of person. I'm more of a hands-on person.
>
> *[Malika, high school junior]*

Low-level codes:
"I need help studying"
"I only study for 30 minutes"
"I'm not the paper type of person"
"I'm more of a hands-on person"
Low-level coding summary: In the text, Malika described the challenges she experienced with academic preparation for college so much that she is questioning whether she is prepared to attend.

Step Three: Development of High-Level Codes and Master Codebook

Once low-level codes are established from the rest of the data, similar codes should be grouped together to form a common theme. This theme, which ties the low codes together, are called high-level codes. High codes are not usually developed from the participant's words, but they are still very close to the original text. High codes are larger categories that one might use to develop one's master codebook (Carspecken, 1996). After the high-level coding, I provided a high-level coding summary. Using the same data, here is an example of how to transform the low-level categories to form high-level categories.

In vivo/low-level codes:
"I need help studying"
"I only study for 30 minutes"
"I'm not the paper type of person"
"I'm more of a hand-on person"

High-level categories (for master codebook):
Perception of Self
Cultural Capital (Bourdieu, 1979/1984)
Habitus (Bourdieu, 1979/1984)

    High-level coding summary. Possible high-level codes for this data might be *perception of self, cultural capital* and *habitus*. In this illustration, *perception of self* was selected because it summarized how Malika described her academic performance. This code is also broad enough to allow other data to be captured here that may include more information about Malika's academic experiences as well as the perceptions from other participants who were self-reflective. In the larger study, *perception of self* was coded when students described their performance, personality or behavior.

Bourdieu's concepts of *cultural capital* (knowledge, skills, abilities) and *habitus* (students' aspirations or possible actions) are other high codes that should be considered for this text. Malika recognized that 30 minutes of study time was generally not enough to do well in school, especially in college. Malika may also have been intimidated by the academic expectations she would face in college so she perceived herself to be more comfortable utilizing hands-on skills that were non-academic. Malika's hands-on skills demonstrate that she *does* have cultural capital, just not the kind that will be valued in helping her get into college. Therefore, she does not have a college-going habitus and may not have believed that she belonged in college. In this illustration, high codes are formed and can be used to develop your master codebook. In the master codebook, Bourdieu's concept of *cultural capital* would be used to code larger quantities of data whenever a participant described their academic experiences and performance.

Step Four: Data Management and Data Organization

Since qualitative data analysis is an iterative process (Merriam, 2009), I continued to develop the codes relative to the data and its potential connection to all of Bourdieu's theoretical concepts as part of the codebook. Developing a codebook helps facilitate the organization of the data, especially in larger projects with multiple participants and research sites. Once the master codebook is developed, it may be helpful to use a coding software such as NVivo or Deduce for data organization and data management (Weitzman, 2000). In this step, one would import data into the database of choice and use the high categories identified in the master codebook to further analyze the data. Utilizing a database software provides an efficient way for pulling a large amount of text based on a high category or theme.

Discussion and Future Application of Proposed Technique

By the time many students enroll in high school, they are far along in their educational trajectories, which is likely to heavily influence their college choices. Some students who graduate from high school will enroll in a top-tier four-year college, while others will enroll in a two-year school or community college. Others may not choose college at all because they enter the workforce or the military. Finally, some students may leave high school without a degree. The differences in these educational trajectories, especially the decision to enroll in college, are often linked to social inequalities, and to what Bourdieu (1979/1984) would call social reproduction. Applying the concepts of Bourdieu's theoretical apparatus to qualitative data analysis offers one useful way of shedding light on the systemic barriers that frame the education system that is not linked to one's individual motivation or cognitive ability.

Future applications of Bourdieu's work should include all four concepts of his theoretical apparatus (cultural capital, social capital, habitus and field), otherwise it might lead to a deficit view, which would be a misinterpretation of his work. Bourdieu's intent was for each of these concepts to function together in order to offer a more complete representation of how systems, structures, and processes afford particular advantages to certain groups in social settings such as educational institutions (Winkle-Wagner, 2010). The use of social reproduction theory memo analysis would also work well when analyzing other forms of data (e.g. field notes, discourse analysis, life history) that seek deeper meaning about people's experiences and the world around them. Future research applying social reproduction to qualitative analysis might also emphasize the role of other socially constructed barriers (e.g. race and gender) or the intersection of all three as cause for the persistence of systemic inequality across our education system. Finally, Bourdieu's theoretical apparatus may not be useful for most quantitative data or research focused on generalizing across populations. Bourdieu's concepts emphasize that the reproduction of inequality often happens in a more covert manner and below the level of consciousness, which would be difficult to examine using large data sets or statistical models.

References

Bailey, T., & Morest, V. S. (2006). *Defending the community college equity agenda.* Baltimore, MD: Johns Hopkins University Press.

Bourdieu, P. (1979/1984). *Distinction: A social critique of the judgment of taste.* R. Nice (Trans.). Cambridge, MA: Harvard University Press.

Bourdieu, P. (1986). Forms of capital. In J. E. Richardon (Ed.), *Handbook of theory for the sociology of education* (pp. 241–258). Santa Barbara, CA: Greenwood Press.

Bourdieu, P., & Passeron, J. C. (1977). *Reproduction in education, society, and culture.* Beverly Hills, CA: Sage Publications.

Bragg, D. D., & Durham, B. (2012). Perspectives on access and equity in the era of (community) college completion. *Community College Review, 40*(2), 106–125.

Brown, E. (2015). In 23 states, richer school districts get more local funding than poorer districts. *The Washington Post.* Retrieved from https://www.washingtonpost.com/news/local/wp/2015/03/12/in-23-states-richer-school-districts-get-more-local-funding-than-poorer-districts/?utm_term=.6cdba0203e5a#graphic

Carspecken, P. F. (1996). *Critical ethnography in educational research: A theoretical and practical guide.* New York: Routledge.

Darling-Hammond, L. (2010). *The flat world and education: How America's commitment to equity will determine our future.* New York: Teachers College Press.

Dika, S. L., & Singh, K. (2002). Applications of social capital in educational literature: A critical synthesis. *Review of educational research, 72*(1), 31–60.

Kim, D. H., & Schneider, B. (2005). Social capital in action: Alignment of parental support in adolescents' transition to postsecondary education. *Social Forces, 84*(2), 1181–1206.

Ladson-Billings, G. (2006). From the achievement gap to the education debt: Understanding achievement in US schools. *Educational Researcher, 35*(7), 3–12.

Lipman, P. (2004). *High stakes education: Inequality, globalization, and urban school reform.* New York: Routledge Falmer.

Lipman, P. (2013). *The new political economy of urban education: Neoliberalism, race, and the right to the city.* New York: Taylor & Francis.

MacLeod, J. (2018). *Ain't no makin' it: Aspirations and attainment in a low-income neighborhood.* Routledge.

Marx, K. (1963). Early writings. Edited and translated by T. B. Bottomore. New York: McGraw Hill Education.

McCoy, D. L., & Winkle-Wagner, R. (2015). Bridging the divide: Developing a scholarly habitus for aspiring graduate students through summer bridge programs participation. *Journal of College Student Development, 56*(5), 423–439.

Merriam, S. (2009). *Qualitative research: A guide to design and implementation.* San Francisco, CA: Jossey-Bass.

Miles, M. B., & Huberman, A. M. (1994). *Qualitative data analysis: An expanded sourcebook.* Thousand Oakes, CA: Sage Publications.

Mullen, A. L. (2010). *Degrees of inequality: Culture, class, and gender in American higher education.* Baltimore, MD: Johns Hopkins University Press.

Musoba, G., & Baez, B. (2009). The cultural capital of cultural and social capital: An economy of translations. In *Higher education: Handbook of theory and research* (pp. 151–182). New York: Spring Press.

National Center for Education Statistics (2015). *School district current expenditures per pupil with and without adjustments for federal revenues by poverty and race/ethnicity characteristics.* US Department of Education, Education Finance Statistics Center. Retrieved from https://nces.ed.gov/edfin/Fy11_12_tables.asp.

Orfield, G., & Lee C. (2005). Why segregation matters: Poverty and educational inequality. Cambridge, MA: Harvard University, The Civil Rights Project. Retrieved from: http://www.civilrightsproject.harvard.edu.

Perna, L. W., & Titus, M. (2005). The relationship between parental involvement as social capital and college enrollment: An examination of racial/ethnic group differences. *The Journal of Higher Education, 76*(5), 485–518.

Reardon, S. F., & Owens, A. (2014). 60 years after Brown: Trends and consequences of school segregation. *Annual Review of Sociology, 40*, 199–218.

Reavis, T. B. (2017). *College choice interrupted or facilitated: A qualitative case study examining how social class and schools structure opportunity for students in urban high schools.* Doctoral dissertation, University of Wisconsin-Madison.

Shapiro, T. M. (2004). *The hidden cost of being African American: How wealth perpetuates inequality.* New York: Oxford University Press.

Swartz, D. (1997). *Culture and power: The sociology of Pierre Bourdieu.* Chicago, IL: University of Chicago Press.

Weitzman, E. A. (2000). Software and qualitative research. In N. K. Denzin & Y. S. Lincoln (Eds.), *Handbook of qualitative research* (pp 803–820). London: Sage Publications.

Winkle-Wagner, R. (2010). Cultural capital: The promises and pitfalls in education research. *ASHE Higher Education Report, 36*(1), 1–144.

6

ANSWERING THE METHODOLOGICAL "CALL" TO POSITION COMPLEX BLACKNESS IN CONVERSATION *WITH* HERMENEUTIC PHENOMENOLOGY

Steve D. Mobley, Jr.

Theory: Critical Hermeneutic Phenomenology

Type of qualitative data: Unique "Texts," e.g. television scripts, poetry, art, and music lyrics

New data analysis technique: Hermeneutic Phenomenological-Critical Analysis

---

(Re)Creating A Scholarly Space While Traversing the "Rare"

> When a Black man is willing and able to quote and use European philosophy in his efforts to name his oppression and proclaim his existence, then he is surely starting something and should be watched.
>
> *(Fanon, 1952/2008)*

I open this chapter with an epithet from Frantz Fanon (1952/2008) because his words profoundly contextualize the spirit of how I position my research *and* methodological stance(s) in tandem with my lived experience(s) as a Black man who holds myriad oppressed identities. Frantz Fanon was an African philosopher, phenomenologist, and critical theorist whose pioneering philosophical contributions were quite influential for his time because he was unafraid to confront the existence of colonialism and anti–Black racism and its residual effects on Black communities across the diaspora (Gordon, 2015). As a Black scholar who engages phenomenology, which I define below as both methodology[1] *and* philosophy, his work functions as a vital foundation for me. In particular, Fanon's book *Black Skin, White Masks* (1952/2008) serves as a textual embodiment of Black scholarly resistance and transgression against a philosophical canon largely dominated by White Eurocentric interpretations. One of the major issues that I found during my early engagement with "foundational" phenomenological philosophy was that it was limited to a specific cultural parity and dominated by White male lenses. However, Fanon questions these philosophical texts in order to situate the lived experiences of Blacks who reside in an anti-Black world (Mahendran, 2007). During my engagement with *his* brand of phenomenology, it was encouraging to encounter a Black philosopher who was "doing" the work that I was attempting to. There are not many examples that place Blackness in conservation with European/White phenomenological philosophy *and* challenge it with Black anti-essentialist narratives as well. Within my work, I deliberately contextualize Black experiences that lie on the margins. I too take an anti-essentialist *and* intersectional approach that seeks to highlight the depth and uniqueness of Black experiences within higher education while also underscoring the ways in which Black students experience intra-racial tensions.

Within this chapter I introduce a much needed forum to (re)create a scholarly space for critical qualitative researchers who seek to (un)cover the myriad complexities that are apparent amongst Black communities within post-secondary educational spaces. As a critical scholar who engages research *with* and not *on* his people, I understand that I must approach my work with both care *and* humility. I have been given the platform to question and seek truth; *everyone* is not granted this freedom. This chapter offers a different perspective that illuminates how one can utilize hermeneutic phenomenology and then connect it to critical theories and approaches in order to investigate the lived experiences of Black students who are present within post-secondary environments.

Specifically, I use hermeneutic phenomenology[2] in a critical manner in order to explore the many nuances that are apparent within historically Black college and university environments (HBCUs)[3]. While there is an abundance of new research on Black colleges, there is a void that is present. There is a lack of diversity among the methods used to examine these institutions and their students. Furthermore, it has been rare for HBCU scholars to prominently feature *and* deeply reflect on why and how they choose the research methods they utilize to (re)present and portray these distinct higher education environments and their students.

There are complex identities that lie within HBCU contexts *and* the researchers that choose to answer the "call" to study these higher education environments. The intersections of many oppressed identities (e.g. race, class, gender, and sexuality) lie in the margins of HBCU communities *and* their researchers. An intense yet fascinating relationship is present between that which is being researched and the researcher. Within this chapter I assert myself as a critical researcher who studies HBCU environments and explicitly underscore my positioning as a scholar who does not claim to be "value free" in my positioning (Green & Winkle-Wagner, 2015). This stance is key. "Critical researchers often claim a value orientation that takes a direct stance toward social inequity and oppression, where researchers outwardly claim a position against oppression" (Green & Winkle-Wagner, 2015, p. 224). As this body of research evolves, it will be vital for HBCU scholars to bring their methodological voices to the forefront. These vigilant narratives can be used to ensure that thoughtful HBCU research will continue to be produced. Overall, this chapter highlights the nuanced and compelling research environment that was made available to me. As I have *un-covered* and answered the *un-answered* during my phenomenological journey, within this chapter I now (re)turn to how I engaged *this* philosophical method.

Seizing the Opportunity to Reveal Phenomenology's Critical Features

> Phenomenology means . . . letting be seen . . . that which shows itself, just as it shows itself from itself.
>
> *(Heidegger, 1962/2008, p. 58)*

> Human life escapes us if we try to capture it from a theoretical, objectivizing attitude.
>
> *(Safranski, 1998, p. 146)*

Phenomenology is a "freeing" methodology—a raw, yet sensitive approach that gets inside phenomena. "Modern thinking and scholarship is so caught up in theoretical and technological thought that the program of a phenomenological human science may strike an individual as a breakthrough and a liberation" (van Manen, 2007, p. 9). Rather than *tell* the reader *what* they should *believe* about a phenomenon, phenomenology seeks to *show* and engage so that one may deeply feel the experience, continue to question, and further explore the possibilities. As such:

> Phenomenology is best understood as a radical, anti-traditional style which emphasizes the attempt to get to the truth of matters, to describe phenomena, in the broadest sense as whatever appears in the manner in which it appears, that is as it manifests itself to consciousness, to the experiencer.
>
> *(Moran, 2000, p. 4)*

Phenomenology allows the phenomenologist to resist methodological seductions that are often preoccupied with what is correct or incorrect (Hultgren, 1995). I use phenomenology to discover that which is limited and (un)explored within higher education research.

Phenomenology's strength is that it fuels the researcher's passion while also recognizing their integral role in the research process. When applied critically, phenomenology has the power to liberate and empower one's research inquiry to critique ideologies that are apparent in the status quo (Blockett, 2017). In a relinquishment from objectivist research practices that often (re)move the researcher from that which they are researching (Blockett, 2017), I chose phenomenology—and it chose me as well.

"An interpretation of human existence cannot be neutral, dispassionate theoretical contemplation, but must take into account the involvement of the inquirer in the undertaking" (Moran, 2000, p. 197). This method is unafraid to call attention to aspects of our lives that are often neglected by empiricism, in particular the background assumptions that we all bring as we seek to better understand particular phenomena (Moran, 2000). Questioning the rigid confines that reside within the empiricism that permeates many qualitative traditions is a foremost tenant of most critical approaches. "Thus it becomes clear that in every understanding there remains something unexplained, and that one therefore must ask about what motivates every understanding. This changes the entire concept of interpretation" (Spiegelberg, 1982, p. 281). Phenomenological research is always a project of someone: a real person, who seeks to draw upon individual, social, and historical life circumstances to make sense of a certain aspect of human existence (van Manen, 2007). These ideas reflect the values that one regularly adopts when "doing" critical hermeneutic phenomenological work:

> Researchers are grounded in philosophical paradigms in which they situate themselves and their work. These paradigms literally *inform, govern, and limit* their work. Thus, choosing a philosophical paradigm to address my topical interests was not an accidental choice. I thought it over carefully and considered my options.
>
> *(Brimhall-Vargas, 2011, p. 149)*

No research methodology, either qualitative or quantitative, or research paradigm provides "perfect" entry into research. But, as scholars we are provided the privilege to choose our research journeys.

My study, *Difference Amongst Your Own: The Lived Experiences of Low-Income African-American Students and Their Encounters with Class within Elite Historically Black College (HBCU) Environments,* utilized *hermeneutic phenomenology* as a critical qualitative methodology that has rarely been used in the fields of higher education and student affairs. This study is critical in nature because it deliberately challenges and questions positivistic research practices that often inhibit researchers to be freed from research environments that seek to confine and inhibit evocative research exploration(s). In adopting this epistemological stance, I make it apparent that my work seeks visible and emancipatory pathways for Black individuals and our communities (Stewart, 2017). *Difference Amongst Your Own* directly confronts the impact that social class differences have on the undergraduate experiences of low-income African-American students who attend *elite HBCUs*.[4] "Just because the phenomena are mostly not immediately given [i.e., a special method for gaining access to our experience and making it explicit] is needed" (Heidegger, 1962/2008, p. 59).

This phenomenological study drew upon various sources to bring forth mutual understanding. I was able to summon extant higher education research, African-American fiction, poetry, television sitcoms, cinema, and even song lyrics to bring the reader into the phenomenon. The foundational philosophical views of Martin Heidegger, Hans-Georg Gadamer, and Edward S. Casey also served as a strong basis for this work. However, it was also extremely important to me that I placed the previously mentioned philosophers in conversation with Black voices as I was exploring a particular facet of the Black higher education experience. I chose to feature Black philosophers including Lewis Gordon and Frantz Fanon. In placing "Blackness" directly in the center of *Difference Amongst Your Own,* I intentionally showed that "there is no one phenomenology."

"There Is No One Phenomenology": Recognizing Distinction

In the summer of 1927 Martin Heidegger offered a course at the University of Marburg entitled *Die Grundprobleme der Phänomenologie,* translated into English as *The Basic Problems of Phenomenology.* He emphatically declared during one of his lectures:

> There is no such thing as the one phenomenology. We shall maintain that phenomenology is not just one philosophical science among others, nor is it the science preparatory to the rest of them; rather, the expression "phenomenology" is the name for the method of scientific philosophy in general.
>
> *(Heidegger, 1927/1982, p. 24).*

More than 80 years after Martin Heidegger declared that there is no one phenomenology, there is still tremendous misunderstanding surrounding this methodology. A variety of research methods have become popular over this period of time including ethnography, grounded theory, and phenomenology (Denzin & Lincoln, 2000). This is especially true in higher education and student affairs scholarship.

While phenomenology has gained familiarity in higher education and student affairs research, it is often portrayed homogeneously in this body of work. Furthermore, phenomenology is a term that has been and is often (mis)represented in education research (Arminio & Hultgren, 2002). Phenomenology and hermeneutic phenomenology are often (mis)used, erroneously conflated, and/or referred to interchangeably without questioning any distinction between them within education scholarship (Laverty, 2003). It is essential to draw distinctions within this methodological approach. Failure to highlight phenomenology's inherent philosophical and interpretive differences as a methodology and philosophy diminishes the work of those who choose to "do" phenomenology *and* the impact of their scholarship. Neglecting to recognize the nuances inherent in phenomenology as both methodology and philosophy further lends to the confusion surrounding its existence.

A Difference in Philosophic Foundations

> What is phenomenology? There is a difference between comprehending phenomenology intellectually and understanding it from the inside as it were.
>
> *(van Manen, 1984, p. 36)*

Edmund Husserl is credited as being the foremost founder of phenomenology. He criticized the social sciences for their attempts to apply natural science methods to their respective fields, and deemed these acts as erroneous (Bell, 1991). Husserl also felt that the social sciences failed to recognize that they dealt with living subjects who were impacted by their environments (Moules, 2002). Thus, he created what we now know in a broad sense as phenomenology.

Phenomenology is essentially the study of lived experience or the life world (van Manen, 2007). Husserl believed that we could effectively grasp the essences of our lived experiences through the processes of "reduction" and "bracketing." "Bracketing" is the act of suspending the impact of the outer world, as well as the researcher's individual beliefs about the phenomenon, in order to see it clearly (Husserl, 1970). Husserl viewed "reduction" as the thought of the singular, or one essence of an experience that is brought forth. Husserl saw the reduction process as an end itself (Moran, 2000; van Manen, 2007). The hermeneutical approach, however, offers a different entry into this methodology.

Hermeneutic phenomenology is a human science—a stark contrast to the Husserlian approach that centers "reduction" and "bracketing." Human science research always explores the structures of meaning of the lived *human* world (van Manen, 2007). Phenomenology is a rigorous human science because it investigates the way that knowledge comes into being and clarifies the assumptions upon which all human understandings are grounded (Moran, 2000). Martin Heidegger and Hans-Georg Gadamer transformed phenomenology and introduced hermeneutics into its interpretive process. While the idea that one should "bracket" one's prior interpretations in phenomenology had become commonplace, Heidegger believed that the phenomenologist could not "bracket" oneself from phenomena and that the act of "reduction" was limiting. He nullified any distinction between the individual and their experiences, and interpreted them as interrelated and unable to exist without the other. This perspective maintains that one cannot stand outside the pre-understandings and historicality of one's experience (Heidegger, 1962/2008).

Gadamer was also concerned with Husserl's beliefs regarding the role of the researcher in phenomenological inquiry and his notions of subjectivity. Like Heidegger, he, too, believed that phenomenology's in-depth descriptive work must retain the cultural, social, and historical forces that shape our experiences (Vessey, 2007). Gadamer firmly asserted that there is no pure perception, and that "reduction" and "bracketing" further remove us from the phenomena we wish to uncover. "There is a gap in Husserl's phenomenology between what it seeks to grasp, its essences, and the actual state of affairs it attempts to explain" (Vessey, 2007, p. 16). To Husserl, phenomenological investigation was not the viewing of many essences of lived experiences, but a conduit to encounter their limits and finitude (Spiegelberg, 1982). It appears that Husserl eventually began to engage in the very acts that he first challenged.

(Re)Moving the Enigma from Hermeneutic Phenomenological Inquiry

Hermeneutic phenomenology centers on the subjective experiences of groups and individuals in an attempt to disclose the world as experienced by those being studied through their life-world stories (Kafle, 2013). Stated previously, in direct contrast to Husserlian phenomenology, the biases and assumptions of the researcher are not bracketed or set aside; rather, they are included and essential to the interpretive process. While "doing" this method, the researcher is acknowledged as a necessary conduit who provides considerable thought to one's own experiences, and as one who explicitly maintains the ways in which one's position impacts the issues being researched (van Manen, 2007; Moules, 2002).

> To approach phenomena without presuppositions of any kind, to "bracket" them, as Husserl hoped to do, is, in the first place inadvisable, and in the second impossible. Inadvisable because it would involve discarding not only the errors but the wisdom of our tradition; Impossible because without thoughtful insights, there can be no genuine thinking about, and thus no serious approach to the phenomenon in any event.
>
> *(Bontekoe, 1996, pp. 63–64)*

This ideal mirrors the reflexive practices that are often adopted within critical qualitative approaches. Pillow (2003) contends that reflexivity allows critical researchers to be "critically conscious through personal accounting of how [their] self-location (across for example, gender, race, class, sexuality, ethnicity, nationality), position, and interests influence all stages of the research process" (p. 178). Reflexivity thus becomes a vital forum whereby research is produced that poses questions about interpretation and is understood as an ongoing self-awareness during the research process (Pillow, 2003). Overall, phenomenology as methodology and philosophy acknowledges in a critical way that we live in a world of relationships that *must* be recognized. When interpreting our existence with relation to our place with others and in place(s), there is an ever-present knowing that we must acknowledge our existence and how we relate to these entities during the research process.

This brand of phenomenology imparts a research methodology that directly confronts the rigid confines placed upon us by empiricism.[5] Since its beginning, phenomenology as a whole has attempted to correct the problems of educational conformity that students and scholars pervasively endure. Phenomenological inquiry, especially hermeneutic approaches provide researchers with a sense of scholarly nonconformity.

Furthermore, *Dasein* is a fundamental concept in hermeneutic phenomenology— a Heideggarian term used to portray that entity or specific aspect of our humanity which is able to wonder about its existence and inquire into its own being (Heidegger, 1962/2008; van Manen, 2007). *Dasein* encompasses our relation to others, the manner in which we "see" ourselves and our existence in the lifeworld. Like my phenomenon it has *not* been easily captured.

> The concept of *Dasein* is fundamental to hermeneutic phenomenology for without our capacity to wonder, human beings would not be able to interpret experience in the world, nor would we even be called to question, and being called to question is what allows hermeneutic phenomenology to exist.
>
> *(Eddy, 2008, p. 116)*

It is evident that "being" is an intricate human state. While considering the tenets of *Dasein*, Moran (2000) contends that phenomenologists have the potential to "overcome the strait-jacket of encrusted traditions . . . this also means rejecting the inquiry by externally imposed methods" (p. 5).

Hultgren (1995) further confirms that when one chooses to engage phenomenology, *especially* hermeneutic phenomenology, there is considerable tension that has to be reconciled; especially considering that one is leaving a *familiar* paradigm and entering into a *new* one. This distinction is key, especially to those higher education and student affairs scholars and scholar practitioners who make the choice to engage these critical approaches when researching topics that derive from personal connections to the communities and institutions to which they belong. Those in our field who choose to "do" this work will have to leave the comfort of tradition and choose the (un)familiar. As a qualitative inquiry, hermeneutics is often "othered." This is unfair. Instead of embracing the rigor of this method, positivistic researchers often choose to remain heavily influenced by theoretical, prejudicial, and suppositional intoxication (van Manen & Adams, 2010). The criteria or standards that are imposed upon qualitative researchers pose limits on how and what we study and the methods we choose to engage.

(Re)Claiming HBCUs Hermeneutically *and* Phenomenologically

I researched a phenomenon that I once lived. During my undergraduate years as an African-American low-income student I came face to face with social class in a unique manner during my attendance at an elite HBCU. My college years had a critical impact on my development and shaped how I view others and the world in which we live. It was my intrigue and passionate wonder about my undergraduate encounters that fueled and drove my desire to uncover the lived experiences of others who had these encounters, but, in a phenomenological manner. Desire is a particular attentiveness and special concern with an aspect of life. "One cannot legitimately study human existence without remembering that desires and values emanate from him and shake the contours of investigation" (Gordon, 1995, p. 9). Without desire there is no real motivation to question (van Manen, 2007).

My phenomenon of pursuit has not been prominently featured in higher education scholarship. This experience is absent and sorely understudied. Thus, I had to renew contact with this highly nuanced and complicated experience in an existential manner. I had to (re)turn and consume myself with every "thing" that resembled and disclosed this phenomenon to me. Merleau-Ponty (1962) stresses that "turning to the phenomena of lived experience means re-learning to look at the world by re-awakening the basic experience of the world" (p. viii). Why is this necessary? Where must one go to be re-awakened? Husserl provides a complex answer.

In phenomenological inquiry Husserl calls for the human science researcher to return to the *things themselves* (Steeves, 2006). Phenomenologists have a particular attitude and attentiveness to the things of the world in which their phenomenon lives and breathes (Merleau-Ponty, 1962). Van Manen (1984) expresses that:

> Phenomenological research requires of the researcher that [they] stand in the fullness of life, in the midst of the world of living relations and shared situations . . . It means that the researcher actively explores the category of lived experience in all its modalities and aspects.
>
> *(p. 38)*

When "doing" this work, phenomenologists must become full of the world and full of the lived experience that they are studying. As such, I could not rely solely on academic literature, I had to engage the "life-world" and summon every "thing" that resembled HBCU environments, Blackness, and Black intra-racial class differences. As phenomenologists engage the "life-world," they also often recognize the importance of "place" in their studies. Lived experience does not exist in a vacuum and is influenced by many "things."

Embracing "Different" Resources

For the purposes of this book chapter, I highlight how I used television scripts that uniquely illustrated one of the complex manners in which I engaged hermeneutic phenomenology as methodology and philosophy and also showed how my participants experienced intra-racial social class differences within their elite HBCU environments. During my adolescence the television series *A Different World*[6] called to me. It was an escape and provided a way out of an existence that was often painful. Its images are "printed indelibly on [my] brain" and tell a story of *my past*. I associate this series with my childhood hopes and dreams. The fictional depictions that were presented on *A Different World* provided a tangible portrait to me of what HBCU college life resembled.

Upon deciding to explore my phenomenon I knew that it would be essential to (re)turn to *A Different World*. I would need to explore the series and challenge myself to both affirm and critique its impact. What would it mean to (re)turn? To return is to "come back." Its meaning also reveals that in a literal sense it is to "come home." My (re)turn to *A Different World* was a homecoming, a celebration; and like a homecoming celebration I (re)united with old friends and (re)engaged history in the present. While I "knew" *A Different World,* had I seen it *phenomenologically*? How did these images display themselves to me as an adult? "Moving through Phenomenology is the process of letting things manifest themselves" (Heidegger, 1963/2003, p. xiv).

(Re)Engaging "A Different World" and Other "Texts"

Historically Black colleges and universities have had relatively few television representations where they are depicted as organizations committed to the education of African-American students (Parrott-Sheffer, 2008). The television series *A Different World* (1987–1993) was lauded for its "social relevance, uncompromising construction of Blackness (Whiteness was not the normative yardstick), and the ability to use the situation comedy formula as a vehicle to highlight the Black experience in America" (Coleman, 1998, p. 104). Under the helm of Debbie Allen (a Howard University alumna) the series tackled serious issues including race, AIDS, Apartheid in South Africa, and—to varying degrees—intra-racial class difference within the African-American community. This show was one of my first glimpses into HBCU student life and fundamental to my college choice process; however, I now view its images with different lenses.

A Different World aired for six seasons; however, the series was void of a character who came from a low-income background until its fifth year. This representation was eventually adjusted and "Lena James" portrayed by actress Jada Pinkett-Smith was added to the cast in 1992. The character "Lena James" shows this phenomenon. Although Lena James is a fictional representation of a low-income student within the HBCU context, I bring her plot to the forefront of the phenomena of intra-racial class conflict within HBCU communities because her storyline represents a prevailing tension present within this study.

Her moments on *A Different World* convey the tensions that are present when low-income and middle-/upper-middle-class students come together within a private, selective HBCU context. During her time on the show it was made obvious that Lena James wrestled with both her academic and socioeconomic identities. This conflict plays out in a sobering manner in an episode entitled *Do the Write Thing*. The following scene depicts the tensions that Lena had with her social class standing at her elite HBCU when her father visits campus.

Grover James:	Hey baby-girl . . .
Lena James:	Hey Grover . . . Look, I just want to explain the essay tonight, I didn't . . . *[Grover interrupts]*
Grover James:	It's alright. You did what you had to do to stay in school. Besides you never would have won any awards writing about me.
Lena James:	I didn't say that.
Grover James:	You didn't have to. I may not have been Ward Cleaver, but I wasn't Eldridge either. What was that Black Panther stuff?
Lena James:	Like you just said, I had to do what I had to do to stay in school, I guess it's just getting by.
Grover James:	*[Grover walks over to Lena to embrace her]* Babygirl, I'm so proud . . . *[Lena shrugs away; there is a silence]* and I have to be moving on so um, I just came by to give you this . . . *[Grover pulls out a thick wad of money]*
Lena James:	*[Lena looks at Grover with frustration and sighs]* Where did you get that? The track?
Grover James:	Hey, don't ask questions you know the answer to!
Lena James:	Well I don't see the point in taking it! You'll just call me in two weeks, in trouble, *again* and ask for it back!
Grover James:	It seems like both of us get into sticky situations from time to time!
Lena James:	Yeah? Well when does it end? The hustling? The gambling? You can't keep living like this! I can't keep living like THIS!
Grover James:	Baby, we always got by . . .
Lena James:	*[shouting]* Well I am sick of getting by! I scammed my way into this school with that Engineering scholarship and I got caught! I'm busted and I am tired of lying!
Grover James:	Yeah? Then why did you accept the Journalism scholarship?
Lena James:	*[Lena begins to cry]* Because I am just like you!
Grover James:	Baby, you don't have to be like me! Lena what did you say in that essay? Something like, create your own destiny

	and make your name count. Baby if you can make that up, you can make it true.
Lena James:	It's easier said than done.
Grover James:	Well, I hope I taught you more than "three card Monty." It's on you baby girl. *[Grover hugs Lena and puts the money in her pocket]* Take care and look I'll call ya in a couple of weeks alright? You know you my one and only? I love you. *[Grover exits scene]*
Lena James:	*[Lena turns away and begins to cry some more]* I love you too Grover. *[end of scene]*

(West & Sallid, 1992)

Lena constantly negotiated how she would reconcile both her socioeconomic and academic identities. She was constantly aware that differences were apparent between herself and her peers. When low-income students encounter elite institutions of higher education they experience change and transformation. How do these students make meaning of these changes? They also face feelings of insecurity and uncertainty (Reay, 2005). It has also been revealed that there are consequences for low-income students who choose to attend elite universities (Jetten, Iyer, Tsivrikos, & Young, 2008). "[They] face dilemmas including the ability to maintain connections to one's social background, including family, friends and the wider community" (Reay, Crozier, & Clayton, 2009, p. 1105).

"Analyzing" Lived Experience(s)

Using *A Different World* as text revealed so much. It presented the nuance that was apparent in the life-world of my phenomenon *and* the philosophy inherent in my chosen methodology. Lena James' experiences conveyed the complicated relationships that African-American low-income students have with their elite HBCU environments—especially how their pasts meets their present. In this section, I present how I was able to use this text to "show" this phenomenon. In my efforts to "show" my process, it must be made clear that there is immense research freedom that lies with the phenomenologist. The "critical" nature of this method as methodology and philosophy is that it challenges the "scientific method" often engrained when teaching research methods. The activities that I highlight are not specific steps to be completed in a rigidly direct or sequential fashion. Within this approach, methodological paths cannot be exclusively determined by inflexible signposts (van Manen, 2007).

Using *Dasein* to Illuminate Being in Hermeneutic Phenomenology

A critical element of *Dasein* is its manner to always be in a world—*Dasein* is world-involved and world-disclosing (Heidegger, 1962/2008). What is the "world?"

World in this instance is a context or environment where myriad meanings reside (Heidegger, 1962/2008). The "world" in this study is the elite HBCU campus and the society that the students who live this phenomenon encounter. Both are intricately intertwined with self and history. Due to the aforementioned and because my phenomenon was sorely understudied, I had to summon a source from the *life-world* to aptly "show" this phenomenon.

First, *Dasein* for Lena, her being in the world, during her time as a low-income African-American student at an elite HBCU, was unique. It was *her* experience. This scene discloses how she encountered intense environmental pressures that stemmed from her class status and even the manner in which she performed "Blackness" in her elite HBCU environment. These interactions generate several questions. Why was Lena dishonest? Was she ashamed of her background? Did she feel forced to fabricate a past in order to fit within her new setting?

In this example, *Dasein* reveals not only one's "being," but their relationships to others as well. In (re)engaging *A Different World*, I was allowed to embrace the complex manner of my chosen phenomenon—I engaged being, in its time *and* in its place. Many nuances were provided. The philosophy illuminates an innovative perspective of how I was able to engage this work phenomenologically. How can this philosophy further be placed into conversation with Black philosophers?

Using Fanon to Move Toward a Critical Hermeneutic Phenomenology

Fanon called attention to the way that Blacks are often represented with broad and sweeping generalizations that are void of the rich intersections that are inherent in Black communities. Black identity is complex. It is far from a monolithic experience and has much more to do with cultural identity and legacy as opposed to an identity based on merely skin color (Mobley, 2015). It was absolutely necessary to place his Black philosophy in conversation with the Whiteness present in the "traditional" foundational philosophers who pervade this tradition. His work allowed me to further "show" this phenomenon. When "doing" this work it is imperative to deliberately choose "texts" and additional philosophers of color who can be placed in tandem with one's phenomenon of pursuit.

For instance, the central questions and nuances that accompany the fictional Black models in *A Different World* evoke debates surrounding "What is Black?" or rather "What *should* be deemed as *Black?*" within the American societal context. These same questions are pervasive within previous educational scholarship. "Negro experience is not a whole, for there is not merely one Negro, there are Negroes" (Fanon, 1952/2008, p. 136). Researchers have constantly attempted to define and (re)define Black communities. These individuals who thrive, dwell, and exist within their oppressed identities are often placed into a "Black Box."

My hermeneutic phenomenological exploration confronts the mainstream notions of heterogeneity that are held by both Black communities and those within the majority. Placing the Black narratives that were present in *A Different World* in conversation with White *and* Black philosophers was vital to my phenomenological exploration. Also, summoning Lena's story was important for *this* human science research inquiry. It provides immense context. To gain a deeper understanding of how class manifests within elite HBCU environments, a clearer picture of how African Americans exist within American higher education social structures was absolutely necessary (Sanders-McMurty, 2007).

(Re)Turning To Soul(ful) (Re)Search

An intense facet of phenomenology is the strength that lies in the possibilities of the impossible. When one chooses to "do" hermeneutic phenomenology, there is a knowing that while many questions shall be answered, they will undoubtedly be coupled with infinite possibilities for further questioning once inquiry is "complete." My hope is that in my "showing" phenomenology within this chapter that those who come into contact with this work will be prompted to explore and question further—that they, too, will be called to action. This *action* will be critical for those critical researchers who seek to engage in soul(ful) projects. The preparation and execution of human science research is "soulful" in its efforts to bring many meanings of life's phenomena to our reflective awareness (van Manen, 2007).

Gordon (2000) contended that "there is something peculiar about how Blacks are studied which requires reflection on one's method more so than one would with normative populations" (p. 69). The major problem that often arises when studying African-American communities is the failure of researchers to understand and provide a sense of humanity to Black populations. Higher education scholarship often adopts deficit-laden perspectives and has used negative Black stereotypes inherent in society to glean resonance and produce knowledge that continues to "other" and further relegate Black communities to the margins. "One might think that such an error could easily be alleviated by merely studying [African Americans] as human beings" (Gordon, 2000, p. 71). Why aren't Black communities explored honestly and respectfully? Is their humanity always lost? Is it easier to be led by destructive assumptions when engaging Black research topics?

> The [act] of lumping all Negros under the designation of "Negro people" is to deprive them of any possibility of individual expression. What is thus attempted is to put them under the obligation of matching the idea one has of them.
>
> (Fanon, 1969, p. 17)

"Scientific approaches" permeate higher educational research. "A convenient model of an exact discourse now exists. Its objects of study amount to which one can work within the confines of 'all there is'" (Gordon, 1995, p. 51). The "exact" is confining, and "convenient models" should be challenged. This chapter challenges the overt and covert "standards" that often make researchers feel trapped or stifled in their efforts to "accurately" conduct research. Senior and junior scholars should never have to wonder: "Am I too close to my academic interests? Why do I have to separate *myself* from *my* research in order to achieve scholarly validation? How can I do the questions in my head justice when I do not relate to the methods associated with *accurately* finding the answers?" I hope that upon reading this chapter that those who choose to "do" phenomenology will find comfort in being presented with another critical option to engage their work—even when the landscape may seem confining or void of perspectives that resonate with them or those communities they desire to (re)search.

Notes

1 "Method" often refers to research procedures and the seeking of "exact" knowledge (Madison, 1988). My use of methodology is centered on one's ability to be reflective, insightful, sensitive to language, and constantly open to the experience(s) that are being explored during their (re)search process(es) (van Manen, 2007).
2 As research methodologies, phenomenology and hermeneutic phenomenology have fundamental similarities and differences that derive from their philosophical foundations (Laverty, 2003). These nuances will be expounded upon within this chapter.
3 The Higher Education Act of 1965, as amended, defines an HBCU as: "any historically Black college or university established prior to 1964, whose principal mission was, and is, the education of Black Americans" (White House Initiative on Historically Black Colleges and Universities, 2017).
4 Institutions that are considered *elite HBCUs* are a subjective grouping of Black colleges and universities. Scholars have deemed them with this designation due to their highly credentialed faculty members, prominent alumni in various fields, and the social statuses of their students (Mobley, 2015).
5 There are numerous stances surrounding what constitutes "rigorous" qualitative research. Many of the positions that offer ways in which to conduct "good" qualitative inquiry are heavily influenced by positivistic viewpoints that often deem critical approaches as "less than" due to their questioning and rejection of "the epistemological whiteness and racial bias that dominates research conducted in the Western European/US tradition" (Stewart, 2017, p. 286).
6 *A Different World* is an American television sitcom which aired for six seasons on NBC (from September 24, 1987–July 9, 1993). It is a spin-off series from *The Cosby Show* chronicling the lives of students at Hillman College, a fictional historically Black college (HBCU) in Virginia (La Deane, 1992).

References

Arminio, J. L., & Hultgren, F. H. (2002). Breaking out from the shadow: The question of criteria in qualitative research. *Journal of College Student Development*, *43*(4), 446–460.
Bell, D. (1991). *Husserl*. New York: Routledge.
Blockett, R. (2017). "I think it's very much placed on us": Black queer men laboring to forge community at a predominantly White and (hetero)cisnormative research institution. *International Journal of Qualitative Studies in Education*, *30*(8), 800–816.

Bontekoe, R. (1996). *Dimensions of the hermeneutic circle*. Atlantic Highlands, NJ: Humanities Press International.

Brimhall-Vargas, M. (2011). *Seeking personal meaning in new places: The lived experience of religious conversion* (Doctoral dissertation, University of Maryland, College Park). Retrieved from ProQuest Digital Dissertations. (3461496).

Coleman, R. M. (1998). *African-American viewers and the Black situation comedy*. New York: Garland Publishing.

Denzin, N. K., & Lincoln, Y. S. (Eds.). (2000). *Handbook of qualitative research* (2nd ed.). Thousand Oaks, CA: Sage.

Eddy, W. (2008). *Re-dis-covering identity: A phenomenological study exploring the ontological complexities of being gay* (Doctoral dissertation, University of Maryland, College Park). Retrieved from http://drum.lib.umd.edu/handle/1903/8547

Fanon, F. (1952/2008). *Black skin, White masks* (R. Philcox, Trans.). New York: Grove Press.

Fanon, F. (1969). *Toward the African revolution: Political essays*. New York: Grove Press.

Gordon, L. R. (1995). *Fanon and the crisis of European man: An essay on philosophy and the human sciences*. New York: Routledge.

Gordon, L. R. (2000). *Existentia Africana: Understanding Africana existential thought*. New York: Routledge.

Gordon, L. R. (2015). *What Fanon said: A philosophical introduction to his life and thought*. New York: Fordham University Press.

Green, A., & Winkle-Wagner, R. (2015). A three way analysis of diversity in HBCUs: Contemplating how diversity of methodologies and researcher backgrounds influences interpretations of diversity data. In T. N. Ingram, D. F. Greenfield, J. D. Carter, & A. A. Hilton (Eds.), *Exploring issues of diversity within HBCUs* (pp. 223–244). Charlotte, NC: Information Age Publishing.

Heidegger, M. (1927/1982). *Die Grundprobleme der phänomenologie* (A. Hofstadter, Trans.). In A. Hofstadter (Ed.), *The basic problems of phenomenology* (p. 328). Bloomington, IN: Indiana University Press.

Heidegger, M. (1962/2008). *Being and time* (J. Stambaugh, Trans.). Albany, NY: State University of New York Press.

Heidegger, M. (1963/2003). *Preface/Vorwort* (W. Richardson, Trans.). In W. Richardson (Ed.), *Through phenomenology to thought* (p. xiv). The Netherlands: Nijhoff.

Hultgren, F. H. (1995). The phenomenology of "doing" phenomenology: The experience of teaching and learning together. *Human Studies, (18)*4, 371–388.

Husserl, E. (1970). *Logical investigations* (J. N. Findlay, Trans.). New York: Humanities Press.

Jetten, J., Iyer, A., Tsivrikos, D., & Young, B. M. (2008). When is individual mobility costly? The role of economic and social identity factors. *European Journal of Social Psychology, 38*(5), 866–879.

Kafle, N. P. (2013). Hermeneutic phenomenological research method simplified. *Bodhi: An Interdisciplinary Journal, 5*(1), 181–200.

La Deane, A. (1992). 'Different World' goes beyond realm of 'sitcom'. Retrieved from http://articles.latimes.com/1992-01-13/entertainment/ca-145_1_difficult-world

Laverty, S. M. (2003). Hermeneutic phenomenology and phenomenology: A comparison of historical and methodological considerations. *International Journal of Qualitative Methods, 2*(3), 21–35.

Madison, G. B. (1988). *The hermeneutics of postmodernity: Figures and themes*. Indianapolis, IN: Indiana University Press.

Mahendran, D. (2007). The facticity of blackness: A non-conceptual approach to the study of race and racism in Fanon's and Merleau-Ponty's phenomenology. *Human Architecture, 5*, 191–204.

Merleau-Ponty, M. (1962). *Phenomenology of perception*. London, UK: Routledge & Kegan Paul.

Mobley Jr, S. D. (2015). *Difference amongst your own: The lived experiences of low-income African-American students and their encounters with class within elite historically Black college (HBCU) environments* (Doctoral dissertation, University of Maryland, College Park). Retrieved from ProQuest Digital Dissertations (3725526).

Moran, D. (2000). *Introduction to phenomenology*. New York: Routledge.

Moules, N. J. (2002). Hermeneutic inquiry: Paying heed to history and Hermes – an ancestral, substantive, and methodological tale. *International Journal of Qualitative Methods*, *1*(3), 1–21.

Parrott-Sheffer, A. (2008). Not a laughing matter: The portrayals of Black colleges on television. In M. Gasman, & C. L. Tudico (Eds.), *Historically Black colleges and universities: Triumphs, troubles, and taboos* (pp. 207–222). New York: Palgrave.

Pillow, W. (2003). Confession, catharsis, or cure? Rethinking the uses of reflexivity as methodological power in qualitative research. *International Journal of Qualitative Studies in Education*, *16*(2), 175–196.

Reay, D. (2005). Beyond consciousness? The psychic landscape of social class. *Sociology*, *39*(5), 911–928.

Reay, D., Crozier, G., & Clayton, J. (2009). 'Strangers in paradise'? Working-class students in elite universities. *Sociology*, *43*(6), 1103–1121.

Safranski, R. (1998). *Martin Heidegger: Between good and evil*. Cambridge, MA: Harvard University Press.

Sanders-McMurty, K. (2007). *"Linked together in service": A history of education and philanthropy among the Black elite: The Links, Incorporated, 1946–1996*. Unpublished doctoral dissertation, Georgia State University, Georgia.

Spiegelberg, H. (1982). *The phenomenological movement*. The Hague, Netherlands: Martinus Nijhoff.

Steeves, H. P. (2006). *The things themselves: Phenomenology and the return to the everyday*. Binghamton, NY: State University of New York Press.

Stewart, D. L. (2017). Trans*versing the DMZ: A non-binary autoethnographic exploration of gender and masculinity. *International Journal of Qualitative Studies in Education*, *30*(3), 285–304.

van Manen, M. (1984). 'Doing' phenomenological research and writing: An introduction. *Phenomenology and Pedagogy*, *2*(1), 36–39.

van Manen, M. (2007). *Researching lived experience: Human science for an action sensitive pedagogy*. Albany, NY: State University of New York Press.

van Manen, M., & Adams, C. (2010). Qualitative research: Phenomenology. In E. Baker, P. Peterson, & B. McGaw (Eds.), *International Encyclopedia of Education, Volume 6* (pp. 449–455). Oxford: Elsevier.

Vessey, D. (2007). Who was Gadamer's Husserl? *The New Yearbook for Phenomenology and Phenomenological Philosophy*, *(7)*, 1–23.

West, J. E. (Writer), & Sallid, O. (Director). (1992, April 2). Do the write thing [Television series episode]. In T. Werner, C. Mandabach, & M. Carsey (Producers), *A Different World*. Los Angeles, CA: NBC.

White House Initiative on Historically Black Colleges and Universities Website (2017). Retrievedfromhttps://sites.ed.gov/whhbcu/one-hundred-and-five-historically-black-colleges-and-universities/

7

THINKING WITH QUEER OF COLOR CRITIQUE

A Multidimensional Approach to Analyzing and Interpreting Data

Reginald A. Blockett

Theory: Queer of Color Critique, Quare Theory, and Queer Critical Theory
Type of qualitative data: Critical Ethnography
New data analysis technique: Queer of Color Analysis
Substantive topic in education: Black queer men's worldmaking practices

The number of empirical studies exploring the lived experiences of lesbian, gay, bisexual, transgender, and queer (LGBTQ) students of color, specifically Black queer and transgender students, in college has increased significantly over the past decade (Blockett, 2017; Goode-Cross & Good, 2008, 2009; Means & Jaeger, 2013, 2015; Nicolazzo, 2016; Patton, 2011, 2014; Patton & Simmons, 2008; Squire & Mobley, 2015; Strayhorn & Tillman-Kelly, 2013). Scholars have effectively responded to the call for increased qualitative inquiries on the diverse lives of LGBTQ students (Renn, 2010). Each of these studies contributes to the production of knowledge examining the lives of LGBTQ students of color, specifically considering the impact of their identity on college-choice, gender and sexual performance, marginalization and isolation, and interpersonal relationships and kinship networks. While scholars have worked to produce rigorous and sound naturalistic inquiries, there is seemingly a void in the methodological and theoretical undertakings of studies seeking to analyze the sociocultural experiences of queer and transgender students of color. In this chapter, I contend with the analytical tensions and complications of employing critical and postmodern theoretical frameworks to conduct data analysis. Drawing on data from a multi-year critical ethnographic study of Black queer men participating in a college peer-support group, I employ queer of color critique as a theoretical framework, specifically ideas within Black queer studies, critical race theory, and concepts from sexuality studies. I offer a multidimensional analytical technique, first incorporating methods congruent with critical ethnography like meaning field analysis and recon-structive horizon analysis, then by plugging-in my theoretical framework using a technique I refer to as queer of color analysis to interpret data (Carspecken, 1996). This technique is especially useful for inquiries aiming to unearth the nuanced experiences of LGBTQ students of color, specifically Black queer men (BQM).

Queer of Color Critique

Quare Theory

This analysis technique employs interdisciplinary frameworks espoused in queer of color critique, which is an epistemological (way of knowing) and theoretical per-spective that advances intersectionality. Intersectionality is a way of thinking that considers overlapping identities and overlapping systems of oppression (Collins, 1993; Crenshaw 1989, 1991). Queer of color critique derived in part from queer theory, which is a postmodern theory that critically examines homophobia and heterosexism experienced by sexual minorities and seeks to understand normative and deviant behavior related to sexual orientations and identities (Ferguson, 2004; Means, 2013). Several scholars have reimagined the use of queer theory to critique its neglect of an analysis on racial subjectivity across LGBTQ identities (Ferguson, 2004; Johnson, 2005; Muñoz, 1999). While queer theory provides a necessary lens to examine prevailing structural issues like the ideology that heterosexuality is normative, referred to as heteronormativity (Jagose, 1996), it fails to situate race as a central formation alongside that of sexual orientation. Johnson (2005) critiqued traditional queer theory, suggesting "queer theory has often failed to address the material realities of gays and lesbians of color" (p. 129). Johnson continued his critique stating, "Beyond queer theory's failure to focus on materiality, it also has failed to acknowledge consistently and critically the intellectual, aesthetic, and political contributions of nonwhite, non–middle-class gays, bisexuals, lesbians, and transgendered [sic] people in the struggle against homophobia and oppression" (p. 130). Moreover, through a reconceptualization of queer theory, Johnson offered "quare theory," from the southern African-American vernacular for queer, which foregrounds the ways in which lesbians, bisexuals, gays, and trans-gender people of color come to sexual and racial knowledge.

Means (2013) and Means and Jaeger (2013) instituted quare theory into higher education research with their studies on Black gay men in college. Means and Jae-ger recommended that future research on sexually minoritized students of color:

> Should consider the use the quare theory framework to understand the col-legiate experiences of students in academic spaces, student organizations,

and other spaces and areas of interest in higher education. Quare theory intentionally calls our attention to how race, gender, class, sexual orientation, and other identities intersect to shape one's social location.

(p. 135)

I advance the use of quare theory as a core framework in analyzing the collegiate experiences of Black queer men in a peer-support group. While quare theory works to explain cultural phenomena experienced by Black LGBTQ people, the framework does lack in its ability to analyze institutional structures that facilitate student development and engagement. For this reason, I couple quare theory with another critical theory rooted in intersectionality, queer crit.

Queer Crit and Disidentifications

Expanding the terrain of critical race theory, Delgado and Stefancic (2010) explained that queer crit "examines the interplay between sexual norms and race" (p. 94). Understanding and analyzing at the intersection of race and sexuality has been explored by several critical scholars in education (Blockett, 2017; Misawa, 2010; Patton, 2011). Misawa (2010) outlined six contributions of queer crit, which are: (1) centrality of the intersection of race and racism with sexual orientation and homophobia; (2) challenge to mainstream ideologies; (3) confrontation with ahistoricism; (4) centrality of experiential knowledge; (5) multidisciplinary aspects; and (6) a social justice perspective. Queer crit exposes institutional structures that diminish the conditions for Black queer student success. For example, a queer crit analysis of campus LGBTQ centers and Black culture centers on college campuses would question the need of sanctuary for students who are both LGBTQ and Black. Queer crit recognizes the implicit violence in creating spaces that affirm students' sexual identity solely and not their racial identity simultaneously, and vice versa. The use of each theory – quare theory and queer crit – highlights the scholarship and knowledge production cultivated by a lineage of queer of color critiques. Theorizing around the constructs of race, gender, and sexuality, Muñoz's perspectives on disidentifications rounds out the critical interdisciplinary frameworks used in the analytic techniques described in this chapter.

Muñoz's (1999) theory of disidentification is central to understanding the labor that queers of color endure as they create new politics, possibilities, and futurities. This cultural phenomenon, which Muñoz referred to as queer worldmaking, is a set of "oppositional ideologies that function as critiques of oppressive regimes of 'truth' that subjugate minoritarian people" (p. 195). Queer worldmaking involves the deployment of new cultural forms to resist prevailing ideologies and expectations typically rooted in normativity. I see queer worldmaking as the epistemological (way of knowing), discursive, and performative politics that Black queers engage as they destabilize compulsory heterosexual and White racial homogenous spaces and locations into anti-oppressive, sexually heterogeneous counterpublics (Berlant & Warner, 1998). In her ethnography of dance culture in New York as a response to the HIV/AIDS epidemic, Buckland (2002) described queer worldmaking as "a production in the moment of space of creative, expressive, and transformative possibilities" (p. 4). Accordingly, I use queer worldmaking to analyze and interpret data and unearth the ways in which Black queer and trans* collegians reconstitute dominant power structures as they come to know their racial, gender, and sexual identities. In the following section, I describe the multidimensional analytical framework employed to understand the sociocultural experiences of Black queer men.

Analytical Framework

I conducted a multidimensional approach to data analysis to thickly describe the speech acts and cultural phenomena I witnessed during data collection with queer students of color. Data analysis was conducted using methods congruent with critical ethnography. In the larger study, I used techniques such as meaning field analysis, and reconstructive horizon analysis (Carspecken, 1996; Madison, 2012). In meaning field analysis, I examined participants' individual speech acts, both verbal and non-verbal, to gain a better understanding of the significance. Carspecken (1996) suggested the use of meaning field analysis to allow the researcher to construct a variation of possible meanings present in the speech acts made by participants. For example, if one participant explains that they can foresee themselves being lifelong friends with other peer group members, the meaning field analysis would extrapolate that:

> [this participant has established a strong connection with other group members]
> AND
> [they plan to have certain friends in their lives forever]
> AND/OR
> [they have no intention at this time in losing contact with peer group members]

The meaning field analysis of speech acts, along with non-verbal cues like head nods and smiles by other group members, captures the range of possibilities and can be coded in various ways during data analysis.

In reconstructive horizon analysis, speech acts are analyzed to reveal claims of identity, as well as objective, subjective, and normative-evaluative meanings (Carspecken, 1996). These claims are analyzed for both their foreground and background meaning and are useful in bringing to bare participant's values and identity. Carspecken explained that this method is useful for researchers interested in thickly analyzing the primary record (observation transcript and fieldnote) to reconstruct meaning and claims made by study participants. Objective claims are those made by participants where a concrete, measurable truth can be derived. Subjective claims are those statements that arise from feelings or emotions. Carspecken described normative-evaluative claims as those made "about what is proper, appropriate and conventional" (2006, p. 83). Lastly, identity claims are specifically analyzed in critical qualitative inquiry to garner how participants might describe themselves, their peers, and/or their counterparts. Table 7.1 below illustrates a sample reconstructive horizon analysis using the same speech act as above wherein a participant stated that they could see themselves being lifelong friends with other peer-support group members.

These analytic techniques used in critical ethnography methodology are advantageous for researchers working with groups of participants, such as the Black queer men in the peer-support group (Carspecken, 1996). The analytic techniques above were useful in terms of identifying meaning and describing values embedded in truth claims made by participants.

I then interpreted the data using the substantive theory described earlier in this chapter, including theoretical and analytical perspectives on intersectionality (Carbado, 2013; Collins, 1993; Crenshaw, 1989, 1991), queer of color analysis which critiques heteronormativity and racialized homophobia (Cohen, 1997; Ferguson, 2004, 2005; Johnson, 2005) and hegemonic gender and sexual performance and embodiment (Bailey, 2013; hooks, 2004; McCune, 2014; Johnson, 1995, 2005; Muñoz, 1999). These theories attempt to describe and explain the life worlds and conditions of those who experience racial, gender, and sexual marginalization, specifically Black queer men's subjectivity. I drew on the theoretical perspectives of these studies to critically analyze the social, cultural, and educational experiences of Black queer men in college, a process

TABLE 7.1

	Objective Claims	Subjective Claims	Normative – Evaluative Claims	Identity Claims
Foreground	The peer-support group provides a space for friendship and community	Other peer-support group members have a desire to maintain lifelong friendships	LGBTQ students ought to be involved in peer-support groups to gain friendships	LGBTQ students and communities participate in peer-support groups
Background	LGBTQ students who do not have friends or community can find them in peer-support groups	LGBTQ students feel their best when they can make friends with other queer students	The friendships should be strong enough that they will last far beyond your years in college.	LGBTQ students specifically, yearn for a sense of community

that Jackson and Mazzei (2012) refer to as "plugging in." The plugging-in technique involves three specific strategies: (1) disrupting the theory/practice binary by putting philosophical concepts to work; (2) purposefully and transparently connecting specific theoretical concepts (e.g. critique of heteronormative illogics or queer worldmaking) to questions used in the thinking through of analysis; and (3) working the same data chunks repeatedly to create new knowledges that do not reify the theory/practice binary (Jackson & Mazzei, 2013). In doing so, I extracted the worldmaking practices (Berlant & Warner, 1998; Buckland, 2002; Goodman, 1978) deployed by Black queer men as they survive and persist in a predominantly White and heterocisnormative[1] Midwestern research university.

Unlike conventional qualitative analysis procedures, the process of "plugging in" theory does not rely on coding and thematic grouping. Instead, the researcher draws from the theoretical perspective to analyze data. Nicolazzo (2017) found this analytical method useful in their study of trans★ collegians where three central tenets of Critical Trans★ Studies were employed to analyze ethnographic data alongside study participants. Here, I "plug in" core concepts of quare theory, specifically as study participants address the demarcation of their varied material conditions as they come to know racial, sexual, and gender performance in college. I also conduct data analysis by thinking with queer of color critique and its contribution to understanding queer worldmaking and disidentifications. Rather than sifting through the raw data to generate coding structures, I collapsed the theory/practice dichotomy and drew direct connections between my data that spoke to the theoretical perspective and vice versa. For example, below, you will find raw data in the form of speech acts where participants describe concepts that have been theorized. These data-rich speech acts are not dilapidated into a code or combined into a theme; rather, they are fortified into a finding.

The analysis presented in this chapter illuminates the dynamic ways in which Black queer men contest normativity by composing new life-worlds that are not undergirded by stagnant ideologies of gender and sexuality. Goodman (1978) suggested that the ways of worldmaking involve five processes – composition and decomposition, weighting, ordering, deletion and supplementation, and deformation – each of which are processes in the production of life-worlds. He explained, "the making of one world out of another usually involves some extensive weeding out and filling – actual excision of some old and supply of some new material" (p. 14). For Goodman, worldmaking relies on the ability to augment, detach, and at times remove aspects of particular life-worlds in order to produce an innovative and more accurate representation, both discursively and materially.

Muñoz (1999) viewed worldmaking as a deconstruction of dominant paradigms and worldviews by dilapidating gender and sexual practices highlighted by heteropatriarchal hegemony (the power structure that defines gender and sex in particular ways and prioritizes men and masculine performances) and a complete abandonment of racialized heterosexual performances that center straightness,

Whiteness, and cisnormativity. Muñoz coined this worldmaking process for queers of color as disidentification – the extent to which racial, gender, and sexual minoritized persons disengage from dominant cultures and construct their own culture. Jourian (2017) mobilized Muñoz's important work to illustrate the ways trans★ men defy gender norms. He explained, "to disidentify is an agentic political act of resistance that creates new truths rather than either adopting the dominant reality or opposing it entirely" (p. 247). As such, disidentification elucidates performativity as a politic with potential to produce new and counter cultural formations. Muñoz posited that the act of disidentification works to create counterpublics, which he defined as "communities and relational chains of resistance that contest the dominant public sphere" (p. 146). Cultural workers produce counterpublics through a varied and dynamic gender system, kinship networks that extend beyond biological expectations, and performances that reflect actual survival strategies. The outcome is a cultural phenomenon that dismantles hegemonic systems of gender identity and expression, while also creating space for queer and trans★ communities of color to thrive. The following section presents the analysis of the data using the plugging-in method (Jackson & Mazzei, 2013).

Intersectional Analysis

In the project I am considering here, I worked alongside Black queer college men in a peer-support group over the course of two years, conducting observations, interviews, and shadowing. In this section, I draw on data from my multi-year critical ethnography to demonstrate how researchers might link theory to data through the plugging-in approach. The peer-support group provided a space for study participants to transgress normative ideologies around race, sexuality, and gender. In this section, I offer an example of how the aforementioned forms of analysis might play out in the reporting of the data to offer insight into how theories can help point out larger social structural issues. Study participants deployed strategies to overcome marginalization by critiquing systems and processes that sought to streamline their varied subject identities. Speaking on the radical potential of queer politics, Cohen (1997) contended:

> The inability of queer politics to effectively challenge heteronormativity rests, in part, on the fact that despite a surrounding discourse which highlights the destabilization and even deconstruction of sexual categories, queer politics has often been built around a simple dichotomy between those deemed queer and those deemed heterosexual.
>
> *(p. 440)*

Rather than reifying this illogical politic, study participants found ways to move beyond binaries and hierarchies as they came to know a more progressive queer politics that transgressed racialized heterocisnormativity. This is evident in participants' ways of thinking and being that suggest a relinquishment from regulatory ideologies and embodiments aimed at controlling their potentialities as Black queer men. A queer of color analysis of data revealed the labor endured as participants reworked dichotomies, social order, and in particular, compulsory heterosexuality and the various formations derived from the arrangement of heteropatriarchy. Ferguson (2004) reminded us that "racialization has helped to articulate heteropatriarchy as universal" (p. 6). In this order, concepts like masculinity, intimacy, sex and sexual practice, for example, are all measured up against White, heterosexual, capitalist men. As subjects outside of the boundaries and privileges granted to normative gender, racial, and sexual colonialists, Black queer men in this study share their experiences crafting a radical queer politic (Cohen, 1997).

Group members had strong opinions and ideologies about masculinity and masculine identities. Discussions on masculinity were common and occurred throughout the course of my field experiences. During one group meeting in the fall of my first year in the study the conversation was extensively on the topic of masculinity and male privilege. One participant, Angel, and several other peer-group members were thinking about what it means to be masculine, who has access to masculinity, and what traits and characteristics define someone as masculine. One group member mentioned that as a gay man "your masculinity is going to get challenged and you're not going to be able to defend it." This point was affirmed by multiple other group members, several of which shared stories of times where they have had to defend their "masculine-ness" or "maleness" to other men, both gay and straight, and among some women, particularly butch (masculine-performing) lesbian women. Below is a segment of the conversation where Angel shared his perspectives on what it means to be masculine.

Angel:	*I don't know. I think about . . . well when I think about masculinity, I really think about masculinity primarily with two words. Dominance and penetration.*
Several group members:	*Um hum.*
Angel:	*When you think of masculinity within culture. What do masculine people do? They dominate, all the time. And they penetrate. They penetrate their will onto somebody else, they penetrate their ideas onto somebody else. They penetrate . . . other people, physically. You see what I'm saying? So, it's penetrative. Right? And it's dominate because it's penetrative. So, when I think about that I am very − I don't know. I'm very . . . sensitive when people say, "Oh, you're so dominant." I'm like, "Noooo!" That's not at all what I'm trying to do here. I'm trying to accommodate, right, so everybody has the space to talk and to do whatever, right? Because I'm not*

	particularly interested in being super-duper masculine.
	That's not at all really what I'm interested in.
Group member:	Yeah (head nods).

Angel's viewpoint that masculinity is concerned with dominance and penetration illustrates how some queer men have come to understand their heterosexual counterparts. He sees masculine-ness as being bounded to power and superiority, particularly exuding physical, ideological, and political dominance over weaker subjects and populations. His perspective suggest that this sort of domination is embedded within male culture – where men are accustomed to inserting themselves and their logics, even when unwarranted. In this way of thinking, Angel has a hard time imagining himself having access to dominant masculinity as he acclaimed "Noooo" when he was accused by someone he knew. Rather, Angel explains that his interest is to "accommodate" and essentially make space for everyone by not performing a hyper-masculine identity. This demarcation between penetrative, dominating masculinity and the accommodating, space-making masculinity is a similar practice witnessed by McCready's (2010) study participants who also sought to disengage from hegemonic masculinity. Two of McCready's study participants described their experiences as Black gay and gender non-conforming young men who participated in an African Dance Program that was highly populated by Black girls and young women. McCready noted that the young men identified as effeminate and through their participation in the feminized dance group, they worked to "challenge normative notions of masculinity" (p. 83) by making space for diverse masculinities. Similarly, Angel acknowledged his sense of diverse masculinity that does not rely on power and dominance, but instead operates from a more nuanced logic of male-ness, in turn, queering masculinity in the process. This disidentifying act (Muñoz, 1999) challenges the norms and logics bounded to masculine politics and performances that are uninterested in accommodating and space making. As a social construct, masculinity is intended to be mapped onto male bodies and is a critical formation in manliness. As such, for effeminate, femme, gender non-conforming, and gender queer men, like Angel, masculinity presents itself as a site of struggle and limitation. For multiple participants in this study, the project of queer world-making required a collapsing of and complete detachment from heteromasculinity, particularly hegemonic and destructive masculinity, like that which Angel described (hooks, 2004; Haltom & Worthen, 2014). Angel goes on to discuss how he views himself as a feminist and what that means for him in terms of his masculinity and maleness.

Angel:	*I definitely see myself as a feminist. How can you be concerned with male privilege, not looking for male privilege, and call yourself feminist? So, I'm a black–white person? What is that? You know what I mean, so . . .*
Several group members:	(Laughing)

Angel:	You know, or it's like somebody who's in the KKK who's Black . . . what is that?!
All group members:	(Laughing louder)
Shaun:	Right! (Laughing)
Angel:	What is that?

Here, I analyze Angel's linkage between race and gender in his perspectives of what embodied feminist praxis might look like for a Black queer man. His understanding of heteromasculinity is tied to heteropatriarchy and racial superiority. In other words, Angel sees maleness and the performance of masculinity as symbolism of White supremacy, similar to conclusions drawn by scholars around the confluence of heteromasculinity to White racial domination (Carbado, 2013). Smith (2006) argued that "heteropatriarchy is the building block of US empire" (p. 71), wherein settler colonialism and White supremacy work in concert to establish binaries and hierarchies with interest in troubling all non-White, non-straight, and non-male subjectivities.

As a Black queer man and self-identified feminist, Angel sees himself on the fringes of heteromasculinity and thus a casualty of any project that is inherently anti-Black and anti-queer. Smith (2006) makes this point clear, stating "Just as the patriarchs rule the family, the elites of the nation-state rule their citizens. Any liberation struggle that does not challenge heteronormativity cannot substantially challenge colonialism or white supremacy" (p. 72). Angel's rhetorical questioning of "what is that?" is rooted in the very radical queer politics that intends to transgress hegemonic identity categories (Cohen, 1997). The Black queer worldmaking project that I witnessed during my time in the peer-support group operated within this framework and sought to dismantle binaries, hierarchies, and systems of domination, like heteromasculinity, for example. In the following section, I conclude by describing the implications of this particular analytic strategy, particularly when employing critical frameworks like queer of color critique.

Implications for Queer of Color Analysis

Carspecken (1996) reminds the qualitative inquirer that in critical ethnography, "the researcher, including [their] values, is supposed to enter intrinsically and inseparably into the methods, interpretations, and epistemology of critical research" (p. 5). My ways of thinking and identifying as a Black queer man have an impact on my interpretations of the data and subsequent findings. Mobilizing queer of color critique in this study unearths the dynamic sociocultural experiences of Black queer men as they navigate campus environments and institutional policies and practices that place them at the margins. The data analysis techniques carried out in this chapter extrapolate how Black queer men in college experience racism, homophobia, and heterosexism and these issues would not be as clear without the theoretical underpinnings and analytic techniques. While participants were able to persist in their graduate and undergraduate degree programs, they found themselves experiencing marginalization and isolation in social and academic spaces. In turn, these Black queer men forged their own sense of community as they disidentified with both their Black heterosexual cisgender peers, and their White queer peers. They made clear that they expected more from administrators who often placed the burden of space making on marginalized students. Several implications for current and future research and data analysis derived from this study.

First, for qualitative studies with prolonged engaged fieldwork, it is important to understand how the researcher shows up in the field. I lay out a number of strategies and protocols related to the conducting of fieldwork. However, determining when and how to enter the field is a decision the researcher must consider. I was able to join the peer-support group given my identities as a queer man and student at the time of data collection. This experience allowed me to establish rapport with group members and eventually recruit them as research participants. This critical strategy also allowed me to fully engage with participants on a deeper level, eventually developing strong friendships with a number of the group members. This was most useful in generating rich and trustworthy data both inside and outside of the peer-support group meetings. It is not enough for a researcher to maintain the "objective observer role" of conventional ethnographic studies. Conversely, by completely participating alongside study participants in the field, the critical ethnographer is allowed to co-witness key cultural formations, like coming to know disidentifications.

Second, putting queer of color analysis to work requires an analytical framework where data can be studied through a theoretical lens that critiques racialized heteronormativity and contests the limits of status-quo ideologies. In other words, by thinking with queer of color critique and plugging in (Jackson and Mazzeik, 2012) the core concept of disidentification, critical inquirers are equipped with tools to analyze queer worldmaking practices as they are produced by cultural workers attempting to re-work abrasive, marginalizing publics like predominantly White and largely heterocisnormative postsecondary institutions. The consequence of neglecting to carry the theoretical framework throughout the study, specifically in the data analysis phase, runs the risk of misinterpreting and misrepresenting a cultural phenomenon. Moreover, incompetent researchers might reify illogics that participants are attempting to dismantle. That is, researchers who do not adequately incorporate theory throughout the research may work to reinforce stereotypes and oppression. Not only would this experience be harmful to individual participants, but it might also risk the study's ability to produce catalytic validity (Lather, 1986; Lincoln & Guba, 1985). In this respect, employing queer of color analysis has the potential to augment the discursive and material conditions for Black queer men.

Finally, a queer of color analysis makes clear the specific type of racism that derives from homonormative (norms of what it means to be homosexual) racialization within queer communities (Ferguson, 2005). Several participants focused on visibility of queer subjects, particularly Black queers, suggesting that Black queer men value their legibility as Black *and* queer. Ferguson (2004) eluded to this in his queer of color critique, stating "The racialization of Mexican, Asian, Asian American, and African American labor as contrary to gender and sexual normativity positioned such labor outside the image of the American citizen" (p. 14). Ferguson's critique centers on the racialization of queer subjects bounded to colonization, capitalism, and heteropatriarchy. Homonormative racialization positions the LGBTQ community as explicitly White, which makes space to theorize all other racial subjects through a White cultural gaze. What the Black queer men in this study experienced was a campus climate where Black queer male subjects were effectively erased and therefore not seen as an underserviced subculture. By resisting these normative readings of the LGBTQ community as solely White, study participants essentially formed their queer world by centering their Black queer culture.

Note

1 The prevailing ideology implied in higher education policy, practice, and pedagogy that straight cisgender performances are normal.

References

Bailey, M. M. (2013). *Butch queens up in pumps: Gender, performance, and ballroom culture in Detroit.* Ann Arbor, MI: University of Michigan Press.
Berlant, L., & Warner, M. (1998). Sex in public. *Critical Inquiry, 24*(2), 547–566.
Blockett, R. A. (2017). "I think it's very much placed on us": Black queer men laboring to forge community at a predominantly White and (hetero)cisnormative research institution in the Midwest. *International Journal of Qualitative Studies in Education, 30*(8), 800–816. http://dx.doi.org/10.1080/09518398.2017.1350296
Buckland, F. (2002). *Impossible dance: Club culture and queer world-making.* Middletown, CT: Wesleyan University Press.
Carbado, D. W. (2013). Colorblind intersectionality. *Signs, 38*(4), 811–845.
Carspecken, P. (1996). *Critical ethnography in educational research: A theoretical and practical guide.* New York: Routledge.
Cohen, C. (1997). Punks, bulldaggers, and welfare queens? The radical potential of queer politics. *GLQ: A Journal of Lesbian and Gay Studies, 3*(4), 437–465.
Collins, P. H. (1993). Toward a new vision: Race, class, and gender as categories of Analysis and Connection. *Race, Sex and Class 1*(1), 25–45.
Crenshaw, K. (1989). Demarginalizing the intersection of race and sex: A black feminist critique of antidiscrimination doctrine, feminist theory and antiracist politics. *The University of Chicago Legal Forum, 1989*, 139–167.
Crenshaw, K. (1991). Mapping the margins: Intersectionality, identity politics, and violence against women of color. *Stanford Law Review, 43*(6), 1241–1299.
Delgado, R., & Stefancic, J. (2010). *Critical race theory: An introduction* (2nd ed.). New York: New York University Press.

Ferguson, R. A. (2004). *Aberrations in black: Toward a queer of color critique*. Minneapolis, MN: University of Minnesota Press.

Ferguson, R. A. (2005). Race-ing homonormativity: Citizenship, sociology, and gay identity. In E. P. Johnson and M. G. Henderson (Eds.), *Black queer studies: A critical anthology* (pp. 52–67). Durham, NC: Duke University Press.

Goode-Cross, D. T., & Good, G. E. (2008). African American men who have sex with men: Creating safe spaces through relationships. *Psychology of Men & Masculinity, 9*(4), 221–234. doi:10.1037/a0013428

Goode-Cross, D. T., & Good, G. E. (2009). Managing multiple-minority identities: African American men who have sex with men at predominately white universities. *Journal of Diversity in Higher Education, 2*(2), 103–112. doi:10.1037/a0015780

Goodman, N. (1978). *Ways of worldmaking*. Indianapolis, IN: Hackett Publishing.

Haltom, T. M., & Worthen, M. G. (2014). Male ballet dancers and their performances of heteromasculinity. *Journal of College Student Development, 55*(8), 757–778.

hooks, b. (2004). *We real cool: Black men and masculinity*. New York: Routledge.

Jackson, A.Y., & Mazzei, L. A. (2012). *Thinking with theory in qualitative research: Viewing data across multiple perspectives*. New York: Routledge.

Jackson, A. Y., & Mazzei, L. A. (2013). Plugging one text into another: Thinking with theory in qualitative research. *Qualitative Inquiry, 19*(4), 261–271.

Jagose, A. (1996). *Queer theory*. New York: New York University Press.

Johnson, E. P. (1995). Snap! Culture: A different kind of "reading". *Text and Performance Quarterly, 15*(2), 122–142.

Johnson, E. P. (2005). "Quare" studies, or (almost) everything I know about queer studies I learned from my grandmother. In E. P. Johnson & M. G. Henderson, *Black queer studies: A critical anthology* (pp. 124–157). Durham, NC: Duke University Press.

Jourian, T. J. (2017). Trans* forming college masculinities: Carving out trans* masculine pathways through the threshold of dominance. *International Journal of Qualitative Studies in Education, 30*(3), 245–265. doi: 10.1080/09518398.2016.1257752

Lather, P. (1986). Issues of validity in openly ideological research: Between a rock and a soft place. *Interchange, 17*(4), 63–84.

Lincoln, Y. S., & Guba, E. G. (1985). *Naturalistic inquiry*. Beverly Hills, CA: Sage Publications.

Madison, D. S. (2012). *Critical ethnography: Method, ethics, and performance* (2nd ed.). Los Angeles, CA: Sage Publications.

McCready, L. T. (2010). *Making space for diverse masculinities: Difference, intersectionality, and engagement in an urban high school*. New York: Peter Lang.

McCune, J. R. (2014). *Sexual discretion: Black masculinity and the politics of passing*. Chicago, IL: University of Chicago Press.

Means, D. R. (2013). *Demonized no more: The spiritual journeys and spaces of Black gay male college students at predominantly white institutions* (published doctoral dissertation). North Caroline State University, Raleigh, NC.

Means, D. R., & Jaeger, A. J. (2013). Black in the rainbow: "Quaring" the Black gay male student experience at historically Black universities. *Journal of African American Males in Education, 4*(2), 124–140.

Means, D. R., & Jaeger, A. J. (2015). Spiritual borderlands: A Black gay male college student's spiritual journey. *Journal of Student Affairs Research and Practice, 52*(1), 11–23.

Misawa, M. (2010). Musings on controversial intersections of positionality. In V. Sheared and associates, *The handbook of race and adult education* (pp. 187–200). San Francisco, CA: Jossey-Bass.

Muñoz, J. E. (1999). *Disidentifications: Queers of color and the performance of politics*. Minneapolis, MN: University of Minnesota Press.

Nicolazzo, Z. (2016). 'It's a hard line to walk': Black non-binary trans★ collegians' perspectives on passing, realness, and trans★-normativity. *International Journal of Qualitative Studies in Education, 29*(9), 1173–1188.

Nicolazzo, Z. (2017). *Trans★ in College: Transgender Students' Strategies for Navigating Campus Life and the Institutional Politics of Inclusion*. Sterling, VA: Stylus Publishing, LLC.

Patton, L. D. (2011). Perspectives on identity, disclosure and the campus environment among African American gay and bisexual men at one historically Black college. *Journal of College Student Development, 52*(1), 77–100.

Patton, L. D. (2014). Preserving respectability or blatant disrespect? A critical discourse analysis of the Morehouse Appropriate Attire Policy and implications for intersectional approaches to examining campus policies. *International Journal of Qualitative Studies in Education, 27*(6), 724–746.

Patton, L. D., & Simmons, S. (2008). Exploring complexities of multiple identities of lesbians in a Black college environment. *Negro Educational Review, 59*(3–4), 197–215.

Renn, K. A. (2010). LGBT and queer research in higher education: The state and status of the field. *Educational Researcher, 39*(2), 132–141. doi:10.3102/0013189X10362579.

Smith, A. (2006). Heteropatriarchy and the three pillars of white supremacy: Rethinking women of color organizing. *The Color of Violence: The Incite Anthology* (S. Falcon, Ed.). Cambridge, MA: South End Press, pp. 67–73.

Squire, D. D., & Mobley Jr, S. D. (2015). Negotiating race and sexual orientation in the college choice process of Black gay males. *The Urban Review, 47*(3), 466–491.

Strayhorn, T. L., & Tillman-Kelly, D. L. (2013). Queering masculinity: Manhood and Black gay men in college. *Spectrum: A Journal on Black Men, 1*(2), 83–110.

8

GLOBALIZATION, HIGHER EDUCATION, AND CRISIS

A Model for Applying Critical Geography toward Data Analysis

Chelsea A. Blackburn Cohen

Theory: Critical Geography
Type of qualitative data: Interviews
New data analysis technique: Critical Geography Analysis
Substantive topic in education: Higher education responding to displaced academics

---

The globalization of higher education is in no way a new or under-researched phenomenon. Since the mid-1990s, an international turn in all corners of the modern university has become commonplace, evident in the surge of student and scholar mobility, the establishment of cross-border research networks and strategic partnerships, the increased rate of higher education participation worldwide, competition in global university ranking systems, and the rise of global/intercultural rhetoric in university mission statements (Altbach, 2015; Knight, 2008; Marginson, 2016). Yet this focus on the tangible, on the measurable aspects of how a university is adapting to remain relevant in today's international knowledge economy, is limited in its failure to connect what constitutes the "global." That is, while the international buzz grows, attention to major crises that affect an international higher education community remain unacknowledged. The inattention to global crises ushers an essential question about the purpose and role of higher education in contemporary society. An historical account of the literature suggests that the university ought to promote humanitarianism, democratic ideals and world citizenship, rhetoric that largely mirrors what we see today (Holian, 2008).

This chapter argues that within an era in which institutions in the United States espouse rhetoric of the global, we are less willing, less able, and less empowered to respond to global crises that have historically warranted our attention. While the goal of this chapter is not to demonstrate empirical findings, it aims to offer an example for future research to employ critical geography toward the analysis of data. As is demonstrated here, critical geography is used to explore the internationalization of higher education and the contributions the theory has made toward conceiving of mattering spaces, demonstrating how the era of globalization has impeded the ability of higher education institutions to address and respond to humanitarian crises of a global scale. In so doing, people, their knowledge and ideas, and potential contributions are organized into mattering spaces.

This chapter examines these relationships and how they unfold amidst crisis: specifically, the state of education for the largest refugee population since World War II, largely those fleeing the conflicts plaguing Syria. Key insights are drawn from strands of critical geography, which offer productive ways of thinking about relations across space, place, and time (Massey, 2005). Application of these theories are particularly important to the analysis of historical data on the refugee crisis during and after World War II and the response of higher education institutions in the *pre*-globalization era. Such a critical analysis of historical response offers an essential backdrop to understanding how the era of globalization has altered the ability of higher education to respond to crisis and illuminates new ways of thinking about the mattering spaces formed both directly and indirectly as a result. In so doing, a critical geographical approach toward qualitative data analysis is presented for future scholarly inquiry.

Overview of Critical Geography

Despite a long history of critical thinking in geography, the use of the term "critical geography" reflects a rather recent development in thinking and scholarship (Bauder & Engel-Di Mauro, 2008). Considered "both an approach to scholarship and a practice of scholarship," major influences in the area of critical geography can be traced back to the thinking of Karl Marx, Pierre Bourdieu, and Michel Foucault (Bauder & Engel-Di Mauro, 2008; Blomley, 2006). As a major figure within French Marxist theory in the 1930s, Henri Lefebvre became a foundational thinker for the future of critical geography in his theorization of space. This mid-century thinking in terms of spatiality focused on the effects of capitalism on the city, the urbanization of consciousness, the capacity of capitalism to eradicate difference (Soja, 1989). Emerging in the 1970s, geographers with a critical bent began forging intellectual pathways to elevate issues related to civil rights, pollution, and war. Toward the end of the 1980s, critical geography took hold, with attention toward "questions of culture, representation and identity, as well as an alertness to the multiple and imbricated geographies through which oppression and domination are produced" (Blomley, 2006, p. 89).

Geography as a discipline consists of two major subfields, physical and human geography. Critical geography is represented by a larger group of strands of human geography that, in essence, seek to understand how places affect and are affected by each other (Knox & Marston, 2010). Critical geography most often examines social, economic, environmental, political, historical and/or human relationships in contexts often described through notions of power, space, place, and time (Blomley, 2008; Escobar, 2001; Grossberg, 2013; Massey, 2005; Mouffe, 2013; Wills, 2013). The major tenets of critical geography—an acute attention to material practices of power and power dynamics (Grossberg, 2013; Massey, 2005), a social justice orientation (Cumbers & Routledge, 2013; Smith & Desbiens, 2008), and a focus toward emancipation, consciousness, and change (Blomley, 2006; Soja, 1989) reflect larger concepts of critical scholarship.

In the present moment, scholars argue that critical geography's "intellectual territory has become less certain" (Blomley, 2006, p. 89) and that it lacks a "distinctive theoretical identity" (Hubbard, Kitchin, Bartley, & Fuller, 2004, p. 62). A partial contribution to the ambiguity of critical geography's application can be observed in the various ways in which globalization has been theorized and defined, as well as its implications for geographical study. Though the conceptualization of globalization is routinely up for debate (Robinson, 2007), its prominence in academic as well as everyday rhetoric reflects the societal transformations in the mid-1990s with the formation of the World Trade Organization (WTO) and the establishment of the General Agreement on Trade in Services (GATS) (Smith & Desbiens, 2008). These developments are now largely seen in academic literature across many disciplines as the birth of a neoliberal globalization. While one may be forced to choose a particular manifestation of globalization, for instance, economic globalization, for geographers, the globalization era in general has been described as "a speeding up of things" and characterized in terms of its relation to time and space (Blomley, 2006; Knox & Marston, 2010). Whether the relationship between notions of time and space can vary from one of a *time–space distantiation* (where formerly independent bodies interact across vast distances), to that of a *time–space compression* (where speed–distance replaces physical distance) (see Harvey, 1989), it is agreed upon that our previous understandings of relations across time and space are inalienably changed (Blomley, 2006; Hubbard *et al.*, 2004).

The insights that critical geography has offered in its questioning of globalization are of particular importance and largely inform the analysis offered here. The critical geography scholarship that addresses the human experience of globalization can be envisaged as falling into three major themes: imagination, manifestation, and contradiction. This *imagination* is often in reference to what globalization might firstly imply—free trade, unbounded space, the interconnectedness of social relations and "a geography of borderlessness and mobility" (Massey, 2005, p. 86)—among other optimistic narratives (Grossberg, 2013; Hubbard *et al.*, 2004; Mouffe, 2013; Smith & Desbiens, 2008). Meanwhile, *manifestation* themes account for the ways in which this positive view of globalization disregards the stark inequalities it is known to produce in a "geography of border discipline" (Massey, 2005, p. 86; Mouffe, 2013). The theme of *contradiction* essentially highlights this disjuncture between the imagined and how it manifests, accounting for its unfolding in relations, while arguing that these contradictions are central to maintaining the established orders of power. Massey (2005) offered a gripping assessment of globalization that is particularly useful and highlights the above themes:

> And so in this era of 'globalization' we have sniffer dogs to detect people hiding in the holds of boats, people dying in the attempt to cross frontiers, people precisely trying to 'seek out the best opportunities.' That double imaginary, *in the very fact of its doubleness,* of the freedom of space on the one hand and the 'right to one's own place' on the other, works in favor of the already-powerful. Capital, the rich, the skilled . . . can move easily about the world, as investment, or trade, as sought-after labor or as tourists; and at the same time, whether it be in the immigration-controlled countries of the West, or the gated communities of the rich in any major metropolis anywhere, or in the elite enclosures of knowledge production and high technology, they can protect their fortress homes. Meanwhile the poor and the unskilled from the so-called margins of this world are both instructed to open up their borders and welcome the West's invasion in whatever form it comes, and told to stay where they are.
>
> *(p. 87)*

Critical geography's attention toward globalization and to space, place, and time is especially helpful when seeking to problematize the ways in which globalization is constructed as an all-encompassing narrative. No matter the domain in which it appears, the popular rhetoric of globalization is prone to emphasize an imperialist stance where it is deemed "'natural' for there to be winners and losers in an evolving society (and hence the idea that capitalism is natural)" (Hubbard *et al.*, 2004, p. 211). This optimistic capitalist orientation, representative of the *imagination* context of globalization, has most powerfully endured across political landscapes, though there has also been a turn toward the critical since the 2008 economic crisis and the rise of alt-right ideology in the United States.

These developments have been particularly interesting in the context of higher education, where globalization has forced it to become more independent from government and competitive in a market-like environment (Altbach, 2001). Critical geography offers numerous avenues for nuanced insight into the internationalization strategies most universities are scrambling to achieve, not to mention dominating global rankings systems to attract foreign faculty and high fee-paying international students (Altbach, 2015; Hazelkorn, 2014). However, critical geography has largely been ignored in higher education scholarship despite its easily discernable contributory power (Marginson & Pusser, 2012; Pasque, Carducci, Kuntz, & Gildersleeve, 2012).

Globalization, Higher Education and Crisis

As described earlier in the preceding sections, the last quarter century of globalization has marked a major change for higher education institutions throughout the world. Despite the global emphases that have become commonplace across colleges and universities—and spill easily off the tongues of their recruiters—there has been a serious lack of attention to crises that impact higher education communities around the world (more accurately in certain global spaces). For the context of this chapter and to illustrate the application of critical geography toward data analysis, the crisis of mass displacement is used.

The massive displacement as a result of the Syrian Civil War marks the largest humanitarian crisis since World War II (Zavis, 2015). Acknowledging the important lessons that can be gleaned from history, a consideration of the relationship between higher education and crisis of a comparable global scale offers a particular merit for this analysis. Additionally, analyzing the role of higher education in addressing the devastations of World War II—referred to here as the *pre-globalization era*—opens an analytic window through which to consider globalization as an independent variable in understanding how space, time, and geographies of responsibility are understood.

Application of Critical Geography for Data Analysis

In what follows, I present an approach toward data analysis as linked to critical theory. This technique uses document analysis to examine relevant historical and present-day text excerpts that address globalization, higher education, and the nature of crisis. The approach as elaborated below is best suited for the analysis of data that examines the relationship of globalization and its developments to a particular sociopolitical phenomenon.

Coding Themes

I first used the three themes of *Imagination, Manifestation,* and *Contradiction* driven by critical geography to understand the hopes and limitations characteristic of the globalization era, followed by the concepts of *space* and *place* applied to both eras. These themes were then presented across *time*. For a broader application, the theme *Imagination* refers to that which is considered ideal. In this sense, the optimistic narratives of any new development could represent *Imagination*, whether that might be a new policy or political, economic, or social agenda. At the other end of the spectrum is the theme of *Manifestation*, which represents what the ideal has in turn become. An example of both *Imagination* and

Manifestation might be applied toward a new capitalist framework, where the imaginative narratives hinge on the ideals of meritocracy, an optimistic concept that argues that one can achieve social and economic advancement relative to the amount of labor they invest. *Manifestation*, then, would highlight the realities of a capitalist framework in terms of meritocracy, for instance, how one person may work harder than another but will not achieve the same amount of social and economic advancement. Finally, *Contradiction* can be defined as the ways in which the ideal is not met. In following with the above example, *Contradiction* would be used to examine this discrepancy, for those who are not born with the right social, cultural, and/or political capital to begin at the same rung of the ladder as others, highlighting the *who* (marginalized people) and the *why* (discriminatory policies preventing social and economic advancement of certain populations).

As relevant to this project, application of these themes for data analysis aids in understanding how globalization may be constructed and communicated as a narrative (*Imagination*), how it might play out on the ground (*Manifestation*), and what that means and to whom (*Contradiction*). These themes are particularly useful for data analysis relative to the impacts of globalization. Due to the nature of these themes and their articulation of how a new organizing principle might be imagined versus its reality—for example, the equitable ideals of meritocracy in a capitalist system—it is limited in its scope to analyze topics beyond such far-reaching phenomenon like globalization or capitalism, but might prove useful for valuable insights into new political movements or ideologies or economic interventions.

The Analytic Approach: Coding

The use of this analytical approach involves a six-step process. It is worth reiterating that when choosing data sources, it is necessary to choose "before" data and "after" data to understand the impacts, if any, of the phenomenon under study as an independent variable. Data sources including but not limited to interview data, focus groups, meeting minutes, conference proceedings, and/or news articles are likely to offer the richest context for analysis using critical geography, especially those that are considered alongside a historical approach that traces developments over time.

Step 1: Low-level coding. To illustrate, application of these three themes for data analysis first begins with deriving low-level codes from chosen text excerpts specifically representative of the globalization-era phenomenon. Low-level coding is a type of coding "that falls close to the primary record and requires little abstraction" (Carspecken, 1996, p. 146). The example below represents one of two samples of text in reference to the ongoing crisis in Syria in the globalization (the "after") era. This text is an excerpt from an interview with a Syrian academic, Dr. Oula Abu-Amsha, who fled the country in 2012:

Leaving my academic network in the country made me feel lost and alone, I had very few contacts outside Syria that I tried to put to work. I wanted to be involved in giving back education to Syrian youth but . . . things don't work this way! Even if you feel that you have something to give, the global system that pretends to take care of my people in distress won't let you in. I've met many wonderful people in the last few years. They are all willing to help, but the system doesn't easily make place to outsiders like me.

(O'Keeffe & Pásztor, 2016, p. 199)

Low-level codes: feelings of loss leaving academic network; few social contacts outside Syria; desire to give back education to Syrian youth; things don't work this way; global system pretends to care; global system won't let you in; people willing to help but the system doesn't let them; the system does not make place for outsiders.

Step 2: High-level coding. For the second step of this analysis technique, these low-level codes are then transformed into high-level codes that reflect a higher level of inference (Carspecken, 1996). This higher inference requires checking back with low-level codes to ensure that the inference has not distanced itself too far from the original text.

Step 3: Imagination, Manifestation, and Contradiction themes. The resulting high-level codes are then assigned to the themes of *Imagination, Manifestation* and *Contradiction* as the third step demonstrated below.

Imagination high-level codes: desire to educate Syrian youth
Manifestation high-level codes: leaving academic network as loss (of place); social connections bound to space; things don't work this way; global system won't let you in.
Contradiction high-level codes: global system pretends to care [but doesn't]; global system doesn't let people help [who want to]; global system does not make place for outsiders [only insiders].

Space and *Place*, concepts naturally articulated through critical geography, are simplified for the use of data analysis into the following characterizations. Mouffe (2013) asserts that *Space* is a product of both material practices of power and relations and struggles. *Space* has a density and substance of its own, constituted through flows and interactions (Massey, 2005), and is both emergent and real (Grossberg, 2013; Lefebvre, 1991). For this analysis, though *Space* is shaped by practices and ideologies, it refers specifically to the material and tangible, whether that may be a nation, an institution, a boundary, or a border.

Place, on the other hand, refers to the more abstract nature of experience. *Place* is the context of lived reality (Grossberg, 2013; Massey, 2005) and created by social, political, and economic relationships (Wills, 2013). Places are not demarcated by boundaries; they are located within "webs of relations and practices" and consist of articulations of "investment and belonging, attention and mattering, pleasure and desire, and emotions" (Grossberg, 2013, p. 37). *Place* can have multiple meanings and experiences. As it pertains to this analysis, it is helpful to think of *Place* as "a sense of place," emphasizing the *sense*—the meaning-making of being in a particular place—whether that may be a social network, the feeling of home, the feeling of belonging, the feeling of fear or loss.

Step 4: Space, place, and time: high-level coding. To honor critical geography's tradition of challenging notions of space, place, and time, excerpts separately representing rhetoric on globalization, higher education, and crisis are analyzed across time, namely, texts were derived from both the globalization era and the *pre*-globalization era. After the initial coding of the globalization-era texts into *Imagination, Manifestation,* and *Contradiction,* a second round of coding is performed so that the low-level codes could also be assigned to categories of *Space* and *Place,* representing the fourth step in this analytical technique. For the previous example of Dr. Oula Abu-Amsha, the *Space* and *Place* high-level codes are presented below.

> **Space high-level codes:** social connections bound to space; global system won't let you in; global system doesn't let people help [who want to].
> **Place high-level codes:** leaving academic network as loss of place; global system does not make place for outsiders.

This process of coding for *Space* and *Place* is also applied toward the *pre*-globalization-era texts so that conceptions of space and place (and how they may or may not have changed) can be analyzed over time. Following is an example of this *pre*-globalization-era coding scheme from a 2008 address "Liberty and Fear: Reflections on the New School's Founding Moments (1919 and 1933)", by Ira Katznelson, a professor at Columbia University.

> The early New School's assertive modernism and muckraking spirit represented the most attractive pole of American culture, one at odds with the era's most ugly and violent features, signified by lynching and a resurgent Ku Klux Klan, the closing of the immigration gate, quotas on university admissions, and smug celebrations of speculative wealth. Not surprisingly, the institution was immediately controversial. [From the beginning] it was attacked for advancing radical and subversive ideas.
>
> *(Katznelson, 2009, pp. 403–404)*

Low-level codes: The New School's assertive modernism; The New School's muckraking spirit; two poles of American culture; The New School at odds with era's most ugly and violent features; era of lynching and resurgent Ku Klux Klan; era of closing immigration gate; era of quotas on university admissions; era of smug celebrations of speculative wealth; The New School as controversial; The New School attacked for radical and subversive ideas.

Space high-level codes: The New School's assertive modernism and muck-raking spirit; New School as controversial; New School attacked for radical and subversive ideas.

Place high-level codes: two poles of American culture; New School at odds with era's ugly and violent features (lynching, Ku Klux Klan, closing immigration gate, quotas on university admissions, inequality/speculative wealth).

GLOBALIZATION

Imagination

Context: Globalization as free trade; free trade as mobility; free trade as inherently good; unbounded space as inherently right; free trade as moral virtue; global travel and networks increase diversity and interaction; global travel and networks as facilitating enriched understanding of the world and new ideas

Higher Education: Globalization helps HE sector grow; HE vital in knowledge economy; HE as globalized

Crisis: Desire to educate Syrian youth

Manifestation

Context: Global space power; global space as incontrovertible; globetrotters inhabit familiar places in global spaces; globetrotters avoiding spaces of cultural diversity; interactions with 'Others' as functionality; global openings of our territories and places does not necessitate meaningful interaction

Higher Education: HE as private good and commercial transaction; decreased government investment; HEIs to compete for their own funding; commercialization and privatization of knowledge; decreased public funding, service and support

Crisis: Leaving academic network as loss (of place); social connections bound to space; things don't work this way; global system won't let you in; Syrian universities closed or operating at limited capacity; students and professors risk their lives; students traverse checkpoints; there are hidden costs of war; education is the hidden cost of this war

Contradiction

Context: Immigration as exception; asylum-seekers as bogus; economic migration as unwarranted; unequal properties of capital mobility; contested access to capital; those in diverse/global spaces isolate in pockets of safe familiarity

Higher Education: HEIs need to think less like educational institutions; global/commercial pressure threatens HE

Crisis: Global system pretends to care [but doesn't]; global system doesn't let people help [who want to]; global system does not make place for outsiders [only insiders]; student space for IDPs; universities can't house students; students risk military service and repercussions

FIGURE 8.1

Step 5: Context, higher education, crisis sub-themes. After assigning high-level codes to their respective themes in both the globalization and *pre-globalization-era* texts, codes are labeled into sub-themes of *Context, Higher Education,* and *Crisis* to reflect their relevance to each domain so that upon final analysis, impacts of globalization can be traced toward each area under investigation.

Step 6: Codebooks. In the final step, all of the resulting themes from the coding process are assembled into three codebooks: one representing the three themes relevant to globalization, one for notions of space over time, and another for place over time. The three codebooks—encompassing all ten text excerpts under analysis from a larger empirical study—are shown and discussed below.

In the globalization codebook, the positive ideals of free trade, mobility, and an overall openness dominate the *Imagination* landscape. *Manifestation* codes uncover the underbelly of these ideas, especially when considering the movement of persons—referred to above as 'globetrotters' who, while traveling extensively for business, education, or trade, are likely to avoid spaces of cultural diversity where meaningful interactions are more likely to occur. Higher education's emphasis on and support of the public begins to diminish; in the crisis category, higher education in Syria emerges as unsafe, subjected to military use and the dissolution of academic networks. The *Contradictions* that arise unveil the differential rights to mobility, a lack of openness, and the notion that higher education institutions ought to think less like educational institutions. We see the global system emerge as a form of oppression that "pretends to care but doesn't" and "won't let people help who want to".

Future applications of data analysis technique. In applying the above codebook framing to other research areas, it is helpful to consider which relationships have the most potential to reveal meaningful findings. For instance, while the themes of *Imagination, Manifestation,* and *Contradiction* would apply to other studies investigating some sociopolitical or economic intervention, the three sub-themes of *Context, Higher Education,* and *Crisis* may not. In following with the ongoing example of a capitalist intervention and the ideals of meritocracy, it might be most appropriate to supply *Context* as the first sub-theme (as context in and of itself helps situate the landscape of the phenomenon under study within each domain). In the above example, *Higher Education* is used to better understand the relationship between globalization and higher education. So, if one might want to investigate a capitalist intervention it might be best to use a second sub-theme of *Economic Advancement* or *Social and Economic Advancement* (depending on the type of intervention). It is helpful to think of this second sub-theme as the key dependent variable under investigation. Finally, the third sub-theme of *Crisis* (above), might well work for the capitalist intervention example (for instance, if one were investigating a capitalist intervention in the aftermath of crisis; see Naomi Klein, 2007), or on the other hand, a sub-theme of *Equality* might work more broadly as well.

Space and Place

The two codebooks below allow introspection into how the era of globalization has impacted conceptions of space and place in societal contexts, higher education and crisis. In terms of *Space* (see Figure 8.2 below), one can see a development over time where space in the *pre*-globalization era appears to be more boundary-specific. However, this understanding lacks the stark "geometries of power" as observed by Massey (2005), where the nature of global space is one of power, incontrovertibility and constituted by uneven flows. The spatial context of higher education suggests that while fostering world citizens have been present in missions in both eras, the age of globalization witnesses the "intrusion of the marketplace" into higher educational institutions and defines knowledge as an increasingly vital yet private good. In terms of *Space*, there are little conclusions to be drawn from the category of crisis. This limitation is perhaps an oversight in the coding process or technique, or possibly a matter of the small amount of text under analysis.

Interesting parallels begin to emerge when considering the relation of *Place* over time (Figure 8.3). For instance, note the "two poles of American culture" that appear immediately in the *pre*-globalization context cast a striking resemblance to many of the controversies and inequities that plague the current period

PRE-GLOBALIZATION ERA		GLOBALIZATION ERA
SPACE		SPACE
Context: U.S. did not suffer loss equal to Europe; U.S. expected to help with post-war efforts		**Context:** Global space as incontrovertible, power; free trade as right to mobility but unequal properties of capital mobility
Higher Education: Emergence of new university model (the New School)—to commit to humanism and democratic ideals, foster world citizens—albeit at times controversial and attacked for radical ideas; public and private HEIs expected to embrace new responsibilities to a new world		**Higher Education:** Marketplace intrudes campus; higher education as "private" good; public universities lack state funds; regulations promote privatizing knowledge; higher education provides society's new knowledge; Syrian universities closed or operating at limited capacity; student and faculty traverse areas of high risk; student space for IDPs; universities cannot house students; universities aren't safe
Crisis: Displaced persons unwilling to return home, unable to settle elsewhere		**Crisis:** Space as unbounded but social connections bound to space; global system doesn't let people help who want to, doesn't let you in

FIGURE 8.2

PRE-GLOBALIZATION ERA

PLACE

Context: U.S. open to understanding existing order; internationalism as means of realizing humanist ideal; two poles of American culture; America's ugly features (lynching; Ku Klux Klan, closing immigration gate, quotas on university admissions, speculative wealth)

Higher Education: U.S. HEIs ready to advance domestic social reform, readjustments to established order; UNRRA university product of post-war moment; temporary solutions result in new imagination of higher education in post-war world; New School at odds with era's ugly and violent features; world citizenship implies zeal for world service; cannot repeat historic mistakes of HEIs' ignorance/unawareness of services it should render under changing circumstances

Crisis: DPs stranded between past and future

GLOBALIZATION ERA

PLACE

Context: Global openings do not guarantee meaningful interaction; economic migration as unwarranted; globetrotters inhabit spaces of familiarity; 'Others' rendered invisible without dialogue; immigration as different geographical imagination

Higher Education: Leaving academic network as loss of place; university and military disconnect; education as hidden cost of this war; growing commercialization of higher education; higher education institutions need to think more like businesses; higher education institutions need to think less like educational institutions; commercialization of knowledge influences missions; global and commercial pressure threatens higher education; decreased ability for higher education institutions to provide service; higher education as pivotal in globalizing environment

Crisis: asylum-seekers as bogus

FIGURE 8.3

of life in the United States. (This is not explicitly represented in the codebook, though widening the scope of analysis would easily lend to this conclusion.) What can be seen in the globalization era is that *Place* absorbs a character that lacks any sense of genuineness. Higher education appears to move from a heightened sensitivity and relationship to war, to a current era where it is seen as vital to societies, but there is little to no mention of its engagement with any sort of conflict, despite its increasingly global nature. As it pertains to crisis, the *pre*-globalization era codes suggest displaced persons were lost and stranded—literally and metaphorically—whereas now these communities are seen as unjust, "bogus" and shut out.

The Analytic Approach: The Final Codebook

Once these individual codebooks are analyzed, salient codes are reorganized into one final codebook to offer a holistic evaluation of how higher education's attention and response to crisis has or has not changed as a result of globalization. While the previous analyses offer more nuanced insights to the *Imagination*,

HIGHER EDUCATION AND CRISIS

U.S. did not suffer as Europe, but expected to assist with post-war efforts. New higher education institutions emerged (the New School, UNRRA) to commit to democratic ideals and foster world citizens. Higher education institutions expected to embrace new responsibilities to a new world. Higher educations to disrupt the era's ugliest features. Mobility of displaced scholars integral in establishing new institutions and creating new knowledge in the U.S.

GLOBALIZATION

Higher education fuels society in a knowledge economy, but regulations promote privatizing knowledge. Higher education as "private" good, marketplace intrudes campus. Global and commercial pressure threatens higher education. Decreased public funding for higher education; institutions need to compete for resources. Higher education institutions need to think less like educational institutions and more like businesses.

HIGHER EDUCATION AND CRISIS

Syrian universities closed or operating at limited capacity; Syrian universities unsafe. Displaced scholars feel loss of academic network and social connections. Decreased ability for higher education institutions to provide service. **Education as the hidden cost of this war.**

FIGURE 8.4

Manifestation, and *Contradiction* aspects of globalization, the final codebook (Figure 8.4) exposes a more central and defining truth: whereas in the past, higher education was involved and embraced new responsibilities in the context of crisis, in the current age it has no apparent engagement. Put simply, in the *pre*-globalization era, education was an *aid* to war; in the current era, education is the *cost* of war.

Future Directions for Proposed Technique

Using critical geography as a foundation for data analysis reveals the unfolding of policies or interventions over time and their impacts on various webs of relations that may look or operate differently across space and place. Considerations of space and place offer nuanced insights that other data analysis techniques may miss: in particular, juxtaposing the movement or transformation of space alongside the lived context of reality that characterizes *Place* and the multitude of ways it can be experienced. Opening up this window into lived realities allows the researcher to trace more fully the seemingly unlimited scope of impacts and experiences related to a new or emerging social, political, or economic phenomenon.

With a larger research scope for the future coding for critical geography by enhancing data analysis with *Space* and *Place* over time might prove helpful for future projects and researchers as new global and local realities continue to shift. As our imagination of concepts like capitalism or meritocracy or war have changed since the "opening up of the world," so, too, have our understanding and engagement with them. It is imperative—as critical scholarship suggests—that the emerging relationships of power and resulting inequalities be investigated, questioned, and reimagined for a more just, equitable, and peaceful future.

References

Altbach, P. G. (2001). Higher education and the WTO: Globalization run amok. *International Higher Education, 23*(1), 2–4.

Altbach, P. (2015). Perspectives on internationalizing higher education. *International Higher Education, 27*.

Bauder, H. & Engel-Di Mauro, S. (2008). Introduction: Critical scholarship, practice and education. In H. Bauder & S. Engel-Di Mauro (Eds.), *Critical geographies: A collection of readings*. Kelowna: BC, Canada: Praxis ePress.

Blomley, N. (2006). Uncritical critical geography? *Progress in Human Geography, 30*(1), 87–94.

Blomley, N. K. (2008). Activism and the academy. *Critical geographies: A collection of readings*, 28–32.

Carspecken, P. F. (1996). *Critical ethnography in educational research: A theoretical and practical guide*. New York: Peter Lang.

Cumbers, A. & Routledge, P. (2013). Place, space and solidarity in global justice networks. In D. Featherstone and J. Painter (Eds.), *Spatial politics: Essays for Doreen Massey*, 213–223. London: Wiley-Blackwell.

Escobar, A. (2001). Culture sits in places: Reflections on globalism and subaltern strategies of localization. *Political Geography, 20*(2), 139–174.

Grossberg, L. (2013). Theorising context. *Spatial politics: Essays for Doreen Massey*, 32–43. London: Wiley-Blackwell.

Harvey, D. (1989). Time–space compression and the postmodern condition. In *The condition of postmodernity: An enquiry into the origins of social change*, 284–307. Malden, MA: Blackwell.

Hazelkorn, E. (2014). Reflections on a decade of global rankings: What we've learned and outstanding issues. *European Journal of Education, 49*(1), 12–28.

Holian, A. (2008). Displacement and the post-war reconstruction of education: Displaced persons at the UNRRA University of Munich, 1945–1948. *Contemporary European History, 17*(2), 167.

Hubbard, P., Kitchin, R., Bartley, B., & Fuller, D. (2004). *Thinking geographically: Space, theory, and contemporary human geography*. New York: Continuum.

Katznelson, I. (2009). Reflections on the new school's founding moments, 1919 and 1933. *Social Research*, 395–410.

Klein, N. (2007). *The shock doctrine: The rise of disaster capitalism*. New York: Henry Holt and Company.

Knight, J. (2008). *Higher education in turmoil: The changing world of internationalization*. Rotterdam: Sense Publishers.

Knox, P. L., & Marston, S. A. (2010). *Human geography: Places and regions in global context* (5th ed.). Essex, UK: Pearson.

Lefebvre, H. (1991). *The production of space* (Vol. 142). Blackwell: Oxford.

Marginson, S. (2016). High participation systems of higher education. *The Journal of Higher Education, 87*(2), 243–271.

Marginson, S., & Pusser, B. (2012). The elephant in the room: Power, politics, and global rankings in higher education. In M. N. Bastedo (Ed.), *The organization of higher education*, 86–117. Baltimore, MD: Johns Hopkins University Press.

Massey, D. (2005). *For space*. Thousand Oaks, CA: Sage.

Mouffe, C. (2013). Space, hegemony and radical critique. *Spatial Politics: Essays for Doreen Massey*, 19–31. London: Wiley-Blackwell.

O'Keeffe, P., & Pásztor, Z. (2016). Syrian academics in exile. *New Research Voices, 1*(2), 1–202.

Pasque, P., Carducci, R., Kuntz, A. & Gildersleeve, R. (2012). *Qualitative inquiry for equity in higher education: Methodological innovations, implications, and interventions*. San Francisco, CA: Wiley.

Robinson, W. I. (2007). Theories of globalization. *The Blackwell companion to globalization*, 125–143. London: John Wiley & Sons.

Smith, N., & Desbiens, C. (2008). The international critical geography group: Forbidden optimism? *Critical Geographies: A Collection of Readings, 18*, 39–44.

Soja, E. W. (1989). *Postmodern geographies: The reassertion of space in critical social theory*. London: Verso.

Wills, J. (2013). Place and politics. In D. Featherstone and J. Painter (Eds.), *Spatial politics: Essays for Doreen Massey*, 135–145. London: Wiley-Blackwell.

Zavis, A. (2015, November 30). What can we learn from Europe's last massive human migration? *The Los Angeles Times*. Retrieved from http://www.latimes.com/world/europe/la-fg-europe-refugees-wwii-20150930-html-htmlstory.html

9

CONTEXT AND MATERIALITY

Inclusive Appropriations of New Materialism for Qualitative Analysis

Barbara Dennis

Theory: Barad's New (Critical) Materialism
Type of qualitative data: Photos
New data analysis technique: Diffractive analysis
Substantive topic in education: Ugandan schools and community spaces

---

I draw on a cluster of concepts within Karen Barad's (2007) New Materialism, to develop a new way of thinking about agency and context in qualitative analyses. The cluster of concepts with which I will be specifically working include "intra-action," "agential cut," "diffraction," and "material," which I define below. In general, Barad's thinking enacts a deconstruction of the binarial space between self and other, in order to develop a more inclusive involvement of the material contexts for the social sciences. Barad is neither the only nor the first person to philosophize about the self–other distinction, but her particular way of doing this can give us new insights for qualitative data analysis. For example, including the material context in our social science could involve articulating how the books and desks in a particular classroom space are part of the social life of the class. These concepts are ways to articulate entanglements of phenomenon – like the ways in which certain kinds of student interactions are made possible in the classroom specifically because of the arrangement of their desks. "*[P]henomenon are the ontological inseparability of agentially intra-acting 'components'*" (Barad, 2003, p. 215, italics in original). We could say that the arrangement of desks, the norms of the class, the teacher's intentions all work together to constitute particular social and learning opportunities. Situated context and rich description, such as noting the arrangement of desks and classroom norms, have been important aspects of all forms of qualitative inquiry, yet even when well described the context is typically unproblematized and not taken up analytically where social action is often enough talked about without reference to the material context. Barad's (2007) theorizing provides a nice springboard for reconstructing context and materiality and transforming those reconstructions into inclusive, open analytic concepts entangled within our interpretations of social action and agency. In this chapter, both context and materiality (which I am using here to indicate actual material substance, but this definition gets nuanced as we go along) are critically examined with the purpose of advancing our analyses of both context and agency. I begin by identifying a problem in the field of qualitative research after which I work with this cluster of new materialist concepts because I think they can help us do a better job understanding the lively nature of material contexts in relation with agency. The bulk of the chapter is devoted to engaging analytically with a photo from some work I am involved with in Uganda. I conclude with a few questions that surfaced for me regarding the concepts.

The Educational Context/Problem

Following Elizabeth St. Pierre's (2008) gesture toward thinking post-qualitatively, contemporary researchers have been encouraged to use theory to call into question taken-for-granted concepts, particularly those concepts whose labor in educational research has moved along without much exploration. One such concept is "context." The relevance of context for truth, ethics, practices, and claims about the self are acknowledged in contemporary educational research, though our conceptions of context itself are left largely unproblematized. Contexts might be described in interactive, socio-cultural, or material terms, but descriptions themselves seem to fall short of their potential. The concept "context" has been structured through contrasts between subject/object, material/social, and condition/action: Context has been written as a static background with human activity as the foregrounded relief. "[W]hat is needed is a robust account of the materialization of *all* bodies—"human" and "nonhuman"—and the material discursive practices by which their differential constitutions are marked" (Barad, 2007, p. 812).

As a physicist, Barad brings a physical orientation that challenges a static, atomistic way of conceptualizing and working with material. Traditional social scientists tend to think of material as context or tool *for* subject activity. This way of thinking requires an unquestioned boundary between subject and object, material and social, condition and action, context and text. A traditional orientation might suppose that the desks in the classroom are material upon which subjects can act. Certainly, it would be difficult to propose any alternative that did not also include this as a possibility, but a critical orientation has the potential to bring about new insights and novel ways of acting, transforming a tiresome status quo into new opportunities. For example, perhaps we can begin to notice the ways in which arrangements of desks and norms for social interaction in the classroom open-up or close-off social learning opportunities. What makes one classroom feel better than another? Through critique, we can refuse the taken-for-granted boundaries along with the descriptions of social life that are rendered through them. In so doing, we create a way to live/be/do differently (St. Pierre 2008). For me, this difference involves trying to better understand the subject/object relationship in newly refined ways.

In the next section, we will look closely at Barad's new materialism and the specific concepts that will lead us to a new way of integrating our descriptions of context with our analyses of agency.

New (Critical) Materialism

To introduce critical materialism, I begin with a description that utilizes the concepts diffraction, intra-action, and agential cut. Next, I establish what is more than critical about new (critical) materialism and identify some key elements of Barad's work that are useful for thinking about context. I conclude this section with a philosophical articulation of the concept "context" using insights of new (critical) materialism.

New materialism resonates with performative theories of truth, in that, *social action* rather than language is the basis for an understanding of and orientation toward social science. Barad writes, "The move toward performative alternatives to representationalism shifts the focus [of social science methodology] from questions of correspondence between description and reality (e.g., do they mirror nature or culture?) *to* matters of practices/doings/actions" (Barad, 2003, 802, italics added). Barad uses this shifting point to invite us into diffractive ways of thinking about our social sciences – thinking the social *with* the scientific toward new possibilities of understanding. Diffraction involves interference that also retains varying effects of difference. "The relation of the social and the scientific is a relation of 'exteriority within.' This is not a static relationality but a doing—the enactment of boundaries—that always entails constitutive exclusions and therefore requisite questions of accountability" (Barad, 2003, 803). The phrase "exteriority within" is meant to indicate that the clear boundaries presumed to distinguish subject from object, text from context and so on are actually porous, re-constitutive, and active, not binarial. The presumed object can be found within the subject. This is what I will use the phrase intra-relational to mean (Dennis, forthcoming). We can think about this with respect to locating our bodies in a desk and understanding that the opportunity of our bodily movement and feeling is now partially bounded by and constituted of its being with the desk. Barad uses the concept of intra-action to indicate that relations are not composed of external, additive, atomistic entities, but instead are internal actions co-constitutive with one another. Relations are thought of as *within* rather than *between* subjects (which is what is typically meant by the word interaction). This relationality is not static, according to Barad, but is instead an active doing – relating (within not between). Barad says that the doing is an enactment of boundaries and I understand that to mean our doing enacts intra-relations, which are always also bounded – constituting inclusions and exclusions. The doing aspect – the enactment of boundaries—leads us to the concept "agential cut" where agency is synonymous with this *doing*. Since the doing includes the material, this notion of agency resists a strict subject/object binary. We bring into being, so to speak, our agency, through our doing *with*. Rather than describe my agency in relation to the desks as teacher (subject) acting on the desks (objects) to arrange them with particular learning goals in mind we can use Barad to describe the arranging as the co-malleability of my teaching and the arrangement of desks in the space. Both my own teaching plans and the situatedness of the desks must be thought together. One could now easily outline the way this particular intra-action establishes boundaries for the way teaching and learning are engaged in this specific moment. In this section of the chapter, I build up these central concepts of Barad's new materialism by locating first its critical potential, engaging with its concept of material, and establishing the relevance of this cluster of concepts for our practical, analytical engagements with "context."

What's Critical About "New Materialism"?

Many writers refer to the cluster of ideas for which Barad's work is centralized as the "new materialism." Braidotti (2006) and Delanda (2015) both began using the phrase "neo-materialism" in the 1990s. Both of them, in different ways, found a need to distinguish between linguistic-centered post-structuralism and materialist-oriented post-structuralism. While much could be said about this distinction, suffice to say here that materialist-oriented post-structuralists (like Foucault) argue that the material world constrains and resources linguistic signification (Olssen, 2003, p. 194). "'Neo-materialism' emerges as a method, a conceptual frame and a political stand, which refuses the linguistic paradigm, stressing instead the concrete yet complex materiality of bodies immersed in social relations of power" (Braidotti interviewed in Dolphijn & van der Tuin, 2012, p. 21). Refusing the linguistic paradigm argues that we cannot take language for granted, but also suggests that we cannot center language in our understanding of social life writ large. You will see below that I take these points up as critiques, without abandoning a communicative ground. Let's look at why I am saying this new materialism is critical.

Barad's particular approach to new materialism is critical in several ways. First of all, Barad critiques the over-reliance on and over-interpretation of language in social science. Relatedly, Barad critiques representationalism and its taken-for-grantedness in common ways of doing social science. It follows, then, that Barad critiques the effects of these ways of thinking, namely she argues that matter has not mattered enough to the social sciences. Barad specifically critiques humanism by articulating a post-humanist account of performativity. This account focuses on the diffractive co-emergence of subjects and material through which agential cuts establish, re-establish, shift, and transform their seemingly inert boundaries as constitutive of the two. Overall, Barad's work explicitly refuses to take for granted the binaries of contemporary social science and, thus, her work contributes to a corpus of critical efforts across a spectrum of entangled domains in physics, queer studies, social science methodology, feminism, and so on.

Kuntz (2015), working with new materialist thought, describes matter as "active, fluid, and productive" and "indeterminate" which "affects the world" (p. 83). He casts truth-telling as materially-situated critique (p. 110). He (2015) articulates an inclusive set of critical ways to enact new materialism through one's research: (1) "understand the means by which otherwise common-sensical rationales develop, producing a host of legitimated practices; and (2) . . . imagine and enable new practices that extend from newly possible forms of knowing" (p. 25).

However, to be perfectly honest, Barad has claimed not to be interested in critique – she considers it over-rated and over-used (Barad interviewed in Dolphijn & van der Tuin, 2012, p. 49). She claims that, "Critique is all too often not a deconstructive practice, that is, a practice of reading for the constitutive exclusions of those ideas we can not do without, but a destructive practice meant to dismiss, to turn aside, to put someone or something down" (Barad interviewed in Dolphijn & van der Tuin, 2012, p. 49). Barad proposed what she calls "a diffractive methodology, a method of diffractively reading insights through one another, building new insights, and attentively and carefully reading for differences that matter in their fine details" (Barad interviewed in Dolphijn & van der Tuin, 2012, p. 50). Diffractive methodology depends on an entangled, internal ethics that deconstructs independence and looks forward through mutuality (Barad 2007). So, in order to call this approach critical and honor Barad's rejection of critique as not good enough, we must not use the word *critical* to refer to a cursory dismantling treatment of ideas or texts. Neither can the word be used as a form of "subtraction, distancing, or othering" (Barad interviewed in Dolphijn & van der Tuin, 2012, p. 49). This orientation compels us to locate ourselves entangled within both the critique and the critiqued and to engaged diffractively with the readings and thinking. For me, this endeavor would be impossible to describe or sustain without also admitting that communicative grounds are implicitly also entangled within.

Selective Description of Barad's New Materialism

Quantum physics has transformed the ways in which physicists do their theoretical and practical work. As a feminist physicist, Barad (2003, 2008) leverages physical insights for social science in order to contribute to feminist social science thinking. To further our understanding of Barad's new materialism, I selectively highlight a few important concepts: diffraction, entanglement as intra-action, and agential cut.

Barad takes up Haraway's (1991) "diffractive" metaphor through quantum physical ways of thinking. This is what she said:

> Diffraction, understood using quantum physics, is not just a matter of interference, but of entanglement, an ethico-onto-epistemological matter. This difference is very important. It underlines the fact that knowing is a direct material engagement, a cutting together-apart, where cuts do violence but also open up and rework the agential conditions of possibility. There is not this knowing from a distance. Instead of there being a separation of subject and object, there is an entanglement of subject and object, which is called the "phenomenon." Objectivity, instead of being about offering an undistorted mirror image of the world, is about accountability to marks on bodies, and responsibility to the entanglements of which we are a part. That is the kind of shift that we get, if we move diffraction into the realm of quantum physics.
>
> *(Barad interviewed in Dolphijn & van der Tuin 2012, p. 52)*

In the above quote, Barad links "diffraction," "entanglement," and "agential cut" while articulating a non-representational definition of objectivity. I want to read Barad's above ideas aloud, with Habermas' (1984/1981) and Carspecken's (2003) perspectives at play. I am going to tease apart the above paragraph and then reflect back on what that looks like materially. I do the teasing apart in order to draw lines around some of the concepts so that their insights might engage our thinking-as-usual (doing what Barad is proposing we do).

"Knowing is direct material engagement . . ." This point suggests that knowing is activity (engagement as an action) that is directly **material** not directly conceptual. To understand this point, I look at some of the other things she says in the paragraph above. A common way of thinking of objectivity and knowledge depends on a sharply bounded disconnection between the subject as knower and the object as known/knowledge. Barad suggests that this is inaccurate. In the above paragraph, Barad argues that ethically, ontologically, and epistemologically the subject and object are **intra-actively entangled** (she uses the word phenomenon to mark this particular entanglement). This **entanglement** is what I think of as the **intra-relation** of subject and object, the within-ness of subject and object as one another – it is not to be thought of as the intertwining of two distinct entities, but rather the absence of such distinctions except when brought about through agential cuts (agency is synonymous with doing). We might think of this within-ness as a momentum yet-to-be differentiated. In practical terms differentiation is the effect of the momentum spun off into a trajectory through **agential cuts**. "[C]uts do violence but also open up and rework the agential conditions of possibility." It takes an agential cut to constitute and acknowledge stark boundaries between subject and object. It seems to me that some agential cuts are habitual, but others have us acting in new ways. We see that an act could always have been otherwise, but given particular interpretive probabilities, agential cuts produce recognizable bounded ranges of possibilities. Agential cuts are not synonymous with straightforward strategic /goal-oriented motivations of an actor. Instead, agential cuts are both the doing and the effect. The act itself cuts into the **ethico–onto–epistemological** entanglement of subject/object (diffraction) and produces effects – effects that cannot be reduced to the linguistic or psychological realms, but rather, as Barad emphasizes, effects that are **material** (meaning they physically exist in time and space as matter). Let's return to the quote at the start of this paragraph. Agential cuts are entangled within our knowledge as direct engagements with material. The agential conditions of possibility have to do with the constitutive conditions within an agential cut.

Barad's ideas about objectivity depend on intra-action. "Objectivity . . . is about accountability to the marks on bodies, and responsibility to the entanglements of which we are a part." Moving away from the traditional way of thinking about objectivity, Barad writes of engaging objectivity by being accountable to its effects (of creating boundaries, defining entities, marking bodies as able, included, and so forth) and being responsible for our entanglements with these marks through our "objective" engagements. This accountability and responsibility let go of the idea that the observer is aloof, disconnected, and individualistically separated from the observation. Barad drew on Bohr's work to propose that the observed object is inseparable from the agencies of observation (p. 814). Habermas's (1984/1981) critical pragmatism locates objectivity in relation (and I think we could use intra-relation) to action-orientations through which objective claims[1] are produced. The claims themselves link the subject and object in action-orientations, while marking the conditions and material specifically relevant for the acting and conditions of possibility.

Here's an example to work through:

> It's the first day of class, the professor walks to the front of the room. Students are sitting, probably in rows, unless the teacher has prepared the room differently. At universities it is rare for a teacher to "own" a room so these spaces are shared and professors with their students have to arrange the room to suit their needs. The teacher is dressed in a brightly colored, semi-casual skirt and sweater. She is wearing her wedding ring and some earrings. As she walks to the front of the room she smiles at

new faces, and greets students she has met before by smiling at them and using their names. She starts talking. She says, "Hi. I am Barbie Dennis and this is a feminist theory and methodology course. To begin with, I would like you to hang your name over the desk so we can start to learn each other's names. In a few moments I am going to ask that we introduce ourselves by providing the name you wish us to use and your preferred gender pronouns. It would also be fun to hear a sentence or two about yourself. I look forward to getting to know you well as the class goes along. As I already said, my name is Barbie Dennis. I use the pronouns she, her, hers.

This paragraph is written from a third-person perspective, the perspective Habermas (1984) associates with objectivity. The focus is on the professor . . . that is, we are not getting an account of what the students are doing. Probably, this focus matches the focus of many people in the room. What the professor does inside the class is intra-actively related with what she does outside the class (in terms of preparation) and with what the students do/are expected to do. This description enacts an agential cut demarcating objectivity from subjectivity and normativity in particular ways. Through this agential cut, objectivity is linked to what one in the room would see and hear if focused on the teacher. To offer up such objective claims is to be "accountable to the marks on the body" (namely, the status/role diffractions and what they require of the bodies in the room), and "responsible for the entanglements" (for example, the subjective,[2] normative,[3] and objective diffractions of the first encounters of a class). Those entanglements can be teased apart analytically, but must be done in a diffractive way, meaning we must use our analysis to locate how aspects of the phenomena are entangled and co-emergent. In the paragraph below, I take the third-person account from above and add in (using parentheses) diffractive aspects of some of the subjective, normative, and objective entanglements energized through this particular agential cutting.

It's the first day of class, ~~the professor~~ (I) walks to the front of the room. ~~Students are sitting, probably in rows, unless the teacher has prepared the room differently.~~ (Rows again. The arrangement of the space demands I start the class from the "front" and that I stand while others are seated.) At universities it is rare for a teacher to "own" a room so these spaces are shared and professors with their students have to arrange the room to suit their needs. (I tend to think of the class as a collection of relationships, but this always also means re-arranging the physical space.) ~~The teacher is~~ (I am) dressed in a brightly colored, semi-casual skirt and sweater. (I want to dress in an inviting way, but, also, show a bit of my personality. And I feel compelled to dress semi-professionally on the first day. Inevitably, I put a lot of thought in to what I wear. [I doubt my male counterparts do this.] Sexism. Leave me alone.) ~~She is~~ (I am) wearing ~~her~~ (my) wedding ring and some earrings. (I don't typically wear much jewelry.) As ~~she~~ (I) walks to the front of the room ~~she~~ (I) smiles at new faces, and greets students ~~she has~~ (I have) met before by smiling at them and using their names. (The recognition of actual faces is important here. The physicality of the students and how they are arrayed in the space is an important part of ritual.) (I feel warmth in my body when I see students in the room, when I see them smile at me.) ~~She~~ I starts talking. (The arrangement of the room is intra-actively related with specific sets of social roles and statuses and it makes possible particular kinds of communicative events. Rows with individual chair-desks all facing the same direction with a large space for teachers at "the front" make it easy for students and teachers to interact one at a time in a teacher-focused way. Individual chair-desks located in a circle around the perimeter of the room make it possible for students to interact with one another and for not all interactions to flow from student-to-teacher, teacher-student. The arrangement of the chair-desks indicates the kinds of interactions I want in the class. My control over the arrangement is part of the intra-relational entanglement.)

What I mean to illustrate above is a way of thinking about objectivity as an active, epistemological-ontological orientation (Habermas, 1984) brought into play through agential cutting. As Barad argues, objectivity is not best described in representational terms. When we engage objectively, we make ourselves accountable to and responsible for specific effects and entanglements. The agential cut of this example results in the effect of classroom organization, material arrangements, and interactions that focus on the professor as lead. This particular agential cut is socially habituated in mainstream US universities. We enact its possibilities or we transgress the habits. A diffractive engagement with objective-describing is critical. Diffraction is a cutting together – where both violence and possibility always are intra-acted. Agency here is the agency of "teacher-in-classroom": the subject (teacher-with-students-in-mind) and object (classroom) are entangled in specific ways through the agential cut. Barad (2003) uses the term *thingification* to talk about the "turning of relations into 'things,' 'entities,' and 'relata'" (p. 804). In my work, I retain the hyphens to indicate the relations and avoid thingifying. By taking seriously intra-activity as an undoing of the subject/object, material/conceptual binaries we recognize the possibility of understanding the material contextual aspects of agency. In the previous example we grasp the subject–subject (teacher–student) intra-action and the subject–object (teacher–classroom) intra-action as they are all entangled (as the first day of class) in producing the effects of classroom engagement-for-learning-sake. In the next section, I develop these insights into analytical orientations.

Analytic Thinking: Understanding Context, Matter, and Agency

It is a significant shift to move away from analyzing data through purely representational terms. My own pragmatic conceptualization of research has been "dialogue" – namely that the research process is an iterative, recursive dialogue, where communication is not conceived of as solely representational. I want to transform my own work and Barad's ideas of agency and matter toward an analysis of agency that is context-inclusive. This effort is much like Barad's (2007) description of a wave, namely, as one wave interferes with/moves through and overlaps with another wave, some of the first wave "remains with the new" after the transformation. The analysis I share would fall under the category of analyses coming to be known as diffractive methodologies.

Any act of analysis is quite explicitly agential cutting. This is unavoidable. Thus, as we move forward with the cutting, we take responsibility for its doing and the effects of the doing, including the responsibility to think differently, undoing habitual, taken-for-granted normalizing. An agential cut constitutes a reality among many realities that might be constituted through different agential cuts in a given event.

What will be produced through the analysis is an entangled account of context, matter, and agency as co-constitutive through the agential cut. We come to see the intra-active relation of matter and agency in new ways when we engage with context as an aspect of the momentum of performance.

An Example

I selected a photo from one of my trips to Uganda. I use this photo in a Mystory (Denzin, 2003) I perform. I have given a lot of thought to this picture. To include it here, I transformed it from color into black and white. The picture must have been taken when I visiting in 2015. One of my friends had recently opened a private primary school in a rural area outside of the capital city, Kampala. His wife, who is in the picture below, is the Director of the School. The school is private in part because it does not meet the requirements to be government certified. The school does not have running water or electricity, but this is not atypical of Ugandan primary schools. My friend and his wife, both educators prior to opening this school, wanted a place where rural children could go to get educated. The Ugandan government does not build schools so there are many rural parts of the country where kids do not have access to schooling. At this time in the school's young history, it did not have its own building and was being housed in an old dairy. The open stalls were used as classrooms. I was asked by my friend and his wife to be the patron of the school. Being the patron of the school involves promoting learning at the school, sharing ideas and materials, contributing to the fiscal well-being and sustainability of the school, and generally supporting the school's promise. I agreed.

When I visit the school, the children perform songs and dances, I meet with the teachers, and I am often fed at my friends' home, I give small talks to the teachers and encourage the students. Inevitably, the moment comes when I give the Director money. In the photo below this is what is happening. I am giving the Director a large, by Ugandan standards, amount of money to support the educational efforts and provide for constructing a compound of school buildings on a nearby site. The photographer must have been my friend, as he had taken up my camera (which I laid on the ground near my purse an hour or so before this photo was taken). I had set the camera down in order to be able to interact with the teachers, children, Madame Director, and the Head Mistress. When I got my camera home, I found it included this particular photo and a number of others that I did not take. Also, though I had a camera, it was nearly always a source of tension for me. I wanted people at the school to know I wanted to remember my time with them. Taking photos of people can be meaningful in that way. However, I was keenly aware of my white-skinned difference and I did not want to be looking at "native" Ugandans from the lens of a camera. Interacting personally with folks was far more important to me. So, on this visit, I had laid the camera down after taking a few group photos. At last, I was happy to find the set of pictures that I had not taken.

Before getting into the analysis, I want to articulate how the philosophical work of new materialism informs my orientation toward the analysis of the photo. The photo will not be treated solely as a representation of an event. Both the photo and the analytic process are performative events – they are doings together. The purpose of the analysis is to open a transformative space for material reconfiguration and dialogue through that which one could call realistic. In describing diffractive analysis, Lenz Taguchi (2012) noted that such efforts rely "on the researcher's ability to make matter intelligible in new ways and to imagine other possible realities presented in the data" (p. 267), managing to

FIGURE 9.1

encounter the analytic event with one's fully corporeality. Specifically, I use the concepts materialization and agential cut to imagine (and put into dialogue) new possibilities of understanding intra-active context and agency. In what follows, I speculate on what might be the most taken-for-granted, habitual interpretation of the photo (I call this "First Read"). Secondly, I trace an analysis process through an iterative agential cut. In this tracing, I will name the agential cut. I use hyphens (Fine, 1994) to articulate the intra-active agency-material relations that emerge when context and agency are located as co-constitutive and when they *transgress* habitual agential cuts. This illustrative agential cut is, again, not to be taken as representative of the possibilities, but rather as a performance of possibility. I conclude this analytic section of the paper with a brief description of other possible agential cuts.

First Read

For academics in Western, privileged work situations, this photo quickly calls to mind the distinct, seemingly intractable binaries between developing third-world countries/first-world countries. The context seems relatively stable. We are seated outside because there is no real "inside" for this event to take place. Here I was, a White lady from a wealthy country, providing financial material to a lady from a poorer country. The wealth redistribution of minuscule proportions on a world stage is playing out in this single picture. The side-by-side seating belies the inequity that has brought the two ladies together, but the other material aspects of the photo speak into that inequity. Note these contrasts:

These contrasts, on first read, indicate the active material contextualization of the event. The binarial conceptualization instantiates a *thingification* of material inequity as representation of world-level social inequity. To complexify this, I am going to add in what is missing from the photo as background to the two ladies and locate some of the "missings" through performative rather than thingified terms.

This first read provides us with interesting dialogue points. There is material *within* the photograph and there are material effects of the photograph itself. The photograph is entailed in the act of establishing the importance of the gift, demarcating the flow of material wealth, answering the trust that was engaged, and holding those involved accountable to the lively relationships.

TABLE 9.1 Money Changing Hands

Dark-skinned body	Light-skinned body
Not adorned	Adorned (with watch)
Each hand involved in different task	Both hands working together
Accepting the reaching in of her light-skinned friend	Reaching into the seated space of her dark-skinned friend
Plastic chair	Wooden chair

Context Matters

Matters of Agency

Money as Material Context	Racialized, Classed Bodies as Material Context of WE
<ul><li>Money moves from country to country, often changing forms.</li><li>Money moves from person to person and that movement is not closely monitored when outside of institutions and is primarily inconsequential to the basic flow of money.</li><li>Money is not found in equal measure around the globe. (Money is concentrated in some places.)</li><li>Institutions monitor amounts of *money more* than they monitor *material money*.</li><li>Money can make purchasing possible. Particular amounts of money can be exchanged for particular goods and services.</li><li>Money can be earned, gifted, traded, withheld and so on, through exchanges.</li><li>Sharing makes mutual equality a possibility when sharing is not the end in itself.</li><li>Money is created from earth resources through nation-states.</li><li>Educating children costs money.</li></ul>	<ul><li>People who live on different continents can work together toward similar goals.</li><li>People of different racial and class backgrounds find their action-orientations harmonized.</li><li>People can move their bodies together, as WE, even when much of their life activities find them seemingly separated.</li><li>Unequal financial distribution does not have to result in unequal sharedness.</li><li>Sharing is not about the transfer from one body to another, it is about con-joined intra-activity with momentum that already assumes the sharing.</li><li>Money is concentrated with some bodies more than others, and that concentration can be described as raced and classed and gendered, etc.</li><li>There are dark and light bodies on the planet. Dark and light bodies are located in different places and have different discursive value.</li><li>Discursive value and social value affect fiscal value.</li><li>We know how to run an effective school.</li></ul>

We can improve the educational opportunities for children (in Uganda)	
<ul><li>We care about children.</li><li>We want good schools for children.</li><li>We want kids to have access to schools</li><li>We do not intend to let the children down.</li></ul>	<ul><li>We are educators.</li><li>We are capable of taking care of the students.</li><li>We are capable of managing money.</li></ul>

FIGURE 9.2

As interesting as this analysis might be, the binarial objectifying is problematic. One crucial way to notice this is my inability to put "women" and "dark-skinned"/"light-skinned" in doing terms. The performance of woman – "womanizing" to re-claim that word – might be easier to articulate than the skinned-ness, but if we link both of these to the performances identified, we begin to see their intra-active, lively relationalities.

Diffractive Analyses

In the first read, I articulated some doings of the photo that specifically put into conversation the material relationships activated through basic binaries of wealth inequity: have-nots and haves. I offer an iteration of a diffractive analysis through which to explore the intra-action of agency and context. In contrast with the first read, I reframe the doing as performances constituted within, across and through the taken-for-granted binaries presented above. I close the section by offering two additional agential cuts to strengthen the illustration.

Marking Material Momentum: Money Transforms

The first agential cut orients through the question: What is the photo doing intra-actively? One of the things the photo does is mark material relationships. In the first read, the doing of the photograph was articulated through a set of binaries that seemed to co-establish material relationships between those who have and those who have not, between the context and the momentum. For this first diffractive analysis, I re-imagine agency and material by un-thinking the distinct boundaries through which the first reading was rendered. This new agential cut focuses my attention on the material momentum of the hands and money. Let's un-think this money as an exchange from one set of hands to another, and, instead think of this as an acting-*with*. This is the first iterative shift in the analysis process – thinking *with* and *we*. The momentum going on in the photo might actually be constituted of moving the world's fiscal material toward a collective responsibility/accountability to educate children through the hands of women (in this case). Contrary to the suggestion of the first read, the money was never "owned" independently by either of the women. The question of whose money is not so relevant through this articulation of reality. Instead the women–money intra-action is part of an ongoing momentum of producing an agency of sharing-together-caring-together for the educative material needs of children. There are new possibilities for imagining the reality of money flowing *with* and *through* a world of conjoined hands. This particular agential cut imagines money as possible material transformation. In other words, the money and the hands are co-constitutively transformed. The money is changed into building supplies, which are fashioned into buildings, which are able to house student learners. The hands are involved throughout the process.

Through this analysis we re-invigorate the context not as passive backdrop for action and intentionality, but as active *within* the action-made-intentional or agency. The agency of sharing-together-caring-together in the service of educating children brings to the foreground a set of objective realities through which we might orient. Though our classed and racial differences are evidenced, their value through this particular agential cut is really more about access on the ground and behind the scenes. It would be possible to engage a tracing of the flow of money and its intra-action with the women (and others with/through whom it flows). The idea is that the world's money can be used for positive or negative effects and that we have a shared responsibility for this . . . not that we have a responsibility for the money we own, but that the money on the planet, made of planetary materials, is ours together, coordinated and claimed, mis-named, and mis-allocated, and beneficial and resourceful.

The binarial differences of the first read are an effect of marking the path of this momentum, but part of what is missing is money-as-potential-for-transformation co-constituted through the hands of engagement – the performance of changing: Changing hands; changing form; changing educational contexts; changing learning opportunities; changing global isolationism; and changing a habitual agential cut of Global-North-Meets-Global-South on the terms of the North and the land of the South.

I, for one, do not see this analysis as separated from the interpretational analysis in an either/or form, but as a both–and opportunity. As we orient through an agential cut, we establish the interpretive parameters and even as we transgress we actively invoke those (habitual) parameters, *thingifications*, through which

TABLE 9.2

WOMEN			
Photographing as school proprietor	Dark-skinned body	Light-skinned body	Donating as caring Americans
Accepting the money	Deserving the money	Appropriating the money	Acknowledging the needs
Photographing the moment	Accepting the money	Giving the money	Supplying some money
Making important the gift	Recognizing the fiscal ability of the givers	Recognizing the need for the money	Trusting the delivery of the money
Planning on developing the school	Promising to manage the money well	Trusting (as if partially owning) the management of the school and its resources to the Director and the Proprietor	Letting go of responsibility

the objective realities get pragmatically performed (and here the idea of co-constitutiveness is crucial). To reconstruct the implicit, possible objective claims (Carspecken, 1996) that would intra-relate to the above analysis, I will emphasize objective action-claims *from within* a contextually inclusive WE performance with agency indicators.

Interpretive claims can only ever partially allude to a richer, more complicated entanglement, but, nevertheless, they are intuitively connected to our understanding of those entanglements. What I have intended to put into dialogue through this analysis is the lively ethico-onto-epistemology of context as it is co-constituted with agency through a very specific agential cut. Any such agential cut actively establishes, with some specificity, interpretive boundaries, boundaries of objective orienting, and the manner of intra-relation through which agency emerges. By relocating context from static, passive background painting to intra-active material with momentum, the entanglements of context and agency emerge for any particular agential cut as it performs reality.

What has been excluded from the analysis performed through this particular agential cut are the children and their educational outcomes. Yet, the children and their educational outcomes are not actually entirely outside this agential cut. For example, Madame Director and I are both educators and we have a keen commitment to the children, imaging ourselves acting on their behalf. Another aspect that has not been included in this agential cut is the way in which the World Bank takes and gives money to poor countries in the name of education while simultaneously profiting off the arrangements (Mayengo, Namusoke, & Dennis 2015).

Other Possible Agential Cuts

For the sake of inviting imagination, I want to just briefly mention two other possible agential cuts through which an analysis might easily proceed. One possibility would be to focus analysis on the material context intra-related with the entanglements of photographer, the photograph, and the photographed. We would begin by noticing the co-performing of photographer, photograph, and photographed. This would open up a transgressive opportunity to establish a relevant reality *through* and *within which* the doing resists, for the moment, the distinction between these as separate entities. Their materiality and not just discursiveness enters the dialogue. Through this agential cut, various audiences of the photograph are excluded . . . the audience of attenders at the event, as well as subsequent audiences across myriad of encounters.

Another possible agential cut would involve orienting ourselves through the "distinctions" between data (photograph) and analysis (product of the researcher's analytic work). This is precisely the kind of diffractive analysis that Lenz Taguchi (2012) performs on a segment of interview data. Lenz Taguchi advised researchers to bring their whole bodies into the analytic experiences, opening one's self up to a wide array of corporeal engagement with the material.

Because I was photographed, though I do not have a memory of the photographing per se, I remember the moment in which the picturing was being done. I remember the smells. I remember the feel of Madame Director's arm. I know how I felt sitting on the good wooden chair, while she sat on the plastic one that could hardly hold her up. I remember how the children touched my hair and called me Mzungu. But these memories do not just stay in my mind. I can feel the warmth of the African equatorial sun in its setting mode, for example. The important point in this agential cut is an awareness of the way the analyst and the data are intra-active and intra-related. What is seemingly excluded through this cut is the way the photo is not just datum. The photo is a collective marker of a cross-cultural, cross-continental friendship, for example – a friendship that tolerates the way money flows through and within it.

Summary

Analysis depends on researchers taking agential cuts *from within* the data. Using the concept agential cut speaks into the traditional separation of researcher and data. The first analytic read produced a series of interconnected binaries through action orientations. The diffractive analysis puts forward an understanding of the intra-active nature of both material context and agentic possibilities. This approach offers performative engagement with a blurred entangled context–text, subject–object. By describing both the first read and the diffractive analysis readers can grasp differences. "Diffraction as a methodology is about studying how differences get made in such a process and the effects that differences make; what is excluded and how these differences and exclusions matter (Barad, 2007: 30)" (Lenz Taguchi, 2012, p. 271).

Conclusion

This chapter was an opportunity for me to play *with you* drawing forward a cluster of concepts from Barad's new materialism *through* my own understandings of Habermas (1984) and Carspecken (1996, 2003). My purpose was to transform the taken-for-granted status quo of context description as backdrop for active and agentic subjects while also grasping the co-constitutiveness of agency. To do this, I turned to a cluster of philosophical concepts emerging from Barad's new materialism. This is a preliminary effort and many questions remain. Lenz Taguchi (2012) conducted a much more embodied approach to analysis. In what ways is that a problem for the analysis I performed? What are the theoretical problems with reading Barad through a communication action theoretical way of thinking? How do these problems manifest in the analysis? To be sure, my taking up of these concepts illustrates an early understanding on my part. There will be much to learn by refusing and resisting the crevices I create and the fissures of which I am unaware, even though the process has opened up for me new ways of taking seriously context-agency.

Notes

1 Objective claims are claims oriented through questions of what works and what things are in a presupposed objectively existing external world. These claims assume that, in principle, an other using the same definitions and orientation toward measurement could validate the claim.

2 According to Habermas (1984/1981) and Carspecken (1996), subjective claims are claims to truth that orient toward a presupposed internal world of the subject about her feelings, inclinations, states of mind and so on to which she, in principle, has privileged access. Validity of subjective claims rests in part on the honesty and authenticity of the subject.

3 Normative claims are those that are oriented through a social community's sense of itself and how individuals within the community would be expected to treat one another as well as the shared values held by community members. These claims are validated by invoking other normative and evaluative claims within the community, ultimately suggesting that the claim in question is valid because it is worthy of our community's assent (Carspecken, 1996).

References

Barad, K. (2003). Posthumanist performativity: Toward an understanding of how matter comes to matter. *Signs: Journal of Women in Culture and Society, 28*(3), 801–831.

Barad, K. (2007). *Meeting the universe halfway: Quantum physics and the entanglement of matter and meaning.* Durham, NC: Duke University Press.

Barad, K. (2008) Queer causation and the ethics of mattering. In N. Giffney & M. Hird (Eds.), *Queering the non/human.* Hampshire, UK: Ashgate Publishing Limited.

Braidotti, R. (2006). Posthuman, all too human: Towards a new process ontology. *Theory, Culture & Society, 23*(7–8), 197–208.

Carspecken, P. (1996). *Critical ethnography in educational research: A theoretical and practical guide.* New York: Routledge.

Carspecken, P. (2003). 'Occularcentrism, phonocentrism, and the counter enlightenment problematic: Clarifying contested terrain in our schools of education', *Teachers College Record, 105*(6), 978–1047.

Delanda, M. (2015). The new materiality. Special Issue. *Architectural Design, 85*(5), 16–21.

Dennis, B. (forthcoming). Working without/against a compass: Ethical dilemmas in educational ethnography. In D. Beach, C. Bagley, and S. Marques da Silva (Eds.), *Handbook on ethnography of education.* Hoboken, NJ: Wiley Press.

Denzin, N. (2003). *Performance ethnography: Critical pedagogy and the politics of culture.* Thousand Oaks, CA: Sage Publications.

Dolphijn, R., & van der Tuin, I. (2012). *New materialism: Interviews and cartographies.* Ann Arbor, MI: Open Humanities Press.

Fine, M. (1994). Working the hyphens: Reinventing the self and other in qualitative research. In N. Denzin, & Y. S. Lincoln (Eds.), *Handbook of qualitative research* (pp. 70–82). Thousand Oaks, CA: Sage.

Habermas, J. (1984/1981). *Theory of communicative action, Volume One: Reason and the rationalization of society* (Thomas McCarthy, trans.). Boston, MA: Beacon Press.

Haraway, D. (1991). *Cyborgs, simians, and women: The reinvention of nature.* New York: Routledge.

Kuntz, A. (2015). *The responsible methodologist: Inquiry, truth-telling, and social justice.* Walnut Creek, CA: Left Coast Press.

Lenz Taguchi, H. (2012). A diffractive and Deleuzian approach to analyzing interview data. *Feminist Theory, 13*(3), 265–281.

Mayengo, N., Namusoke, J., & Dennis, B. (2015). The testimony of neoliberal contradiction in education choice and privatization in a poor country: The case of a private, undocumented rural primary school in Uganda. *Ethnography and Education, 10*(3), 293–309.

Olssen, M. (2003). Structuralism, post-structuralism, and neo-liberalism: Assessing Foucault's legacy. *Journal of Education Policy, 18*(2), 189–202.

St. Pierre, E. (2008). Decentering voice in qualitative inquiry. *International Review of Qualitative Research, 1*(3), 319–336.

SECTION III

Critical Theories and Data Analysis in Institutions and Policies

INTRODUCTION

Christina W. Yao

Educational institutions in the United States, both in structure and policies, are situated in a colonial legacy that permeates all aspects of academic life including research and scholarly inquiry. However, perpetuating existing colonial academic structures in research is problematic, particularly with today's pressures of multiple current events, political actions, and global issues (e.g., Charlottesville race rally,[1] changing DACA policies,[2] etc.) affecting policies, people, and priorities in education. At the same time, the maintenance and (re)production of traditional forms of knowledge and research methods are inherent in current practices in social research. Most troubling is the research training for nascent scholars, most of which emphasizes the positivistic search for validity and unbiased truth in educational inquiry. However, the rigidity in research training often minimizes how social research traditionally privileges dominant ideologies and perspectives. As such, a new discourse is needed on how to utilize critical theories beyond simply as an identified framework, or more commonly, as an afterthought. The promises of liberatory practice from the use of critical theories must be realized beyond naming a framework for a research study; rather, using critical theories must move into analysis and praxis throughout the research process. Thus, this section makes a significant contribution to social researchers on how to apply critical theories and data analysis to institutional representation, policies, and practices. As a result, researchers can engage in and contribute to the emancipatory promises of qualitative research.

In contemporary educational research, critical theories and qualitative research often work in tandem in social research, typically with critical theories informing the research topic and data collection. However, the missing pieces to effective critical qualitative research include techniques on data analysis, interpretation, and implications. Findings and implications effectively distilled from critical data analysis are essential for informing institutional policies and practice. Thus, this section on critical theories and data analysis in institutions and policy is of vital importance in making the explicit connection from *theory* to *research* to *action*, particularly as related to institutional policies and representation.

This section starts with a chapter using postcolonial theory for data analysis. In the chapter, Discourse, Representation, and "Othering": Postcolonial Analysis of Donald Trump's Education Reform, Mercy Agyepong examines the intersection of education and politics through a postcolonial analytical lens. In analyzing Trump's political campaign speech, Agyepong examined how Black and Latinx students are represented and othered in political discourse that was intended as educational opportunities for Students of Color. As illustrated in this chapter, readers will gain insights on how to use postcolonial theory as an analytical tool to understand the multiple meanings and purposes of language, particularly in how Black and Latinx youth are represented in current school choice discourse. Specifically, Agyepong highlights how the "concepts of discourse, representation, and 'othering' allow researchers to interrogate the type of language used by participants, how it is used, why it is used, and its implications." In doing so, the author shares specific techniques in data analysis that unpack embedded messages in narratives related to the politics of school choice.

The effects of coloniality on education are also apparent in Jacqueline M. Forbes' chapter that highlights a Fanonian pedagogical model of analysis on a charter school's video on school success. As stated in her chapter, A Culture of Values: Rethinking School Quality and Culture through Fanonian Critical Theory, charter schools are lauded as solution-based educational options that promote the retention and success of Black students in urban environments. In using Fanon's (1963/2004; 1952/2008) concepts of fabrication and violence, Forbes demonstrates how to "define pedagogical colonization as a parallel relationship that happens in the educational setting" through a thorough video analysis (p. 165). As a result, readers gain insights on how to use a Fanonian coding scheme to analyze and illuminate dominant and oppressive discourse embedded within school practices and communications about Black students.

Rachelle Winkle-Wagner, Thandi Sulé, and Dina Maramba provide an approach for using Critical Race Theory (CRT) as an analytical tool in the chapter, Analyzing Policy Critically: Using Critical Race Theory to Analyze College Admissions Policy Discourse. CRT is heavily used in contemporary education as a conceptual frame that emphasizes several tenets, such as the permanence of racism, importance of counterstorytelling, and the role of interest convergence (Delgado & Stefancic, 2017; McCoy & Rodricks, 2015). A critical component of CRT is the need to be connected to action and praxis; thus, this chapter fills the need for Critical Race Praxis (Yamamoto, 1997) in educational inquiry by providing a systematic analytical approach using CRT in conjunction with critical discourse analysis. In conducting a discourse analysis of the Texas Top Ten Percent Plan, the authors connect the theoretical constructs of CRT with the analysis and interpretation of data, providing readers with insights on making explicit connections throughout qualitative research using CRT.

In the chapter Habermas and Data Analysis in For-Profit Higher Education Institutions, Ashley N. Gaskew applies Habermas' (1987) colonization of the lifeworld to television commercials used as marketing for for-profit institutions. By applying a coding scheme based on the interactions between the system and the lifeworld, Gaskew provides a critical analysis on the University of Phoenix's catchy *More Than Brains v5* commercial. Anyone who has a television set and cable automatically know the sounds and visuals from this commercial that was heavily in commercial rotation. Thus, it is imperative to analyze the video and text in order to understand how this commercial may be influencing viewers through its portrayal of the people and the promises associated with the University of Phoenix. The marketing positionality coding intersects both the visual and the lyrical in an attempt to understand the implicit and explicit messages inherent in the commercial. As a result, readers learn a technique that allows them to situate participants' lifeworlds within a larger system and question the messages that are communicated through educational media marketing campaigns that broadcast into many potential students' television sets.

In the final chapter, Jamila Lee-Johnson and Lora Henderson conduct an analysis of #BlackWomenatWork, Using Social Media to (Re)Center Black Women's Voices in Educational Research. Twitter has emerged as a space for meaningful discourse, most notably through the establishment of "Black Twitter," and this chapter addresses the work challenges of Black women through a critical discourse analysis of a popular hashtag. Layering critical discourse analysis with double consciousness (Du Bois, 1903) in analyzing tweets provides a textual analysis of experiences situated beyond the theoretical "veil." As indicated by this study, Black women experience double consciousness in their workplace, and also through Twitter, which serves as another environment that Black women exist in. Using critical discourse analysis allows an examination of both the *explicit* content of the tweets as well as the *implicit* social structural meanings—all of which are distilled down to 140 characters or less. Thus, this chapter illuminates the complexities of #BlackWomenatWork in tandem with Black women's representation on Twitter, a growing social network space that is now built into the fabric of discourse and representation in contemporary U.S. society.

As illustrated by the five chapters in this section, critical data analysis is imperative when conducting research on historically disenfranchised populations in academic institutions and policy. By using critical theories in tandem with critical analytical approaches, researchers can uncover the explicit and implicit meanings both visible and hidden within qualitative data. In doing so, the linkages between critical theory and interpretation are connected and strengthened, which will hopefully lead to effective and emancipatory implications for institutional practice and policy.

Notes

1 Charlottesville: https://www.nytimes.com/2017/08/13/us/far-right-groups-blaze-into-national-view-in-charlottesville.html
2 DACA: https://www.npr.org/2017/09/05/546423550/trump-signals-end-to-daca-calls-on-congress-to-act

References

Delgado, R., & Stefancic, J. (2017). *Critical race theory: An introduction*. New York: NYU Press.

Du Bois, W.E.B. (1903). *The souls of black folk*. Chicago: A. C. McClurg.

Fanon, F. (1952/2008). *Black skin, white masks*. New York: Grove Press.

Fanon, F. (1963/2004). *The wretched of the earth*. New York: Grove Press. Habermas, J. (1987). *The Theory of Communicative Action*. Boston, MA: Beacon Press.

McCoy, D. L., & Rodricks, D. J. (2015). Critical race theory in higher education: 20 years of theoretical and research innovations. *ASHE Higher Education Report*, *41*(3), 1–117.

Yamamoto, E. K. (1997). Critical race praxis: Race theory and political lawyering practice in post-civil rights America. *Michigan Law Review*. 821–900.

10

A CULTURE OF VALUES

Rethinking School Quality and Culture through Fanonian Critical Theory

Jacqueline M. Forbes

Theory: Franz Fanon's Critical Theory
Type of qualitative data: Videos
New data analysis technique: Fanonian pedagogical colonization coding
Substantive topic in education: School quality and educational success of Black students

---

Historically, critical theory has been understood as the vast collection of counter-hegemonic ideologies that critique systems and structures that perpetuate inequity (Bronner & Kellner, 1989; Crotty, 1998; Kincheloe & McLaren, 2002). In our contemporary context, critical theory helps us identify historical patterns related to racialized identities in our social world, and can be particularly helpful when outlining and challenging disparate outcomes between social groups (Abdel-Malek, 1981; Crotty, 1998; Kincheloe & McLaren, 2002). The collective works of early critical theorists, including Karl Marx, Emile Durkheim, and Antonio Gramsci, have been used throughout the years to help articulate the patterns we observe in our social world (Giddens, 1971). Their contributions to critical theory have been canonized and cited as the intellectual framework that succeeding theorists use to establish critiques of existing power structures and positions of liminality.

At the same time, however, these theorists have been criticized for minimally engaging race within their understanding of social contexts and critical theory (Pasque & Pèrez, 2015; Rabaka, 2010a). Our contemporary social world is highly organized along racial lines, and Black critical theorists have simultaneously pushed the boundaries of critical theory while being pushed to the periphery of the intellectual canon. Audre Lorde (2003, 2012), C.L.R. James (2013), and W.E.B. Du Bois (1903/2008) were contemporaries of canonized theorists, and made important contributions to the critical theory tradition by highlighting the linkages between race and social inequity. In following the tradition of Black critical theorists, contemporary theorists have cited the need for specifically developing and engaging theory that centers Black traditions, histories, and epistemologies.

Critical theory that engages an understanding of Black lived experiences can be used to analyze claims that social institutions make regarding the measures of institutional progress, particularly as it relates to Black people. Frantz Fanon (1963/2004) is one such theorist whose work can be particularly useful in analyzing educational data, particularly in the context of Black students. This chapter aims to demonstrate how to use Fanonian critical theory. This analytical technique is demonstrated through the example of claims that educational institutions make about the success of Black students, but it can be used in additional analyses in the context of Black student education. The first section of this chapter will introduce a Fanonian pedagogical model of analysis, and further explain Fanon's conceptions of fabrication and violence. Using fabrication and violence, the next section of this chapter will introduce a short data excerpt, and illustrate how to code for those concepts using the data excerpt. The final section of this chapter will briefly discuss two contemporary examples of theoretical frameworks that situate critical theory in a Black space.

Fanon's work historicizes and contextualizes longstanding social patterns, and has been used extensively in various disciplines to draw theoretical implications about social conditions—with the exception of the field of education (Leonardo & Singh, 2017). Fanon's analysis of discourse and discursive practice to create a colonized position combined with his theorization on the utility of violence presents a powerful framework in which to understand educative practices as they relate to Black students (Dei, 2010; Leonardo & Singh, 2017).

Developing Fanonian Critical Theory

Frantz Fanon is one of the earliest anti-colonialists and his works are seminal pieces in postcolonial literature (Gibson, 2017; Hiddleston, 2014). His analysis on the psychological and social impact of colonization on the colonized and the colonizer provided important contributions on the framing of Critical Race Theory which is often used as a frame in which to analyze race and racism in education and other disciplines (Seigel, 1968–69). Fanon's most influential works are *The Wretched of the Earth* (1963) and *Black Skin, White Masks* (1967). In both of these works, Fanon explicates how Black people developed an awareness of the social meaning of their own race (Seigel, 1968–69). In *The Wretched of the*

Earth, Fanon begins to deconstruct the psychological implications of colonization on the colonized as well as the colonizer (Fanon, 1963/2004). He continued this work by introducing a new psychoanalytical approach that could be used in a postcolonial context in *Black Skin, White Masks* (Nagy-Zekmi, 2007). Fanon frames his approach as the *"pathology of colonization:"* a perpetual cycle of violent action by the colonizer which dispossesses the colonized of land, resources, and culture. This pathological process is defined by the colonizer's constant awareness of how precarious the balance of power is; at any time, the colonized can recognize the colonizer's exploitation and can revolt against it. To maintain control of the power balance, the colonizer must maintain a constant state of terror and fear against the colonized (Fanon, 1963/2004). In the context of colonization, the colonizer is understood to be white[1] whereas the colonized is understood to be Black. Thus, the colonizing process is simultaneously a restructuring of economic order and a racial project.

Fanon's major works, *Black Skin, White Masks* and *The Wretched of the Earth*, examined the extent to which Black people could resist colonialization even while being forced into colonized positions by the proliferation of white supremacy. He wrestled with conceptions of humanity as applied to Black bodies, and the relationship between whiteness and colonial violence. Thus, his work raised complex concerns about how the colonial agenda could manifest in social institutions.

Using Fanon's theory of colonization as a relationship between the colonizer (the one in power) and the colonized (the one who lacks power), we can begin to define educational colonization as a parallel relationship that happens in the educational setting. Furthermore, we can begin to flesh out the Fanonian concepts of *fabrication* and *violence* within an educational context, and apply them to the relationship between Black students and schools.

Educational Colonization as Fanonian Critical Theory

To the extent that it includes the relational dynamic between teachers and students, the physical arrangement of classrooms, and the determination of what classifies as knowledge, "education is a power-saturated discussion" (Dei & Simmons, 2010, p. xiv). For Fanon, discussions of power were firmly rooted in an understanding of colonization as an iterative process; one that would, over time, continue to adjust itself to maintain the balance of power of the colonizer over the colonized (Browne, 2015; Fanon, 1952/2008; Fanon, 1963/2004). In other words, if the colonial condition is predicated on the oppression of the colonized, the colonizer must use the most effective tool at her/his disposal to maintain control. Thus, the tools that the colonizer uses and how the colonizer uses them can change over time in response to social, economic, or political conditions. Furthermore, Fanon theorized that colonization's success was predicated on the consistent use of colonizing practices, including a carefully crafted fabrication of a colonized subject and the strategic use of symbolic violence against the subject.

Fabrication

Fanon utilizes the Hegelian dialectic[2] to describe the way the colonized psychologically constructs the boundaries of Blackness. He notes that as the white colonizer constructs a pathological image of the colonized, the white colonizer is also working to construct a perfect image of whiteness, and utilizes this image to further set up the colonized as "not that." For Fanon, fabrication is represented as the colonist's insistence on a revision of collective memory of historical events and social identity constructions (Fanon, 1963/2004; Nielson, 2011). The white colonizer works to reduce the colonized into a set of characteristics, wholly disconnecting the colonized from humanity.

One such example can be seen in the "at-risk" educational discourses, whose roots can be traced to the Reagan-era *A Nation at Risk* report (Gardner, 1983). Students who are classified as "at risk" are largely Black students and other students of color, and much of the at-risk rhetoric excludes the historical and social factors that precluded Black students from having access to education. In this case, the *fabrication* presents itself as Black students or other students of color who underachieve, instead of highlighting persisting institutional inequities that cause disparities to exist for Black students and other students of color in education.

In the colonizer's construction of the colonized, natural human complexities are removed, and replaced with a simplified being who is "impervious to ethics, an enemy of values" (Fanon, 1963/2004, p. 6) and lacking in innate moral codes. The colonized is positioned in opposition to rightness, and any cultural behaviors, norms, traditions, and myths associated with the colonized are marked as "innate depravity" (Fanon, 1963/2004, p. 7) and forms of deviance to be eradicated. Created by the colonizer, this pathological image of the colonized, in many ways, becomes the measuring stick against which the colonized is understood. The descriptions of the colonized that the colonizer creates becomes the "livery the Black man has to wear" (Fanon, 1952/2008, p. 17). Fanon also attaches "fundamental importance" to how language is used as a fabrication tool. In an attempt to colonize, the colonizer utilizes language powerfully to distort and destroy the collective memory of the colonized's past, replacing dignity and glory with shame and disorder (Fanon, 1963/2004, pp. 148–149). This reimagining of social history is the foundation on which "the Other" is built. Within a colonialist system, the colonizer constructs the colonized as barbaric, bestial, and in need of rescue from self-inflicted malevolence by the colonist (Fanon, 1963/2004). By constructing the colonized in this manner, the colonizer convinces the colonized of their own inferiority, and creates psychological dependence on the colonizer to impart civility, adequacy, and acceptance (Fanon, 1952/2008; Fanon, 1963/2004).

Violence

"It is the colonist who *fabricated* and *continues to fabricate* the colonized subject" (Fanon, 1963/2004, p. 2), and it is the colonist who uses this fabrication to justify the acts of violence directed toward the colonized. The fabrication sets up an antagonistic relationship between the colonizer and the colonized, in which the colonized is presented as the problem and the colonizer is presented as the solution. "When the colonist realizes it is impossible to maintain domination over the colonies, it decides to wage a campaign in the fields of culture and values" (Fanon, 1963/2004, p. 9). In short, as the colonized resists the colonizer's attempts to define and shape the colonized, the colonizer meets that resistance with violence.

Fanon describes the process of shaping and controlling the colonized's story and identity as a violent, complex, and oppressive one (Fanon, 1963/2004). The colonized internalizes this violent process by adopting inferiority as a constructed identity (Fanon, 1963/2004), but may simultaneously engage in decolonization, resisting the oppressive efforts of the colonizer to create fear and to control the identity and narrative of the colonized. This constant cycle of terror and counterterror, violence and counterviolence (Fanon, 1963/2004) defines a battle between the colonizer and the colonized for control over "overlapping, intersecting, and interlocking systems of domination" (Rabaka, 2010b). In this complex system, the colonizer maintains control by employing colonial strategies. In schools, for example, this form of colonial control can be seen in the implementation of strict behavioral codes that govern how students and staff engage with one another in the classroom and in common areas around the school. Behavioral codes are formed based on the administration's *fabrications* of anticipated or potential student behavior, in which students who resist or transgress behavioral codes can be subject to harsh punitive measures that could be read as violent.

"Fanon argues that the colonizer has structured violence in every institution in the colony and within every aspect of colonial life" (Leonardo & Singh, 2017), and this is where Fanon's insights can be particularly helpful in considering "the normalization of the violence of education" (Dei & Simmons, 2010). In work that engages Fanon for his educational insights, contemporary theorists (Leonardo & Singh, 2017; Dei & Simmons, 2010) connect the processes of standardized testing, tracking, and the school-to-prison pipeline and classifies them as "violent processes" because of their impact on psychologically marginalizing Black students, defining them as a problem (Dumas, 2014) to be solved—or eradicated (Leonardo & Singh, 2017).

Using a Fanonian Approach and Carspecken's Method in Data Analysis

In a political climate amenable to the expansion of new school models and new public–private school partnerships, using critical theory can be particularly helpful in analyzing school quality. For example, in contemporary discussions of public schooling, popular terms including "the achievement gap," "failing public schools," and "school success" are often used to paint a picture of disparate outcomes in urban public schools vs. non-urban schools (Jacob, 2007; Lankford *et al.*, 2002). Within the larger urban education reform movement, charter schools have emerged as a tenable solution to the problem of retaining and graduating Black students in urban environments. In this section, I used data from a marketing video for the Achievement First charter school network as an example of how to apply Fanonian ideas to data analysis. In this example, Fanon's theorizations of *violence* and *fabrication* are used to interrogate charter school quality, and whether or not these models contribute to the miseducation of Black students.

Charter school models like Urban Prep,[3] Achievement First,[4] and KIPP (Knowledge Is Power Program)[5] are recognizable models that are known for their emphasis on standardized testing, highly structured curricula, highly regimented behavior, and hierarchical accountability. This combination of school features, along with such factors as the student–teacher ratio, average student scores' on standardized tests, percentage of seniors who graduate and continue into postsecondary education, and teachers' education level, are associated with school quality (Dondero & Muller, 2012), to which these particular models cite school culture and values as foundational to school quality and student success (Abdulkadiroğlu, Angrist, Dynarski, Kane & Pathak, 2011; Merseth, 2009).

While these schools rely on data-driven and quantitative metrics as ostensibly reliable indicators of school quality, they position school ideology as an equally accurate indicator of school quality by positioning school culture and values as critical to a school's success. Over the years, educational researchers have developed highly sophisticated measures to track test scores and graduation rates, and to measure school quality in order to classify schools as performing well, which serve to assure Black students and parents in urban communities of a school's capability of providing a high-quality education. Yet when we talk about school quality, we often ignore the qualitative counterpart of school ideology,[6] and keep coming back to test scores and graduation rates as the most important indicators of a school's ability to educate Black children in urban communities.

In determining school quality for Black students, theoretical frameworks that engage the Black epistemologies and lived experiences can be particularly helpful. As an example of how this can be helpful, this next section will use concepts derived from Fanonian educational colonization to interrogate the claims made by the Achievement First CEO, Doug McCurry.

Achievement First is a charter school network that has 34 elementary, middle, and high schools in Brooklyn, NY, Providence, RI, and in New Haven, Bridgeport, and Hartford, CT (Achievement First, 2017b). Nearly 12,000 students attend an Achievement First school, of whom 80 percent are first-generation college-going students, 83 percent qualify for free or reduced lunch, and 90 percet are Black and Latinx[7] (Achievement First, 2016; Achievement First, 2017c). The network boasts of strong academic achievement for its students, and notes a 100 percent college acceptance rate among other achievements. The Achievement First website contains several short videos that highlight student achievement, news stories, and snippets from Achievement First's unique school model. The following data excerpt was extracted from one of the videos subtitled, "Follow Achievement First's co-CEO and superintendent, Doug McCurry, as he tours a school and talks about our success" (Achievement First, 2017a).

> **Data Excerpt:** Some kids have very structured and safe home lives; some kids don't, right? And we want to make sure that at our school that they know, that adults will do what we say we're going to do. I think a lot of schools are realizing that they need to root their education in a core set of values that are universal. And I think that comes in two-fold; one, high behavioral expectations. We talk about sweating the small stuff. If we worry about shirttails being tucked in, and the lower grades kids walking in quiet lines and we talk about kids sitting up straight in their desks, tracking the teacher with their eyes. There's a whole set of behaviors that we explicitly teach and that we sweat. But we sweat it in a joyful way. We are unapologetic about teaching the REACH values, which are respect, enthusiasm, achievement, citizenship, and hard work. Basically, when you say those, no one will disagree with those, but what does it mean to teach those explicitly? What does it really mean to hold kids accountable to those? And it's not okay to be disrespectful to your classmates or to your teacher, and we're not just going to punish the heck out of you and hope that you change, but we're also going to explicitly teach those skills as explicitly as we teach reading or history.
>
> *Doug McCurry, Achievement First's co-CEO and Superintendent*

In this example, I utilize Carspecken's method of analysis alongside Fanon's theorizations. Carspecken's analytical method is designed to assess "the significance of activities with respect to the social system at large" (Carspecken, 1996, p. 40), and is useful in research that examines power and equity imbalances. When combined with Fanonian critical theory, this method can be a powerful analytical tool to explicate the connections between power and whiteness and the "legitimizing of Black suffering in the everyday life of schools" (Dumas & ross, 2016, p. 419).

Stage 1: Low-Level Coding

To begin this coding scheme, first start by identifying low-level codes in the data excerpt. Low-level codes are taken directly from the primary text and represent statements of note, patterns, or unusual events (Carspecken, 1996). The low-level codes used here are closely related to the words used in the text at this stage. The following low-level codes were identified from the excerpt for further exploration: "some kids don't," "at school, adults do what we say," "high behavioral expectations." "sweating the small stuff," "there's a whole set of behaviors that we explicitly teach," "hold kids accountable," and "we're going to explicitly teach those skills as explicitly as we teach reading or history." At this stage, the low-level codes represent a broad list of potential statements that it might be useful to use in the next step of analysis.

Stage 2: Meaning Field Analysis

In the next phase of coding and data analysis, one could create broader data meanings by using abstractions and to do this I adapt Carspecken's (1996) meaning field analysis. Carspecken (1996) noted "[meaning field reconstructions] put more words into the actions observed" (p. 97) and increase the "range of possibilities" (p. 97) contained within the data. Select low-level codes from the first stage are brought in here to develop "tacit modes of meaning" (Carspecken, 1996, p. 95) that, when considered within a Fanonian framework, could reveal implied patterns related to educational colonization.

To create a meaning field, the researcher separates parts of the text (or codes) by the words "AND," "OR," or "AND/OR" to demonstrate all the possible meanings embedded in a statement. In this case, "some kids don't" could also mean that student homes are unstable or that student homes are unsafe. "Adults do what we say" could also mean that the adults in students' families are unreliable or that the adults in school are more reliable than the adults in students' homes. "Sweating the small stuff" could also mean "students who commit minor infractions will be held responsible" or "students who commit minor infractions will be held fully accountable." "We're also going to explicitly teach those skills as explicitly as we teach reading or history" could also mean "student behavior is as important as reading or history."

Carspecken (1996) notes that "in everyday situations, one must constantly infer meaning fields from the actions of other people" (p. 99). In this sense, meaning fields are representative of daily events in which we consider intent, motivation, possible outcomes of our actions and the actions of others. In this example, the meaning fields create a set of intentions, motivations, and potential outcomes that can be connected to school settings and students. The meaning field reconstructions create new possibilities for data meanings within a Fanonian analysis of educational colonization, and facilitate important connections when forming high-level codes in the next step.

Step 3: High-Level Coding

After the low-level coding and meaning field analysis (Carspecken, 1996) stages in data analysis, one would begin to develop high-level codes. High-level codes are used to generalize findings, and are abstractions based on meaning fields and low-level codes (Carspecken, 1996). They are highly abstract, yet are "extremely useful for picking up analytic emphases" (Carspecken, 1996, p. 148). In this case, the low-level code "adults will do what we say" and the meaning field "adults in students' families are unreliable" can be abstracted into the high-level code "untrustworthy parents and families." The low-level codes "hold kids accountable" and "sweating the small stuff" along with the meaning field reconstruction "students who commit minor infractions will be held accountable" can be abstracted to the high-level code "teaching submission."

While high-level codes should be used "with caution" (Carspecken, 1996, p. 148), it is important to note that the Fanonian lens of the sociohistorical condition provides an analysis of Black lived conditions that acts as a triangulated data point against which to measure the validity of high-level coding claims.

Step 4: Fanonian Themes

In this last phase of analysis, one would begin to catalogue low-level codes and meaning fields into Fanonian thematic categories:

Fabrication

Using low-level codes, meaning fields, and high-level codes, analyzing for Black student fabrication unearths tacit meanings related to how students are perceived and thus educated within this particular school context. In this case, coding for

---

Black Student Fabrication

Data Example: "Some kids have very structured and safe home lives; _some kids don't_, right? And we want to make sure that at our school that they know, that _adults will do what we say_ we're going to do. I think a lot of schools are realizing that they need to root their education in a core set of values that are universal. And I think that comes in two-fold; one, high behavioral expectations.

Low-Level Codes: Some kids don't; adults will do what we say; core set of universal values

High-Level Codes: Untrustworthy parents and families; Unsafe homes; Low expectations; Black pathology

Meaning Field Reconstruction: Student homes are unstable; student homes are unsafe; adults in students' families are unreliable; adults in school are more reliable than the adults in students' homes

---

FIGURE 10.1

Educational Violence

Data Example: We talk about <u>sweating the small stuff</u>. If we worry about shirttails being tucked in, and the lower grades kids walking in quiet lines and we talk about kids sitting up straight in their desks, tracking the teacher with their eyes. <u>There's a whole set of behaviors that we explicitly teach</u> and that we sweat. But we sweat it in a joyful way. We are unapologetic about teaching the REACH values, which are respect, enthusiasm, achievement, citizenship, and hard work. Basically, when you say those, no one will disagree with those, but what does it mean to teach those explicitly? What does it really mean to <u>hold kids accountable</u> to those? And it's not okay to be disrespectful to your classmates or to your teacher, and <u>we're not just going to punish the heck out of you and hope that you change, but we're also going to explicitly teach those skills as explicitly as we teach reading or history</u>.

Low-Level Codes: Sweating the small stuff; there's a whole set of behaviors we explicitly teach; hold kids accountable; we're going to explicitly teach those skills as explicitly as we teach reading or history

High-Level Codes: Behavioral training; Teaching submission; Asserting dominance

Meaning field: Students who commit minor infractions will be held responsible; Students who commit minor infractions will be held fully accountable; Student behavior is as important as reading or history

---

FIGURE 10.2

Black student fabrication is useful in recognizing the implied identifiers that Mr. McCurry uses to describe the school's students. In the shorter excerpt used above, he builds up to his support for high behavioral expectations for Achievement First students by noting that some children do not have a structured and safe home life nor adults in their lives who keep their word. By setting up his support of high behavioral expectations in this way, Mr. McCurry perpetuates assumptions that low-income and minoritized families—a population that makes up the vast majority of Achievement First families—have low expectations for their children by reinforcing age-old stereotypes about delinquent and pathological Black parents and homes.

Educational Violence

In this case, coding for educational violence allows us to explore themes of dominance and submission in the educational setting. Teaching Black people to obey authority, remain silent, and specific ways to comport oneself hold particular significance as strategies used to maintain white power throughout US American history. By coding for educational violence, the practices of domination and submission that are central to colonization become explicit. Fanon notes that "in capitalist societies, education . . . instills in the exploited a mood of submission and inhibition" (Fanon, 1963/2004, pp. 3–4).

Using Fanon's theories to critically analyze Achievement First claims directly counters dominant, oppressive narratives that are highlighted as integral to the school model's success. Furthermore, this approach intentionally challenges racist and classist underpinnings that appear by identifying, naming, and countering oppression as it manifests in various forms. In short, without the context of Fanon, it is more difficult to make the claim that these schools are not good for Black children, particularly as they present evidence to the contrary using their own metrics.

Conclusion

The struggle for racial equality in schools has a long and troubled history. Local and regional ideologies around race continue to compete to shape national thinking around how and to what extent Black citizens should be educated, and policy was shaped in response to those discourses. In schools, Black students find themselves to be "the problem" (Baldridge, 2014; Dumas, 2016; Leonardo & Singh, 2017), and as the central protagonists in the deficit drama of achievement gaps, failing public schools, and educational inequity. The use of a Fanonian coding scheme to analyze the data can be useful when seeking to examine school claims and practices that are reified through racialized discourse.

In applying this work broadly, researchers, practitioners, and community members concerned with educative practices for Black students might find an analytical framework that provides a mechanism to consider the sub-textual claims used in predominantly Black education environments useful. In Achievement First and similarly modeled schools, the websites are filled with photo op pictures of uniformed Black students graduating from high school and heading on to college at proportionately high rates. However, Fanon's lens forces us to consider why personal style and self-expression are considered antithetical to school success in Black children.

In addition to Fanon's ideas, critical theory rooted in the "discourse of Africana studies" (Rabaka, 2010a, p. 34) can be useful in future research as discursive tools applied in the analysis of the everyday experiences of Black people living within the sociopolitical context of white supremacy throughout the African diaspora. Utilizing Afrocentric theories and epistemologies that explicate how Blackness has functioned within educative contexts broadens the conventional understanding of critical theory as a Eurocentric framework while providing an ideological foundation for critiquing inequitable structures that impact people across the Black diaspora. Africana Critical Theory (Rabaka, 2010a) and Black Critical Theory (Dumas & ross, 2016) are examples of such theories that provide guidance and underscore the importance of centering Black thinkers and intellectual traditions. They are particularly helpful framing models of how to engage Black intellectual tradition to analyze contemporary policies. In recognizing that "White supremacy overlaps, interlocks, and intersects with sexism, capitalism, and colonialism" (Rabaka, 2010a, p. 19), these tenets provide a framework to interpret the results of policies, practices, macrosystems, and educational data. In short, new research that analyzes claims that are made about Black students, schools, and other educative environments could employ these theories that explicitly challenge whiteness and center Black thought and experiences within the framework.

When creating educative practice for Black students, those involved may have narrow definitions of school quality that are limited to high academic achievement and similar relative markers, and using Black theorists who center critical Black epistemologies broadens the scope to consider many more additional markers that include process and rhetoric—not just academic outcome. Likewise, other educative practices defined aculturally and devoid of critical racial analysis result in similar limitations. Fanon's critical theory, and similar theories that engage Blackness with specificity, facilitate a deeper understanding of how Blackness functions in our contemporary social context, and provide an explanatory framework in which to analyze the marginalization of Black students in schools.

Notes

1 In this work, Black is capitalized in its reference to African diasporic people dispossessed of land, culture, and lineage. It is used as a metonym to categorize those who share African kinship legacies. White, as it refers to the hegemonic social structure that engendered this dispossession, is not capitalized.

2 The Hegelian dialectic, as introduced by Hegel in his work *Phenomenology of Spirit* (1998), is understood as the thought practice of working through oppositional ideas until a logical conclusion is reached. Fanon presented the Hegelian dialectic in his chapter on the master–slave relationship in which the master created identity for the slave and parameters for their relationship while the slave created an opposite self-identity, and psychologically rejected the parameters of the relationship that the master created. Agathangelou (2016) refers to Fanon's usage of the concept of dialectics as "the thinkability of politics [including how] political thought frames its most basic problems."

3 You can find Urban Prep at http://www.urbanprep.org/

4 You can find Achievement First at http://www.achievementfirst.org/

5 You can find KIPP at http://www.kipp.org/

6 In the 1960s, Louis Althusser wrote extensively on the topic of ideology, crediting the coining of the term to Destutt de Tracy and Cabanis. He roots its definition in philosophical traditions, and theorizes it as an "imaginary relationship" (Althusser, 1971/2014, p.181) between people and their everyday experiences. It can be understood as the

significance people draw from life events that inform the interpretations of those events. In schools, for example, differences in ideology can be seen in why staff and administrators decide which academic and social codes will govern individual schools, school districts, or school models.

7 Latinx, instead of Latino/a, is used throughout to include students who identify outside the gender binary.

References

Abdel-Malek, A. (1981). *Social dialectics: Civilisations and social theory* (Vol. 1). SUNY Press.

Abdulkadiroğlu, A., Angrist, J. D., Dynarski, S. M., Kane, T. J., & Pathak, P. A. (2011). Accountability and flexibility in public schools: Evidence from Boston's charters and pilots. *The Quarterly Journal of Economics, 126*(2), 699–748.

Achievement First. (2016). *Annual report*. New Haven, CT: Achievement First.

Achievement First. (2017a). "Achievement First Videos." Retrieved from Achievement First Public Charter Schools, http://www.achievementfirst.org/about-us/achievement-first-videos/video/21059/

Achievement First. (2017b). "Achievement First History." Retrieved from Achievement First Public Charter Schools, http://www.achievementfirst.org/about-us/history/

Achievement First. (2017c). "Data Analyst, Team Systems & Data." Retrieved from Achievement First Public Charter Schools, http://www.achievementfirst.org/filead min/af/home/2012_New_Site/7_Careers/2016-17_Job_Descriptions/44247322_ achievement_first_data_analyst_jul_2017_FINAL.pdf

Agathangelou, A. M. (2016). Fanon on decolonization and revolution: Bodies and dialectics. *Globalizations, 13*(1), 110–128.

Althusser, L. (1971/2014). *On the reproduction of capitalism: Ideology and ideological state apparatuses*. Verso Books.

Baldridge, B. J. (2014). Relocating the deficit: Reimagining Black youth in neoliberal times. *American Educational Research Journal, 51*(3), 440–472.

Bronner, S. E., & Kellner, D. (Eds.). (1989). *Critical theory and society: A reader*. Psychology Press.

Browne, S. (2015). *Dark matters: On the surveillance of blackness*. Duke University Press.

Carspecken, P. F. (1996). *Critical ethnography in educational research: A theoretical and practical guide*. Routledge.

Crotty, M. (1998). *The foundations of social research: Meaning and perspective in the research process*. Sage.

Dei, G.J.S. (2010). Rereading Fanon for his pedagogy and implications for schooling and education. In M. Simmons (Ed.), *Fanon and education: Thinking through pedagogical possibilities*, 1–27. Peter Lang.

Dei, G.J.S., & Simmons, M. (2010). The pedagogy of Fanon: An introduction. *Counterpoints*, XIII–XXV.

Dondero, M., & Muller, C. (2012). School stratification in new and established Latino destinations. *Social Forces, 91*(2), 477–502.

Du Bois, W.E.B. (1903/2008). *The souls of black folk*. Oxford University Press.

Dumas, M. J. (2014). 'Losing an arm': Schooling as a site of black suffering. *Race Ethnicity and Education, 17*(1), 1–29.

Dumas, M. J. (2016). Against the dark: Antiblackness in education policy and discourse. *Theory into Practice, 55*(1), 11–19.

Dumas, M. J. & ross, k. m. (2016). "Be real Black for me": Imagining BlackCrit in education. *Urban Education,* 51(3), 415–442.

Fanon, F. (1952/2008). *Black skin, white masks.* Grove Press.

Fanon, F. (1963/2004). *The wretched of the earth.* Grove Press.

Gardner, D. P., Larsen, Y. W., Baker, W., Campbell, A., & Crosby, E. A. (1983). *A nation at risk: The imperative for educational reform* (p. 65). United States Department of Education.

Gibson, N. C. (2017). *Fanon: The postcolonial imagination.* John Wiley & Sons.

Giddens, A. (1971). *Capitalism and modern social theory: An analysis of the writings of Marx, Durkheim and Max Weber.* Cambridge University Press.

Hegel, G. W. F. (1998). *Phenomenology of spirit.* Motilal Banarsidass Publishing.

Hiddleston, J. (2014). *Understanding postcolonialism.* Routledge.

Jacob, B. (2007). The challenges of staffing urban schools with effective teachers. *The Future of Children,* 17(1), 129–153. Retrieved from http://www.jstor.org/stable/4150023

James, C.L.R. (2013). *Beyond a boundary.* Duke University Press.

Kincheloe, J. L., & McLaren, P. (2002). Rethinking critical theory and qualitative research. In Y. Zou & E. T. Trueba (Eds.), *Ethnography and schools: Qualitative approaches to the study of education,* 87–138. Rowman & Littlefield.

Lankford, H., Loeb, S., & Wyckoff, J. (2002). Teacher sorting and the plight of urban schools: A descriptive analysis. *Educational Evaluation and Policy Analysis,* 24(1), 37–62.

Leonardo, Z., & Singh, M. (2017). Fanon, education and the fact of coloniality. In *Policy and Inequality in Education.* Springer, 91–110.

Lorde, A. (2003). The master's tools will never dismantle the master's house. In R. Lewis & S. Mills (Eds.), *Feminist postcolonial theory: A reader,* 25, 27.

Lorde, A. (2012). *Sister outsider: Essays and speeches.* Crossing Press.

Merseth, K. K. (2009). *Inside urban charter schools: Promising practices and strategies in five high-performing schools.* Harvard Education Press.

Nagy-Zekmi, S. (2007). Frantz Fanon in new light: Recycling in postcolonial theory. *Journal of Caribbean Literatures,* 4(3), 129–139. Retrieved from http://www.jstor.org/stable/40986217

National Center for Education Statistics. (2017). *Racial/ethnic enrollment in public schools.* Retrieved from https://nces.ed.gov/programs/coe/indicator_cge.asp

Nielson, C. R. (2011). Resistance through re-narration: Fanon on deconstructing racialized subjectivities. *African Identities,* 9(4), 363–385. Retrieved from http://dx.doi.org/10.1080/14725843.2011.614410

Pasque, P. A. & Pèrez, M. S. (2015). Centering critical inquiry: methodologies that facilitate critical qualitative research. In G. S. Canella, M. S. Perez, & P. A. Pasque, *Critical qualitative inquiry: Foundations and future.* Left Coast Press, 139–170.

Rabaka, R. (2010a). *Africana critical theory: reconstructing the black radical tradition, from WEB Du Bois and CLR James to Frantz Fanon and Amilcar Cabral.* Lexington Books.

Rabaka, R. (2010b). *Forms of Fanonism: Frantz Fanon's critical theory and the dialectics of decolonization.* Lexington Books.

Seigel, J. E. (1968–69). On Frantz Fanon. *The American Scholar,* 38(1), 84–96. Retrieved from http://www.jstor.org/stable/41209632.

11

DISCOURSE, REPRESENTATION, AND "OTHERING"

Postcolonial Analysis of Donald Trump's Education Reform

Mercy Agyepong

Theory: Aime Cesaire and Edward Said's Postcolonial Theory

Type of qualitative data: Political campaign speeches

New data analysis technique: Discourse, representation, and othering coding technique

Substantive topic in education: President Donald Trump's discourse on education reform

---

With approximately 321 million people in the United States in 2015, 13.3 percent and 17.6 percent are Black and Latinx/Hispanic,[1] respectively (U.S. Census Bureau, 2015); the vast majorities of whom live in large urban cities and attend public schools (Anyon, 1997). However, due to institutional inequalities such as unequal school systems, unequal opportunities, and discriminatory practices, Black[2] and Latinx students academically perform at a lower rate when compared to other racial/ethnic groups. Public education and the academic achievements of "urban" students—often used to refer to Black (specifically African American) and Latinx students—to be the focus of many discussions over the decades (Ladson-Billings, 2013; Noguera, 2003). Unfortunately, the underachievement of Black and Latinx students in urban public schools has been, and continues to be, attributed to these students' own lack of educational aspirations and devaluation of education within their communities, to name a few (Anyon, 1997; Noguera, 2003; Lipman, 2011; Valenzuela, 1999).

The low achievement of Black and Latinx students has led to many political debates regarding their educational opportunities. During the 2016 presidential campaign, then presidential hopeful Donald Trump discussed his vision for public education. In this speech (excerpts analyzed below), he advocated for the use of school choice policies to improve the academic achievements of Black and Latinx students in urban cities. As President, he continued to promote school choice as a panacea for the betterment of public education, and Black and Latinx students.

Using postcolonial theory, specifically the concepts of discourse, representation, and "othering," this chapter examines Donald Trump's (2016) vision of education and the claims and promises that he put forth to provide educational opportunities for students of color, especially Black and Latinx students. Furthermore, through analysis of a campaign speech, this chapter will illustrate how postcolonial theory can be used as an analytical and methodological tool for data analysis. Lastly, this chapter will discuss the kinds of data that are better suited for this analytical method and the kinds that are not.

This chapter, and the data analysis technique that I present, are connected to critical theories and methodologies in that they seek to investigate a topic that will lead to critical inquiry regarding educational opportunities for Black and Latinx students, that is, Trump's views on education and its relationship with these historically disenfranchised groups. According to Pasque and Perez (2015), critical inquiry utilizes methodology that aims to "directly address historical, economic, and socio-political issues of oppression and disparities across race, gender, class, sexual orientation, dis/ability, and the intersectionality of diverse identities" (p. 140). Importantly, the goal of critical inquiry is to be a catalyst for social change, social justice, and equity, therefore combating the status quo. The status quo regarding the achievement of Black and Latinx students is that the low academic achievements among these groups is due to their own inability and unwillingness to succeed, violence within their communities, their culture's lack of interest in education, and government-run public education policies. Donald Trump's solution to this problem is school choice, an educational policy that requires the privatization and marketization of public schools (Anyon, 1997; Noguera, 2003; Lipman, 2011).

Postcolonial Theory: Discourse, Representation, and "Othering"

Postcolonial theory is the theoretical and empirical examination of colonialism and imperialism. It is a type of critical theory that was developed by intellectuals from previously colonized countries. Critical theory of society, a school of thought established by the Frankfurt School in 1937, is a theory that "maintains a non-dogmatic perspective which is sustained by an interest in emancipation from all forms of oppression, as well as by a commitment to freedom, happiness, and a rational ordering of society" (Bronner & Killner, 1989, p. 1). Fundamentally rooted in Hegelianism and Marxism, critical theory focuses on interrogating and interrupting power, oppression, and what is known as "truth." Additionally, critical theory takes action by giving voice to the oppressed in an attempt to create a more just society. Ultimately, critical theorists' view society as unjust and in need of change through action and revolution. Applying critical theory to qualitative research is very important. It allows researchers to engage in research that sheds light on disadvantaged groups in ways that do not continue to oppress or disenfranchise such groups; in a way that brings to the forefront the marginalized experiences of these disadvantaged groups.

Postcolonial theory is particularly concerned with the psychological, economic, social, political, and cultural experiences of the colonized from the onset of colonization to the present day. Postcolonial theorists (also referred to as postcolonial critics) examine, analyze, and critique the relationship between the colonized and the colonizer, and also within the colonized group. With its roots in literary theory, postcolonial critical theory shows how harmful educational practice and policy have been for disadvantaged groups through colonialism and the present day. I use the postcolonial concepts of discourse, representation, and "othering" to analyze data in this chapter.

Discourse, Representation, and "Othering"

Discourse is defined as "a group of statements which provide a language for talking about—i.e. a way of representing—a particular kind of knowledge" (Hall, 1996, p. 201) that "shapes perceptions and practices" (Hall, 1996, p. 225). Discourse is the creation and/or perpetuation of a narrative that justifies the need for something. It is a system of statements that creates and shapes assumptions, knowledge, discipline, and values. Discourse occurs through power; those with power define what particular kinds of knowledge are and how to disseminate such knowledge. Discourse shapes the relationships and interactions between those in power and their counterparts (Ashcroft, Griffiths, & Tiffin, 2007; Hall, 1996). Discourse is not merely the construction of language but what the language means and represents. Therefore, discourse and representation often, if not always, work in unison. Representation is "the production of meaning through language," image, etc. (Hall, 1997, p. 16). Representation occurs when people attach meaning to a description, depiction, portrayal, symbols, and imaginations (Hall, 1997).

"Othering,"[3] coined by Gayatri Spivak, is "the process by which imperial discourse creates its 'others' . . . The various ways in which colonial discourse produces its subjects" (Ashcroft et al., 2007, p. 156).[4] "Othering" is the process by which people are situated as different from, and often less than, those in power and those with power. "Othering" is a dialectical process in that as those in power attempt to position the less powerful as "other" and different, they in turn position themselves as "other" and different. However, the "othering" of both groups is oppositional. That is, those in/with power position their counterparts as uncivilized "others," which then positions those in power as civilized "others." The "othering" process occurs through the use of discourse and representation as discussed below.

Aime Cesaire's (1972/2000) critique of colonialism in *Discourse on Colonialism* insists that in order for European imperialists to justify the colonization of the East, i.e. Africans, Indians, and Asians, they had to reinvent the East as barbaric and the West as their saviors. Europeans therefore use psychology, anthropological sociology, geography, and theology to create discourse and representations of non-Europeans as different, which justified the "othering," and therefore subjugation, of these groups during colonialism (Cesaire, 1972/2000). In *Orientalism*, Edward Said (1978), influenced by the work of Cesaire and other postcolonial theorists, also argued that through discourse and representation—literature, journalistic text, political tracts, images, arts, etc., the Western world (i.e., colonizers) reconstructed inaccurate, misleading, and stereotypical misrepresentations of people from the Middle East. These texts and images portrayed the Middle East as exotic, different, uncultured and unintelligent, thus positioning Middle Easterners (the colonized) in opposition to the normal, civilized, and intelligent Westerners (colonizer), therefore, justifying colonialism.

The colonial discourses, part of what Cesaire (1972/2000) called "thingification" of the colonized, positioned the colonizers as saviors and the colonized as barbarians, and therefore inferior and "other." Cesaire (1972/2000) defined "thingification" as the "reinvention of the colonized, the deliberate destruction of the past" (p. 9). Cesaire (1972/2000) added, "I am talking about societies drained of their essence, cultures trampled underfoot, institutions undermined, lands confiscated, religions smashed, magnificent artistic creations destroyed, extraordinary *possibilities* wiped out" (p. 43). "Thingification" reduced the colonized into "things," miniscule objects and laborers, whose job is to serve the colonizers. "Thingification" occurred through the material and cultural destruction of the colonized, in addition to colonial discourse that allowed for the justification of colonization (Cesaire, 1972/2000). These discourses, representations, and "othering," although based on a "mixture of fact and fantasy which constituted late medieval 'knowledge' of the other worlds," were intellectually justified, deemed "the truth," and have been perpetuated throughout history (Hall, 1996, p. 208).

Discourse, Representation, "Othering," and Qualitative Methods

Postcolonial concepts of discourse, representation, and "othering" relate to critical qualitative methods and are particularly useful for data analysis because they allow researchers to understand the experiences of colonial subjects, that is, people who were colonized in the past and continue to be disenfranchised in today's society, such as Black and Latinx students, who would be viewed as colonial subjects via this thinking. Using these concepts forces researchers to interrogate discourses and perceptions that lead to taken-for-granted assumptions about previously colonized groups; perceptions and assumptions that are rooted in the colonial "othering" of these groups through colonial discourse and reimagination/representation. Furthermore, the use of discourse, representation, and "othering" for critical qualitative methods shapes the types of questions asked, who the participants are, how data is collected/ tools for data, and how data is analyzed.

During data analysis, the concepts of discourse, representation, and "othering" allow researchers to interrogate the type of language used by participants, how it is used, why it is used, and its implications. These ideas push researchers to take a critical look at the ways that everyday discourses, ideologies, representations, and interactions between participants influence their perceptions of one another. Likewise, the concepts of discourse, representation, and "othering" force researchers to question their positionality and intentions for their research. Theorists such as Cesaire (1972/2000) and Said (1978) strongly emphasized the ways in which intellectuals and academic work were used to dehumanize and "thingify" the colonial subjects. Therefore, critical qualitative researchers must be very careful about their interactions with vulnerable groups and the way they interpret their data.

Data Analysis and Coding Technique

Below, I illustrate a coding technique based on the concepts of discourse, representation, and "othering" as a way to analyze Donald Trump's speech on education. The raw data that will be used for analysis is an excerpt from Donald Trump's (2016) speech given on September 8, 2016 at the Cleveland Arts and Social Sciences Academy, a K-8 mostly Black/African America (94.1 percent) charter school in Cleveland, Ohio (Cleveland Transformation Alliance, 2017). The data analysis process will involve an inductive approach to analyze emerging themes in the speech (Creswell, 2013) with a specific focus on adapting Carspecken's (1996) meaning field and reconstructive horizon analysis.

Meaning field analysis allows a researcher to identify the range of possible meanings for a part of text (Carspecken, 1996). Reconstructive horizon analysis is the process of interpreting both implicit and explicit validity claims (claims for agreement) based on objective (third-person, multiple people have access), subjective (first-person, limited access), and normative-evaluative (ethical moral) claims within a particular part of speech (Carspecken, 1996). Through a variety of techniques (discussed below), meaning field analysis allows the researcher to reconstruct possible meanings, implicit and explicit, of their primary record, i.e. data (Carspecken, 1996; Korth, 2003). After meaning fields are constructed, reconstructive horizon is important to data analysis as it allows researchers to interpret data from different perspectives and plausible multiple understandings in order to uncover interactions patterns and underlying meanings of interactions. This method also helps to demonstrate ways that the researcher might be surprised by the research, which can be a validation technique. Reconstructive horizon analysis is particularly useful for the analysis of Donald Trump's speech as it allows a researcher to not only analyze what was said directly, in this case the then-presidential candidate's discourse. But, it also clarifies what might have been implied, i.e. "unarticulated factors" and themes in the speech (Carspecken, 1996, p. 42).

Keep in mind that both critical inquiry and postcolonial theory are particularly concerned with and interrogate historical taken-for-granted assumptions (created through discourse, representation, and "othering") and power relations between marginalized groups and those who are privileged. Therefore, regardless of what Donald Trump's intentions were for the speech, it is important to note and critically analyze the power differences (racially and socioeconomically) and different community and school experiences between him and those he is addressing; especially in a speech that is supposed to convey help for the marginalized group. Donald Trump is an affluent White man who attended private school all his life and, in this case, he was addressing low-income, predominantly Black students about public education and their communities. Positioning him next to the students and community that he is addressing, his power status becomes more evident. I separated the coding into cycles as outlined below. Below is a selected excerpt from one of his speeches.

Donald Trump's Speech/Raw Data

There is no failed policy more in need of urgent change than our government-run education monopoly. The Democratic Party has trapped millions of African-American and Hispanic youth in failing government schools that deny them the opportunity to join the ladder of American success. It is time to break-up that monopoly. I want every single inner-city child in America who is today trapped in a failing school to have the freedom – the civil right – to attend the school of their choice. This includes private schools, traditional public schools, magnet schools and charter schools, which must be included in any definition of school choice. Our government spends more than enough money to easily pay for this initiative – with billions left over. It's simply a matter of putting students first, not the education bureaucracy.

Our public schools are failing to put young Americans on a path to success. Meanwhile, we have all seen the tragic rise in crime in these communities – which remains one of the greatest barriers to fostering opportunity and success for America's children. Violent crime rose more than 20% in Los Angeles in 2015. Homicides in Baltimore increased by 63%. There have been nearly 3,000 victims of shootings in Chicago so far this year.

Government is failing our citizens at every level. That is why I am proposing a plan to provide school choice to every disadvantaged student in America. That means parents will be able to send their kids to the desired public, private or religious school of their choice. Altogether, school choice is serving more than 3.4 million students nationwide, charter schools, in particular, have demonstrated amazing gains and results in providing education to disadvantaged children and the success of these schools will be a top priority for my Administration. They also produce competition that causes better outcomes for everyone.

First Cycle of Coding

The first cycle of coding will assign low-level coding (Carspecken, 1996), also known as in vivo coding (Miles, Huberman, & Saldana, 2014). Low-level coding is often short (e.g., 1–5 words) low-inference codes that use exact words or phrases of participants as a way to stay close to the data (Carspecken, 1996). Here is an example of low-level coding on raw data. I chose to analyze the data at the paragraph level; that is, I did not go sentence by sentence. Based on the speech above, the **first cycle codes (low-level codes: LC)** are:

> Government-run education need to change; Government-run education is a monopoly; Government-run education policies have failed students; The Democratic Party has trapped millions of African Americans and Latino youth in failing government schools; The Democratic Party has denied millions of Black and Latinx youth opportunities; Government schools has denied Black and Latinx youth the opportunity to succeed in America; The Democratic Party has prohibited Blacks and Latinx students from quality education; End government-run monopoly; Every inner-city child should have the right to attend the school of their choice; School choice is the solution; Every type of school should be available to inner-city youth; Our government have more than enough money to pay for school choice; Our government should have money to implement school choice.
>
> Our public schools are failing; Young Americans are not succeeding; We have a rise in crime in inner-city communities; We have failing schools and crime-infested inner-city communities; Crime in inner-city communities remains a great barrier to opportunity and success; Crime in inner-city communities is stifling student educational success; Violent crime has risen in inner-city America; Government is failing our citizens at every level; School choice is the solution; I am proposing a plan to provide school choice to every disadvantaged student in America; Parents will be able to send their kids to desired schools; Charter schools are especially successful in providing education to disadvantaged children; The success of charter

schools will be top priority to this administration; Charter schools produce competition that causes better outcomes for everyone.

Second Cycle of Coding

The second cycle of coding will apply the codes that derived from the first cycle of coding (LC) to the themes of discourse, representation, and "othering" (discussed above). It should be noted that some codes might fit with more than one concept. During this process, it is important to pay attention to other important low-level codes that do not fit into the three concepts/themes. I call these codes outstanding codes. Two things can happen at this stage with the outstanding codes: 1) group these outstanding low-level codes into themes of their own and apply these themes to matching postcolonial concepts; or 2) put the outstanding low-level codes side by side with postcolonial concepts and match the codes with the concepts that best fit. The goal is to use postcolonial concepts as themes for data analysis. If, for any reason, there are outstanding low-level codes that absolutely do not fit any postcolonial concepts, then perhaps a new concept can be developed or a new theoretical framework might be needed, especially if postcolonial concepts cannot be applied to the majority of the data collected. To better provide a clear illustration of the following steps of the coding process, I will focus on the concept "Discourse." Remember that discourse is a system of statements that shapes perceptions and practices. It is an instrument of power that is used by those in power to persuade the powerless of their agenda and goals. Again, I did the analysis at the paragraph level.

Coding for Discourse

Here is a demonstration of the **Second cycle of coding for Discourse:**
Government-run education need to change; Government-run education is a monopoly; Government-run education policies have failed students; The Democratic Party has trapped millions of African Americans and Latino youth in failing government schools; The Democratic Party has denied millions of Black and Latinx youth opportunities; Government schools have denied Black and Latinx youth the opportunity to succeed in America; The Democratic Party has prohibited Blacks and Latinx students from quality education; End government-run monopoly; Every inner-city child should have the right to attend the school of their choice; School choice is the solution; Our government has more than enough money to pay for school choice; Our government should have money to implement school choice. Our public schools are failing; Young Americans are not succeeding; We have a rise in crime in inner-city communities; We have failing schools and crime-infested inner-city communities; Crime in inner-city communities remains a great barrier to opportunity and success; Crime in inner-city communities is stifling student educational success; Violent

crime has risen in inner-city America; Parents will be able to send their kids to desired schools; Charter schools are especially successful in providing education to disadvantaged children; The success of charter schools will be top priority to this administration; Charter schools produce competition that causes better outcomes for everyone.

Keep in mind that the second level codes are still low-inference/low-level codes and therefore stay close to the raw data. The codes for discourse in this example exemplify statements that attempt to convince Black and Latinx communities that Donald Trump is an advocate for the betterment of their communities. His discourse frames the government as "the problem" and positions him as "the savior," and suggests that he is part of the communities' fight for quality education.

Third Cycle of Coding

The third cycle of coding is meaning fields. Meaning fields are the act of "articulating [all the possible] meanings that other people in the setting might themselves infer, either overtly or tacitly" from your data (Carspecken, 1996, p. 95). Meaning fields are especially important in the data analysis process because they allow researchers to analyze their data from different validity claims[5] and therefore different ontological perspectives (Carspecken, 1996). During this coding cycle, meaning fields are created for *each concept*. Below is an example of meaning fields for discourse. For the sake of ease of understanding the example, all possible meaning fields for discourse will not be displayed below. However, during data analysis, *all possible meaning fields should be exhausted for all concepts*. This is done by going through the codes and applying possible meaning fields for each. The conjunctions "AND" or "OR" are used when using exact codes from cycles 1 and 2 while "AND/OR" are used for inferences that are a bit removed from the codes. Carspecken (1996) recommended only constructing meaning fields for data that was particularly dense or for which there might be multiple, layered interpretations. With this in mind, I would recommend constructing meaning fields for the outstanding codes that seem to relate to postcolonial concepts such as discourse, othering, or presentation.

Third Cycle of Coding: Meaning Fields (MF) for Discourse

Government-run education need to change AND government-run education is a monopoly AND government-run education policies have failed students AND/OR the Democratic party has failed America AND the Democratic Party has denied millions of Black and Latinx youth opportunities AND/OR the Democratic Party stands in the way of millions of Black and Latinx youth educational success AND/OR we need alternative school options for inner-city kids AND school choice is the solution

AND/OR every student should attend the school of their choice AND/OR the government should fund school choice for disadvantaged students AND/OR I stand with communities of color AND/OR I am here to help Black and Latinx communities and students AND/OR I am the best presidential candidate for disadvantaged communities AND our public schools are failing AND/OR failing schools contribute to failing economies AND/OR school choice will benefit inner-city students and parents AND/OR school choice promotes options and competition AND/OR crime is a problem in inner-city communities AND we have failing schools and crime-infested inner-city communities AND crime in inner-city communities is stifling student educational opportunities and success AND/OR school choice will end crime in Black and Latinx communities AND/OR school choice will increase the academic success of inner-city students AND/OR quality education is every citizen's civil right.

Fourth Cycle of Coding

Through meaning fields, high-level codes can be reached. High-level codes are less obvious, high-inferences codes. These codes are very abstract and can be farther removed from the data. However, they derive from the raw data and can be checked by the lower-level codes. Of course, because it is still an inference, high-level codes cannot be guaranteed to be 100 percent accurate; they could be true, false, right, or wrong (Carspecken, 1996). Illustrated here is an example of high-level coding of discourse.

Fourth Cycle of Coding: High-Level Coding for Discourse

The federal government should not be in charge of education; Corporations should run the education system; We need privatization of the education system; The government has failed Black and Latinx students; A competitive economy will promote success in minority communities; Competition among school types will increase quality of education; Competition among school types will increase achievement for all students; Competition among school types will increase achievement for students of color; Lack of money should not impact students' school choices; The government can't be trusted; The government does not have citizens' best interest; The Democratic Party is against the success of inner-city communities; Inner-city youth are not succeeding because of crime in their neighborhood; Inner-city youth are not succeeding because of their criminal behaviors; I fight for the American people; I am the non-politician that America needs; Black and Latinx people are ruining America; Americans need to be kept safe from Black and Latinx communities; School choice will limit how many Black and Latinx students that I have to help; Blacks and Latinx communities need to help themselves; I need Black and Latinx communities to count on me for help; Black and Latinx communities should be under police surveillance; We need to make Black and Latinx communities safe; School choice will make Black and Latinx students safe; Black and Latinx students school failure is due to the crimes in their communities; School choice will make Black and Latinx communities safer.

Above is an analysis of the raw data (excerpts from a Donald Trump speech) using the postcolonial concept of discourse. I will provide a second example to further demonstrate the data analysis and coding technique discussed in this chapter. This time I will use the postcolonial concept of "othering." As previously stated, "othering" is the process by which discourse and representation are used to reconstruct and position a group of people as different and inferior. Keep in mind that in any given data, the same codes may apply to more than one concept/theme.

Raw Data/Donald Trump's Speech

There is no failed policy more in need of urgent change than our government-run education monopoly. The Democratic Party has trapped millions of African-American and Hispanic youth in failing government schools that deny them the opportunity to join the ladder of American success. It is time to break-up that monopoly. I want every single inner-city child in America who is today trapped in a failing school to have the freedom – the civil right – to attend the school of their choice. This includes private schools, traditional public schools, magnet schools and charter schools, which must be included in any definition of school choice. Our government spends more than enough money to easily pay for this initiative – with billions left over. It's simply a matter of putting students first, not the education bureaucracy.

Our public schools are failing to put young Americans on a path to success.

Meanwhile, we have all seen the tragic rise in crime in these communities – which remains one of the greatest barriers to fostering opportunity and success for America's children. Violent crime rose more than 20% in Los Angeles in 2015. Homicides in Baltimore increased by 63%. There have been nearly 3,000 victims of shootings in Chicago so far this year. Government is failing our citizens at every level. That is why I am proposing a plan to provide school choice to every disadvantaged student in America. That means parents will be able to send their kids to the desired public, private or religious school of their choice. Altogether, school choice is serving more than 3.4 million students nationwide, charter schools, in particular, have demonstrated amazing gains and results in providing education to disadvantaged children and the success of these schools will be a top priority for my Administration. They also produce competition that causes better outcomes for everyone.

First Cycle of Coding

Low-level coding is often short, low-inference codes that use exact words or phrases of participants as a way to stay close to the data.

First Cycle Codes (Low-Level Codes: LC) are

Government-run education needs to change; Government-run education is a monopoly; Government-run education policies have failed students; The Democratic Party has trapped millions of African Americans and Latino youth in failing government schools; The Democratic Party has denied millions of Black and Latinx youth opportunities; Government schools have denied Black and Latinx youth the opportunity to succeed in America; The Democratic Party has prohibited Blacks and Latinx students from quality education; End government-run monopoly; Every inner-city child should have the right to attend the school of their choice; School choice is the solution; Every type of school should be available to inner-city youth; Our government has more than enough money to pay for school choice; Our government should have money to implement school choice.

Our public schools are failing; Young Americans are not succeeding; We have a rise in crime in inner-city communities; We have failing schools and crime-infested inner-city communities; Crime in inner-city communities remains a great barrier to opportunity and success; Crime in inner-city communities is stifling student educational success; Violent crime has risen in inner-city America; Government is failing our citizens at every level; School choice is the solution; I am proposing a plan to provide school choice to every disadvantaged student in America; Parents will be able to send their kids to desired schools; Charter schools are especially successful in providing education to disadvantaged children; The success of charter schools will be top priority to this administration; Charter schools produce competition that causes better outcomes for everyone.

Second Cycle of Coding

In this cycle, I bring in postcolonial concepts of "othering" *and code the LC under the concept.*

- Pay attention to codes that do not "fit" into or disconfirm the concept (outstanding codes) and bring in a new postcolonial concept for these codes.
- Refer back to postcolonial theory for concepts that exemplify these codes or develop a new concept.

Coding for "Othering"

Second Cycle Codes for "Othering"

Government schools have denied Black and Latinx youth the opportunity to succeed in America; The Democratic Party has trapped millions of African-American and Latino youth in failing government schools; The Democratic Party has denied millions of Black and Latinx youth opportunities; Government schools have denied Black and Latinx youth the opportunity to succeed in America; The Democratic Party has prohibited Blacks and Latinx students from quality education; Young Americans are not succeeding; We have a rise in crime in inner-city communities; Violent crime has risen in inner-city America; We have failing schools and crime-infested inner-city communities; Crime in inner-city communities remains a great barrier to opportunity and success; Crime in inner-city communities is stifling student educational success; Charter schools are especially successful in providing education to disadvantaged children; I plan to provide school choice to every disadvantaged student.

Third Cycle of Coding

Meaning Fields (MF) for "Othering"

Government schools have denied Black and Latinx youth the opportunity to succeed in America AND/OR the Democratic Party has failed disadvantaged youth AND/OR the Democratic Party has failed inner-city communities AND the Democratic Party has trapped millions of African-American and Latino youth in failing government schools AND the Democratic Party has denied millions of Black and Latinx youth opportunities AND/OR the Democratic Party stands in the way of millions of Black and Latinx youths' educational success AND/OR Black and Latinx youth are failing, AND/OR we need alternative school options for inner-city kids AND/OR inner-city youth need school choice; AND/OR inner-city youth need charter schools AND/OR I am here to help Black and Latinx communities and students AND/OR I am the best presidential candidate for disadvantaged communities AND/OR failing schools contribute to failing economies AND/OR school choice will benefit inner-city students and parents AND/OR crime is a problem in inner-city communities AND we have failing schools and crime-infested inner-city communities AND crime in inner-city communities is stifling student educational opportunities and success AND/OR Black and Latinx youth live in crime-infested communities AND/OR school choice will end crime in Black and Latinx communities AND/OR school choice will increase the academic success of inner-city students AND/OR quality education is every citizen's civil right AND/OR charter schools will fix the problem in the inner-city.

Fourth Cycle of Coding

High Level Coding for "Othering"

The Democratic Party does not care about Black and Latinx youth; The Democratic Party does not care about Black and Latinx communities; Black and Latinx people are ruining America; Americans need to be kept safe from Black and Latinx communities; School choice will limit how many Black and Latinx students that I have to help; Blacks and Latinx communities need to help themselves; I need Black and Latinx communities to count on me for help; Black and Latinx communities should be under police surveillance; Black and Latinx youth are dangerous; Black and Latinx youth are violent; Inner-city communities are dangerous; We need to make Black and Latinx communities safe; School choice will make Black and Latinx students safe; Black and Latinx students' school failure is due to the crimes in their communities; School choice will make Black and Latinx communities safer; Black and Latinx school failure is rooted in their culture; Black and Latinx school failure is due to their communities; School choice will decrease the issues faced by Black and Latinx communities; I will save Black and Latinx people from a problem that they created.

While I only offered examples from the postcolonial theoretical ideas of discourse and "othering" due to limited space, in data analysis the researcher *must code for all concepts* (discourse, representation, and othering).

Usefulness: Data Analysis and Coding Technique

As illustrated above, postcolonial theory is a useful critical theory for data analysis. The concepts of discourse, representation and "othering," show how language can have multiple meaning and purposes, thus allowing the researcher to examine the explicit and implicit meanings in a data. This is particularly important because human communication and interactions are not only based on what is said and unsaid, but also who says it, why it is said, and to who it is said to. This coding technique allows for hidden and unspoken messages and communication to be brought to light. In the example of the data used in this chapter and the analysis, the narrative of school choice conveys a sense of care for the schooling of Black and Latinx students. However, upon further interrogation, this topic, Trump's advocacy for school choice for Black and Latinx youth, is embedded in historically created and taken-for-granted discourse and assumptions about Black and Latinx students and their communities. Furthermore, when we get past the explicit language used to discuss school choice, this speech has a strong explicit and implicit emphasis on Black and Latinx people as criminals. Without having examined the data alongside postcolonial theoretical ideas, I may have missed this embedded point.

The data analysis and coding technique provided in this chapter is useful for data collected from different types of qualitative research, including ethnography, case study, and phenomenology. Postcolonial theory and the technique shown above is useful for data analysis in studies that focus on educational policies and practices such as school choice, disciplinary practices, tracking, the model minority stereotype, the role of the institution on students of colors' educational success and opportunities, student–teacher relationships, and the inequalities that exist in the education system, to name a few.

This technique is however less useful, but not entirely, in grounded theory research in which the research seeks to build theoretical models or generate theories. In research in which the researcher seeks to formulate an entirely new theory using thematic analysis, that is, discovering emerging themes, patterns, and categories *from* the data, as oppose to entering the coding and data analysis process with concepts/themes in mind and at hand, this technique will be restrictive. In such research, which requires a more open coding process, this technique will likely be less useful. However, if for example, one is attempting to formulate a theory, or improve a theory, based on an already existing theory, the technique in this chapter could be useful.

It is important to note that my decision to use postcolonial theory was reached through a review of literature on school policies, the schooling of Black and Latinx students in the United States, review of Donald Trump's speeches on education during his campaign, and examination of Donald Trump's position in U.S. society. If one does exhaustive and critical review of the aforementioned and follows the technique step by step, this approach could offer rigor and a systematic way to incorporate theoretical ideas into analysis and interpretation. Furthermore, there are some critical theories and concepts that may equally be useful for this type of coding and analysis, and for the speech presented above. In the end, the use of discourse, representation, "othering," and Carspecken's reconstructive analysis is beneficial in understanding Donald Trump's views on Black and Latinx students and communities.

Notes

1 Latinx is used in place of Latinos/as and Hispanics to represent all identities of people from Latin America.
2 On the U.S. Census, Black is a racial category that includes all people with African ancestry except North Africans. However, Black is often used to refer to African Americans.
3 While Gayatri Spivak differentiates between Othering and othering, many postcolonial critics use the spellings interchangeably (Ashcroft *et al.*, 2007), and so will I in this chapter.
4 For an in-depth understanding of discourse, representation, and "othering," refer to Ashcroft *et al.* (2007).
5 For a more in-depth explanation of validity claims, refer to Carspecken (1996).

References

Anyon, J. (1997). *Ghetto schooling: A political economy of urban educational reform.* New York: Teachers College Press.

Ashcroft, B., Griffiths, G., & Tiffin, H. (Eds.). (2007). *Post-colonial studies: The key concepts* New York: Routledge.

Bronner, E., & Kellner, M. (1989). Introduction. *Critical theory and society: A reader.* New York: Routledge, 1–21.

Carspecken, P. F. (1996). *Critical ethnography in educational research.* New York: Routledge.

Cesaire, A. (1972/2000). *Discourse on colonialism.* New York: Monthly Review Press.

Cleveland Transformation Alliance. (2017). Cleveland Arts and Social Science. Retrieved from http://www.clevelandta.org/school/cleveland-arts-and-social-sciences-academy

Creswell, J. W. (2013). *Qualitative inquiry and research design* (3rd Edition). Thousand Oaks, CA: Sage Publications.

Hall, S. (1996). The west and the rest: Discourse and power. In S. Hall, D. Held, D. Hubert, & K. Thompson (Eds.), *Modernity.* Oxford: Blackwell, 185–227.

Hall, S. (1997). The work of representation. In S. Hall (Ed.), *Representation: Cultural representations and signifying practices.* Thousand Oaks, CA: Sage, 15–61.

Korth, B. (2003). A critical reconstruction of care-in-action. *The Qualitative Report, 8*(3), 487–512.

Ladson-Billings, G. (2013). Lack of achievement or loss of opportunity? In. P. L. Carter & K. G. Weiner (Eds.), *Closing the opportunity gap: What America must do to give every child an even chance* (pp. 11–24). Oxford, UK: Oxford University Press.

Lipman, P. (2011). *The new political economy of urban education: Neoliberalism, race, and the right to the city.* New York: Routledge.

Miles, M. B., Huberman, A. M., & Saldana, J. (2014). *Qualitative data analysis: A methods sourcebook* (3rd Edition). Los Angeles, CA: Sage.

Noguera, P. A. (2003). *The trouble with black boys . . . and other reflections on race, equity, and the future of public education.* San Francisco, CA: Jossey-Bass.

Pasque, P. A., & Pèrez, M. S. (2015). Centering critical inquiry: Methodologies that facilitate critical qualitative research. In G. S. Canella, M. S. Perez, & P. A. Pasque, *Critical qualitative inquiry: Foundations and future.* Walnut Creek, CA: Left Coast Press, 139–170.

Said, E. W. (1978). *Orientalism.* New York: Random House.

Trump, D. J. (2016, September 8). "Remarks at the Cleveland Arts and Social Sciences Academy in Cleveland, Ohio," Online by Gerhard Peters and John T. Woolley, *The American Presidency Project.* http://www.presidency.ucsb.edu/ws/?pid=119195.

U.S. Census Bureau (2015). Quickfacts: United States. Retrieved from https://www.census.gov/quickfacts/table/PST045216/00

Valenzuela, A. (1999). *Subtractive schooling: U.S.-Mexican youth and the politics of caring.* Albany, NY: University of New York Press.

12

ANALYZING POLICY CRITICALLY

Using Critical Race Theory to Analyze College Admissions Policy Discourse

Rachelle Winkle-Wagner, V. Thandi Sulé, and Dina C. Maramba

Theory: Critical Race Theory
Type of qualitative data: State policymaking discourse
New data analysis technique: Critical Race Theory Data Analysis Technique
Substantive topic in education: Race-based college admissions discourse

Critical race theory, also called CRT, has been used in educational research for decades in order to explore ways that racism plays out in educational systems (Ladson-Billings, 1998; Ladson-Billings & Tate, 1995; McCoy & Rodricks, 2015). Scholars have used this critical theory as a way to explore topics such as racism in educational practices (DeCuir & Dixson, 2004; Dixson & Rousseau, 2006), racism in teaching (Picower, 2009), racial microaggressions on college campuses (Solòrzano, Ceja, & Yosso, 2000), the experiences of faculty of color (Bernal, & Villalpando, 2002), and racism in educational policy (Gillborn, 2005; López, 2003). Additionally, CRT has been a useful theoretical tool for studies that focus on particular populations of students such as Latino/a students (Sólorzano, Villalpando, & Oseguera, 2005), and African-American students (Harper, Patton, & Wooden, 2009; Howard, 2008). Methodologically, critical race theory has led to approaches such as counterstorytelling where researchers aim at providing a different set of stories and perspectives than what is sometimes dominant in educational spaces (Solòrzano & Yosso, 2001). Yet aside from a few examples where scholars have offered ideas for critical race methodology

(McCoy & Rodricks, 2015; Parker & Lynn, 2002), many studies that use CRT do not provide detailed descriptions of how data were analyzed in ways that connected specifically to the theoretical approach that is offered by CRT. One problem with the lack of emphasis on how CRT might influence data analysis is that sometimes the emphasis on racial analysis disappears (Parker & Lynn, 2002).

In this chapter, we use examples from our studies of race-based college admissions policymaking discourse (Maramba, Sulé, & Winkle-Wagner, 2015; Winkle-Wager, Sulé, & Maramba, 2012; Sulé, Winkle-Wagner, & Maramba, 2017) to offer an analytic approach for using CRT to analyze qualitative data. We start by describing the tenets of CRT and the historical background of the theory. Then, we consider CRT as a way to analyze policy discourse. To do so, we offer a brief contextual background of the Texas Top Ten Percent Plan, which is an alternative to affirmative action or race-based college admissions that has been in place in Texas since 1998. We use examples from our analysis of changes to the Texas Top Ten Percent Plan to demonstrate ways that we would analyze text using CRT.

Critical Race Theory History and Tenets

Critical race theory emerged out of the Civil Rights Movement as a way for legal scholars to examine the role of law in maintaining and creating racial oppression in the United States (Crenshaw, 1995; Delgado & Stefancic, 2017; McCoy & Rodricks, 2015). Scholars like Derrick Bell (1992) and Lani Guinier (Guinier, Torres, & Guinier, 2009) established themselves as leaders in the legal work that demonstrated how laws could work to perpetuate inequality. By the 1990s, scholars in education were applying some of the ideas of CRT to racial injustices in schools and educational institutions (Ladson-Billings, 1998; Ladson-Billings & Tate, 1995; McCoy & Rodricks, 2015).

Among critical race scholars, there are numerous tenets or ideas for what comprises the foundation of critical race theory. Some of these tenets are (Delgado & Stefancic, 2017; McCoy & Rodricks, 2015):

1. The permanence of racism: Critical race scholars maintain the importance of remembering that the United States was founded in racial oppression and White Supremacy (the idea, enacted in policy and institutions, that White people are superior to people of color) because of the genocide of indigenous populations and enslavement of Africans. The endemic nature of racism means that research and practice in education often reinforces the racist foundation of the country (DeCuir, & Dixson, 2004; Ladson-Billings & Tate, 1995; Patton, 2016).

2. The importance of experiential knowledge and/or counterstorytelling: Critical race theorists often point to the importance of experience as a

knowledge-generating activity. Some critical race scholars have identified counterstorytelling as a methodological approach to identify experiential knowledge (DeCuir & Dixson, 2004; Solòrzano & Yosso, 2001). By offering a way for a new form of storytelling, a counterstory from the dominant or mainstream stories, scholars can point to new ways of thinking, knowing, and new practices in education or other social systems. That is, in educational research, it would be necessary to understand experiences within education, particularly the experiences of historically marginalized or oppressed groups, in order to fully understand educational practices, policies, or outcomes.

3. The role of interest convergence in shaping and maintaining oppression: Interest convergence asserts that until White people have some vested interest in addressing racial inequities, those inequities will remain a central feature of society. Bell (1992), the initiator of this idea, maintained that people of color would only make social and economic progress if such progress aligned with the needs of White people. A good example of interest convergence is race-based admissions policy, affirmative action. There was larger support for affirmative action when the major beneficiaries were White women (Guinier et al., 2009). But, once the interests seemed to shift and people of color would be major beneficiaries of affirmative action, there were an increasing number of challenges to race-based admissions policies (Guinier et al., 2009).

4. Whiteness as property: The notion that Whiteness can become property points out the embodiment and physicality of racism (DeCuir & Dixson, 2004; Harris, 1993). Accordingly, oppressive employment, voting, housing, education, banking, and policing practices were legally enshrined to ensure that Whiteness was a profitable investment (Lipsitz, 2006; Shapiro, 2004). Furthermore, Whiteness as an investment is intricately connected to capitalism as it serves to guarantee that White people benefit most from labor exploitation and citizenship (Lipsitz, 2006; Marable, 2002). Thus, critical race theorists make apparent how U.S. education, as a component of Whiteness, both enacts and maintains White domination (Dixson & Rousseau, 2006; Patton, 2016).

5. A critique of liberalism: The concept of liberalism is associated with competition and individuality or the idea that people earn their positions and status in society based on their individual merit. Critical race scholars challenge these ideas maintaining that many people in the United States are given advantages and disadvantages based on ascribed characteristics like skin color. That is, people of color are systematically being kept from social and economic advantages (e.g., social mobility, jobs, educational opportunities) regardless of their merit or ability (Guinier et al., 2009; DeCuir & Dixson, 2004). Also, liberalism embodies the notion of race neutrality that decisions can be made without consideration of a person's skin color or racial background. Critical race scholars challenge colorblindness and maintain that

colorblindness is not only a myth (i.e., people do see color) but that it can result in inequitable policy and practice (Bonilla-Silva, 2017).

6. An intersectional commitment to social justice: A hallmark of CRT is an interest and attention toward understanding that both identities and oppressive forces intersect (Crenshaw, 1991, 1995). That is, people of color in the United States might face oppression based on White Supremacy, patriarchy (the idea, enacted in policy and institutions, that men are superior to women), and classism.

Taken together, the tenets of CRT encourage scholars to consider racial history and to elevate contemporary ways that racial oppression plays out in society. The use of CRT has led to more emphasis on the experiences of students of color in education at all levels and a deeper analysis of ways that policies that might initially seem to be "neutral" might actually perpetuate racism and inequality (McCoy & Rodricks, 2015). From the initial operationalization of critical race theory, there have been adapted theories that emphasize the experiences of other racially marginalized groups such as LatCrit Theory for Latinx people (Solòrzano & Yosso, 2001) and Tribal Critical Race Theory (Brayboy, 2013) for native populations. Both highlight indigenous knowledges and experiences within those communities. Here, we focus on the combined tenets of CRT (Delgado & Stefancic, 2017), recognizing that there may need to be further expansions of the theory for different racial/ethnic groups.

Applying Critical Race Theory to Race-Based College Admissions Policy Discourse

In our collaborative studies, we have used CRT as a way to explore how race does or does not appear in policymaking discussions about college admissions policy (Maramba *et al.*, 2015; Winkle-*Wagner et al.*, 2012). We have also explored public opinions and social media discourse about race-based admissions policy (Sulé *et al.*, 2017). Critical race theory has been useful in our work because it has helped us to elevate the role of race and racism in discourse.

We use CRT in concert with critical discourse analysis (Fairclough, 2001, 2013), a form of thematic analysis of textual data such as public discourse, interviews, focus groups, or social media. Critical discourse analysis (also CDA) is rooted in critical theories and is not a prescriptive analytic approach, at least in the way that Fairclough (2001, 2013) presented it.

Many of our applications of CRT have been related to race-based college admissions policies (affirmative action) and affirmative action alternatives such as the Texas Top Ten Percent Plan (also called The Plan). The Plan in Texas was initiated by the Texas legislature in 1998 in response to a Federal Court decision, *Hopwood vs. Texas,* 1996 by the Fifth Circuit Court of Appeals (Kahlenberg, 1997). The ruling maintained that the use of race and quotas in Texas Law

Schools was no longer legal. The Plan leveraged existing school racial segregation such that any student attending a Texas high school who graduated in the top 10 percent of their high school class would be guaranteed admission to a Texas postsecondary institution (Long, Saenz, & Tienda, 2010). In 2009, the Texas legislature debated a proposed change to the Texas Top Ten Percent Plan which would mandate that only 75 percent of the admitted class at UT-Austin be comprised of students from the top 10 percent of their graduating classes. The remaining 25 percent would be left to the discretion of the university to award admission based on legacy (parents attended the institution), or other forms of merit (music, athletics, leadership, etc.) (Long & Tienda, 2010). We analyzed the discourse that led up to this policy change (Winkle-Wagner *et al.*, 2012). CRT allowed us to consider both explicit and implicit references to race or racism. Specifically, we analyzed for instances where policymakers used the words "race" or "racism" and we crafted a list of race-related terms that were used in place of race/racism such as "diversity" or "discrimination." We also assessed the silences or instances where policymakers implied something about race but did not say the word specifically (Winkle-Wagner *et al.*, 2012, pp. 8–9). Without the use of CRT, we may not have realized that the absence of explicit racial discussion was actually a signal about how race would be considered (or avoided) in the changes to the policy. Below we offer a few examples of the coding technique we developed so that we could analyze qualitative data with specific references and links back to CRT.

A Critical Race Theory Data Analysis Technique

Our article, "When race disappears: College admissions policy discourse in the state of Texas," captures how critical race theory informed our assessment of the discourse in the Texas Top Ten Percent debate (Winkle-Wagner *et al.*, 2012). The CRT analytic technique that we are presenting proceeds with a few steps, outlined below. We recommend using this CRT analytic technique on portions of the data only because it would be very onerous to do this analysis on all data. To select the data that should be analyzed more deeply, it is important to first conduct a more general form of analysis that allows for possible complexities and ideas to emerge from the data. Then, if the data seems to have deeper meaning than is accessible via the first form of coding, it is useful to proceed to coding that connects to critical race theory. The four-step process of data analysis is specified below:

1. **Step 1: Low-level coding:** First, we started with a form of low-level coding that was emergent from the narratives. We created two-to-five word, in vivo codes and codes very similar to the words of the participants. Based on these codes, we then clustered the emergent in vivo codes into categories. The next step in the process was to analyze the quote or text based on the CRT tenets.

2. **Step 2: Select data that needs further analysis:** Based on the low-level codes, there are likely to be data that seem to need further analysis, particularly related to racial issues or other social issues (e.g., gender, socioeconomic status, etc.). During this step, the researcher would select the data that needs to be further analyzed and mark it or separate that data into a separate file for further analysis.

3. **Step 3: CRT question coding:** From the emergent codes, we then offer questions that relate to all six of the CRT tenets, if relevant. For instance, we pose a question or set of questions that relate to the permanence of racism, based on the text and low-level codes. Then, we consider a question or set of questions related to interest convergence, and onward. It might be the case with some data that not all tenets are immediately accessible in the data.

4. **Step 4: CRT narrative analysis:** Based on the questions we posted in the CRT question coding, we write a narrative analysis of the quote or text. As part of this analysis, we identify the primary CRT tenets, if any, that apply to that data. This analysis could appear in findings sections in our papers if relevant to that particular article or paper. Or, the analysis could help to further consider ways that CRT might be evident in the data.

Examples of Critical Race Theory Data Analysis

As an example, we used the following quote in our article, which was from Texas Senator West, an African-American male Democrat who was speaking in opposition to changes to the Texas Top Ten Percent Plan at the time in 2009 (Winkle-Wagner et al., 2012, p. 12):

> **Quote from Senator West:** *"The reality is that the top 10% law that we put into effect is race-neutral, and it judges a child based on the circumstances that a student finds themselves in when they graduate from high school."*
>
> **In vivo codes:** law is race-neutral, judges child on circumstances, graduate from high school
>
> **CRT questions:**

- Permanence of racism (PR code): Can the law be race-neutral because race is embedded in legal history?
- Experiential knowledge (EK code): Do students of color and White students find themselves in the same circumstances?
- Whiteness as property (WP code): Do White students have more access than students of color to being in the top 10 percent?
- Critique of liberalism (CL code): can students be equally judged on high school performance since merit often privileges White people?
- Interest convergence (IC code): Is it still benefitting White people to make a law seem race-neutral?

- Intersectionality (I code): How does race-neutrality relate to socioeconomic backgrounds?

CRT analysis: Primary tenets – PR, CL, IL

- West is using the word "race-neutral" for the Texas Top Ten Percent Plan when race neutrality is a myth, given the way in which racial inequality continues in college access and admissions outcomes (**permanence of racism**).
- It seems that West is trying to create **interest convergence** by making the policy seem race-neutral and as if all students start from the same place and are judged on their merit for college admissions ("based on the circumstances"); he is making a claim to **liberalism** ideas.

In our article, we did not include this exact narrative analysis (Winkle-Wagner *et al.*, 2012). But, this process did help us to identify which CRT tenets, if any, were relevant to the policymaking discourse we were analyzing. The conversation continued with this quote, for which we offer another example of analysis below: Texas Senator Shapiro, a White woman who is a registered Republican colleague to Senator West and who was one of the primary authors on the Bill to change The Plan so that only 75 percent of the incoming first-year class would be admitted as the top 10 percent of their class. Shapiro was responding to West's comment and trying to reiterate the importance of the Texas Top Ten Percent Plan as a race-neutral and merit-based admissions policy (Winkle-Wagner *et al.*, 2012, p. 11).

> **Quote from Senator Shapiro:** *"Performance. So if that student performs, what this Top Ten Percent law enables that student to do if they have the knowledge and the understanding and the resources available, is to determine what state supported institution to go to."*
>
> **In vivo codes:** performance, student performs, if knowledge and resources, determine what institution
> **CRT questions:**

- Permanence of racism (PR code): Do students have access to the same understanding and resources across racial groups? Do students have access to the same support to perform?
- Experiential knowledge (EK code): Would all students of the same ability be able to perform the same way, given that resources and support likely differ?
- Whiteness as property (WP code): Would White students have access to resources and understanding that students of color might not have?
- Critique of liberalism (CL code): Do students have access to the same performance standards? Is their performance in their high school valued in the same way?

- Interest convergence (IC code): Is performance in high school the best way to demonstrate potential for college?
- Intersectionality (I code): Is performance the same across race, class, and gender groups? Are the resources and support for performance the same?

CRT analysis: Primary tenets – CL, PR, I

- Shapiro is emphasizing the way in which the college admission policy promotes performance. Performance is likely related to merit, which is a **liberalism** value.
- Shapiro also references choice in saying that students determine which institution to attend. The notion that students who are have merited admission can freely choose is also a **liberalism** idea.
- In referencing the importance of performance, Shapiro also raised the point about knowledge, understanding, and resources, which brings up the possibility of inequities in support and resources based on race, class, or gender (**intersectionality, permanence of racism**). It is likely that Shapiro raised this issue in an attempt to try to push for a necessary change to the Texas Top Ten Percent Plan.
- By bringing up performance, this could also be a bid for race-neutrality in the discourse (**permanence of racism**). The word "circumstance" is removed from racialized or gendered terminology or references to inequality in the way she used it, also pointing to a claim toward **liberalism** ideas.

In the case of this particular analysis, we did use the final point about the use of "circumstance" in our paper (Winkle-Wagner *et al.*, 2012, p. 11). Conducting this kind of analysis helped us to delve deeper into the discourse and it also aided us in our in-text analysis within our reporting of the data.

Future Applications of CRT to Qualitative Data Analysis

Our CRT analytic technique is particularly useful for data that relates to policies or social issues because there are likely inherently racialized elements (gendered, class-based, etc.) to the way that people discuss policies, processes, practices, or educational outcomes. We maintain that analyzing policymaking discourse, for example, can shed light on larger views and conversations about racial equity (Maramba *et al.*, 2015). We initiated our use of CRT in analysis of policymaking discourse as a way to connect our use of CRT to the legal theory roots of the theory (Delgado & Stefancic, 2017; McCoy & Rodricks, 2015). Additionally, this CRT analytic technique is likely to work well with interview data or focus group data. The main challenge could be in selecting which data to use for further analysis. We recommend tagging data during the low-level coding process so that it is clear that the data might have deeper meaning that needs to be interrogated.

We anticipate that this form of analysis would work well even for data that does not have an explicit reference to race. But, the analysis would focus on more implied claims in that case and it would be important to conduct other forms of analysis to ensure that the inferences being made with the CRT analytic technique were not overly subjective on the part of the researcher. For instance, a researcher would need to compare the inferences made with the CRT analytic technique back to the initial low-level codes to ensure that what is being inferred does relate to the initial statements in the text.

Critical race theory, similar to other critical theories, allows for researchers to connect qualitative data that is collected at the micro-level, about the everyday experiences of people, to be contemplated in relation to larger social systems. That is, by using critical race theory, we are better able to consider how statements or particular discussions/discourse might actually reveal larger social trends relative to race relations, racism, and racial progress (Maramba *et al.*, 2015; Sulé *et al.*, 2017). But the problem with many usages of CRT in educational research, aside from a few examples (McCoy & Rodricks, 2015; Parker & Lynn, 2002) is that the theory is not often well connected to the analysis, findings, and interpretation. The CRT analytic technique that we propose is a way to provide a seamless usage and consideration of race and racism throughout the research project from the research questions that are asked to the theoretical framework, and through the methodology, including the data analysis and interpretations of the data.

References

Bell, D. A. (1992). *Faces at the bottom of the well: The permanence of racism*. Basic Books.

Bernal, D. D., & Villalpando, O. (2002). An apartheid of knowledge in academia: The struggle over the "legitimate" knowledge of faculty of color. *Equity & Excellence in Education*, *35*(2), 169–180.

Bonilla-Silva, E. (2017). *Racism without racists: Color-blind racism and the persistence of racial inequality in America*. Rowman & Littlefield.

Brayboy, B.M.J. (2013). Tribal critical race theory: An origin story and future directions. In M. Lynn & A. D. Dixson (Eds.), *The handbook of critical race theory in education*. New York: Routledge, 88–100.

Crenshaw, K. (1991). Mapping the margins: Intersectionality, identity politics, and violence against women of color. *Stanford Law Review*, 1241–1299.

Crenshaw, K. (1995). *Critical race theory: The key writings that formed the movement*. The New Press.

DeCuir, J.T., & Dixson, A. D. (2004). "So when it comes out, they aren't that surprised that it is there": Using critical race theory as a tool of analysis of race and racism in education. *Educational Researcher*, *33*(5), 26–31.

Delgado, R., & Stefancic, J. (2017). *Critical race theory: An introduction*. NYU Press.

Dixson, A. D., & Rousseau, C. K. (2006). And we are still not saved: Critical race theory in education ten years later. *Race, Ethnicity and Education, 8*(1), 7–27.

Fairclough, N. (2001). Critical discourse analysis as a method in social scientific research. *Methods of Critical Discourse Analysis, 5,* 121–138.

Fairclough, N. (2013). *Critical discourse analysis: The critical study of language.* Routledge.

Gillborn, D. (2005). Education policy as an act of white supremacy: Whiteness, critical race theory and education reform. *Journal of Education Policy, 20*(4), 485–505.

Guinier, L., Torres, G., & Guinier, L. (2009). *The miner's canary: Enlisting race, resisting power, transforming democracy.* Harvard University Press.

Harper, S. R., Patton, L. D., & Wooden, O. S. (2009). Access and equity for African American students in higher education: A critical race historical analysis of policy efforts. *The Journal of Higher Education, 80*(4), 389–414.

Harris, C. I. (1993). Whiteness as property. *Harvard Law Review,* 1707–1791.

Howard, T. C. (2008). Who really cares? The disenfranchisement of African American males in preK-12 schools: A critical race theory perspective. *Teachers College Record, 110*(5), 954–985.

Kahlenberg, R. D. (1997). *The remedy: Class, race, and affirmative action.* Basic Books.

Ladson-Billings, G. (1998). Just what is critical race theory and what's it doing in a nice field like education? *International Journal of Qualitative Studies in Education, 11*(1), 7–24.

Ladson-Billings, G., & Tate, W. F. (1995). Toward a critical race theory of education. *Teachers College Record, 97*(1), 47.

Lipsitz, G. (2006). *The Possessive Investment in Whiteness: How White People Profit from Identity Politics.* Temple University Press.

Long, M. C., & Tienda, M. (2010). Changes in Texas universities' applicant pools after the Hopwood decision. *Social Science Research, 39*(1), 48–66.

Long, M. C., Saenz, V., & Tienda, M. (2010). Policy transparency and college enrollment: Did the Texas Top Ten Percent law broaden access to the public flagships? *The ANNALS of the American Academy of Political and Social Science, 627*(1), 82–105.

López, G. R. (2003). The (racially neutral) politics of education: A critical race theory perspective. *Educational Administration Quarterly, 39*(1), 68–94.

Marable, M. (2002). *The great wells of democracy: The meaning of race in American life.* Basic-Civitas Books.

Maramba, D. C., Sulé, V. T., & Winkle-Wagner, R. (2015). What discourse on the Texas Top Ten Percent Plan says about accountability for diversity. *The Journal of Higher Education, 86*(5), 751–776.

McCoy, D. L., & Rodricks, D. J. (2015). Critical race theory in higher education: 20 years of theoretical and research innovations. *ASHE Higher Education Report, 41*(3), 1–117.

Parker, L., & Lynn, M. (2002). What's race got to do with it? Critical race theory's conflicts with and connections to qualitative research methodology and epistemology. *Qualitative Inquiry, 8*(1), 7–22.

Patton, L. (2016). Disrupting postsecondary prose: Toward a critical race of higher education. *Urban Education, 51*(3), 315–342.

Picower, B. (2009). The unexamined whiteness of teaching: How white teachers maintain and enact dominant racial ideologies. *Race Ethnicity and Education, 12*(2), 197–215.

Shapiro, T. M. (2004). *The hidden cost of being African American: How wealth perpetuates inequality.* Oxford University Press.

Solórzano, D. G., & Yosso, T. J. (2001). Critical race and LatCrit theory and method: Counter-storytelling. *International Journal of Qualitative Studies in Education, 14*(4), 471–495.

Solòrzano, D., Ceja, M., & Yosso, T. (2000). Critical race theory, racial microaggressions, and campus racial climate: The experiences of African American college students. *Journal of Negro Education*, 60–73.

Sólorzano, D. G., Villalpando, O., & Oseguera, L. (2005). Educational inequities and Latina/o undergraduate students in the United States: A critical race analysis of their educational progress. *Journal of Hispanic Higher Education*, *4*(3), 272–294.

Sulé, V. T., Winkle-Wagner, R., & Maramba, D. C. (2017). Who deserves a seat?: Colorblind public opinion of college admissions policy. *Equity & Excellence in Education*, *50*(2), 196–208.

Winkle-Wagner, R., Sulé, V. T., & Maramba, D. C. (2012). When race disappears: College admissions policy discourse in the state of Texas. *Educational Policy*, *28*(4), 516–546.

13

HABERMAS AND DATA ANALYSIS IN FOR-PROFIT HIGHER EDUCATION INSTITUTIONS

Ashley N. Gaskew

Theory: Habermas' Colonization of the Lifeworld
Type of qualitative data: Television advertisements
New data analysis technique: Marketing positionality code; Extension of Carspecken's (1996) Meaning Field and Reconstructive Horizon Analysis
Substantive topic in education: For-profit higher education institutions' recruitment processes

Critical theorist Jürgen Habermas (1987) theorized about the differences and interactions between the system and the lifeworld. The system is the location of publicly held, larger structural concepts such as: the economic system, the system of gender differentiation (e.g., patriarchy where the idea that men are superior to women is embedded in social structure), and the system of racial differentiation (e.g., White supremacy, the notion that White people are superior to people of color, is part of the social structure). The system governs larger interactions with society in a quicker less intimate manner that should require less thought in order to get larger tasks accomplished. On the other hand, the lifeworld accounts for more intimate day-to-day interactions that people have in their lives. This includes close relationships with family and friends, as well as work and school environments. Habermas (1987) argues that the system is colonizing the lifeworld, meaning that system-level concepts are becoming so prevalent that it can be difficult to identify lifeworld ideas. When the system overtakes the lifeworld more intimate forms of living, learning, and communicating can be coopted to be more restricted, less informal, and thus less critical.

For-profit colleges and universities in the United States (U.S.) offer a compelling example of the system colonizing the lifeworld, and I use these institutions and their mass media products as an example of analysis in this chapter. For-profit institutions have a contentious reputation in the field of postsecondary education, the media, and in the general public (Bennett, Lucchesi, & Vedder, 2010; Floyd, 2007). These institutions have lower outcomes measures such as student retention and graduation rates than the non-profit sector (Apling, 1993; Chung, 2008). Additionally, the for-profit sector has higher student loan default rates than the non-profit sector (For Profit U, 2015). Yet these institutions attract historically marginalized and oppressed student groups (Chung; 2008; Illoh, 2016).

In this chapter, I analyze messages that for-profit institutions send through television commercials. For-profit institutions utilize television commercials as mass media communication tools to communicate their identity, purpose(s), and functions in education and society. Their television commercials provide a window into the private for-profit sector to gauge how this sector impacts students, specifically students of color, low-income students, first-generation students, and veteran students (Chung, 2008) who are attempting to gain access to postsecondary institutions and education. Through analysis of the television commercials that proprietary institutions produce as forms of communication, I present an innovative qualitative data analysis technique that is rooted in Habermas' critical theory. I employ Habermas' (1987) critical theory on colonization of the lifeworld (the location of values, cultural norms, and beliefs that people hold close) to the for-profit sector of postsecondary education. I use Habermasian theory as a first step to understand the impact these institutions have on their students. Specifically, by using Habermas' ideas of how the lifeworld is being colonized by external forces, I am able to understand how the education sector encroaches on the lives of students. Given my critical perspective, I am challenging the messages that these institutions are sending their prospective and current students as well as other stakeholders. By using Habermas, I explore the individual as well as system-level processes. This Habermasian analytic technique could be applied to other data such as data that stems from news media, interviews, focus groups, or public policies. In a practical way, this research is timely and crucial so that new ways of analyzing the field of postsecondary education can help understand its changes. I conclude with how my data analysis technique can be used in the future.

Critical Theory: Habermas – Colonization of the Lifeworld

Critical Inquiry

Critical inquiry challenges the dominant hegemonic structures that are in place. It moves beyond describing injustices that exist, and acts to bring and sustain equitable changes to marginalized groups. At a minimum, critical inquiry focuses on the voices and experiences of marginalized groups of people (Canella, Pérez, & Pasque, 2015). It humanizes participants, and puts them in positions of power to have agency in certain areas of their life being researched. Moreover, the voices and perspectives of marginalized and oppressed groups being centered allows the notion of objective research to be rejected. Critical inquiry can lead to emancipation, social action, and eventually social change (Pasque, Carducci, Kuntz, & Gildersleeve, 2012). Habermas is a critical theorist who called for a moral emphasis toward action in critical theory (Pasque *et al.*, 2012).

Habermas

I apply aspects of Habermas' (1987) theory of communicative action. Habermas focuses on social interaction through instrumental and strategic actions of communication. Additionally, he also looks at the mass media forms of communication that deal with markets, money, and power. With communicative action, communication should be orientated towards understanding. For Habermas, an ideal speech situation occurs when both parties are actively listening to each other to understand each other and expand their knowledge and ideas of others. Moreover, ideal speech allows for open dialogue where the words of those engaged in the conversation are truly listened to and heard so that they can be challenged if necessary, and their hermeneutic circle, their understanding of the position of one another, can be expanded. The hermeneutic circle focuses toward understanding the whole through the individual part; in this chapter, analyzing television commercials as an individual part of understanding the larger sector of for-profit education. This form of communication can only occur when all parties involved are willing to participate and the power dynamics are shifted or removed to give everyone as much of an equitable voice as possible. However, the ideal speech situation is constantly at risk of being terminated.

Habermas (1984, 1987), argues that communication is central to human beings and our relationships with one another. Without communication, individuals could not function in society, because we use communication and communication skills to build and maintain relationships with people. These relationships can include: family, friends, significant partners, and religious leaders. In an education context, these relationships can be extended to include: classroom peers, teachers, instructors, administrators, coaches, and others. Habermas (1987) advances Mead's ideal of communication community and says: "This utopia serves to reconstruct an undamaged intersubjectivity that allows both for unconstrained mutual understanding among individuals and for the identities of individuals who come to an unconstrained understanding with themselves" (Habermas, 1987, p. 2). Applying these ideas to education, Habermas would be arguing for the need and necessity of open, fluid, and enhanced education.

With hermeneutic communication, especially in an education context, people engage in dialogue by taking one another's position so that the horizon of communication and understanding is expanded (Carspecken, 1996). This position-taking allows for one to better understand the viewpoint of others. With this form of communication all willing participants knowingly engage in an elevated form of communication that will challenge and expand the horizon of knowledge and communication that exists. Communication plays out in both the lifeworld and system levels.

Defining the Lifeworld

Habermas (1987) expanded upon Husserl and Schutz's notion of the lifeworld. "From a perspective turned toward the situation, the lifeworld appears as a reservoir of taken-for-granted, of unshaken convictions that participants in communication draw upon in cooperative processes of interpretation" (Habermas, 1987, p. 124). In the lifeworld, more intimate forms of communication occur daily and this communication is clear and understood. The lifeworld is the place for the development and use of the skills and competencies used by people in communities to maintain social relationships. The lifeworld is the location of norms, values, and cultural activities. Moreover, the lifeworld can be, in part, associated with some aspects of private life. There are cultural and social understandings of how communication is to occur within the communities in the lifeworld that are reinforced or changed as communication occurs. For example, in family units, the members of a family know how to communicate with each other; there is a shared language and form of communication in the family. This is also true of racial, ethnic, and cultural groups, where there is a shared form of communication that is unique and specific to the members of that community. In the lifeworld, there is a shared understanding of how to navigate day-to-day activities.

This form of communication can also be established in a classroom setting where the instructor and the students discuss and agree on how the classroom is to be organized, structured, and restructured; throughout the duration of the class. Thus, in the lifeworld, the methods of communication are much more fluid and moving as people are negotiating and communicating with one another; and where "taken-for-granted" actions occur, because individuals establish communities with shared sets of values and worldviews to communicate with people they know in structured and unstructured ways. More structured forms of communicating include agreed-upon classroom rules for how students are to talk and engage with one another. Unstructured forms of communication in the classroom include personality traits of students and body language. Habermas (1987) sees the value in this form of intimate communication that occurs in the lifeworld, but also understands that it cannot happen every time we communicate in advanced and complex societies. Habermas puts forth an argument about how the lifeworld and the system can work hand in hand to help people. Or, on the contrary, the system can ultimately take over lifeworld concepts, as I discuss below.

Defining the System

While the lifeworld deals with intimate daily forms of communication, the system handles broad communication in an instrumental way. Essentially all forms of communication cannot have an in-depth level of communication. The system is the "aggregate effects of interest-oriented actions" (Habermas, 1987, p. 116). The system is the location of the larger social structures such as the economic structure, the racial order (e.g., White supremacy or racial history), or the gender order (e.g., patriarchy) that ultimately influence how society functions.

The system is primarily associated with public life. In the system, communication is presented in a simplified and predictable form, where there are understood norms of communication. For instance, when students go to a bookstore to purchase books for class, they exchange the money for the books, little to no communication is needed. The student is not meeting with the book author(s) or the publisher before purchasing the book, the cashier and other patrons are not asking the student why the book is needed to be purchased and how it will add value to the life of the student. A simplified exchange of goods takes place. This type of communication is simple and needed because it helps society to function. The lifeworld allows for more meaningful relationships with a few people, while the system allows individuals to function in a complex society and get tasks done without having to develop those relationships. However, communication in the system can be a coercive power that can restrict and limit communication in the lifeworld under, what I would argue would be, the guise of efficiency.

Moreover, in the system, Habermas argues that money and power can play a large role in establishing power dynamics that can restrict and prescribe the types of communication and interactions that people have with each other. Examples of this type of system coercion include: White supremacy, patriarchy, and capitalism because these systems construct privilege of one voice and exclude others that do not fit the narrative. For example, if an economic system is connected with a racial hierarchy in such a way that some people are economically disadvantaged, this might be an example of ways that the system can become coercive. Capitalism has negatively impacted communities of color in numerous ways; this stems from the inception of slavery when Black people were not paid for their forced labor; and this restriction of equitable pay has continued for generations since slavery (Jones, 1985). From this logic, economic capitalism can be linked to White supremacy because all participating in the labor and economic markets are not competing equitably. This control of capitalism goes unnoticed or largely unchallenged due to the restricted forms of communication; thus, it can seem normal because the lifeworld is unable to push back to the system. Ultimately, Habermas (1987) argues that system influences (e.g., economic structure, racial

order, gender order, etc.) are starting to "colonize" or take over lifeworld structures. In other words, cultural norms, values, and beliefs are starting to be taken
over by the social structural norms.

Colonization of the Lifeworld

The lifeworld and the system can exist separately and still be connected to
each other to help people carry out the tasks of their daily lives. However, the
problem arises when the system tries to colonize the lifeworld. When colonization occurs, people allow the social, economic, and administrative rules from
the system to overtake the norms of communication that are occurring in the
lifeworld, otherwise referred to by Habermas (1987) as communicative rationality. This colonization prohibits people from understanding or questioning
the rules that govern their actions (Habermas, 1987). During this process of
colonization, the lifeworld and how it functions and operates becomes muddled. Thus, the rules that govern the lifeworld are no longer clear and an individual cannot understand or effectively use the communicative rationality; the
nature of communication is altered and becomes simplified so that individuals'
hermeneutic horizons are not being expanded. By not understanding their
communicative rationality people cannot question it, challenge it, or critique
it (Habermas, 1987). I would argue that this process can happen so slowly that
one may not even know that their communicative action and rationality has
even been displaced. With colonization of the lifeworld, the ideal speech situation cannot occur because communication is muddled and restricted.

The process and aftermath of colonization of the lifeworld weakens individual freedom because the lifeworld becomes a means to an end (Habermas,
1987). Instead of the lifeworld being a place where individuals can challenge
the system, the system consumes the lifeworld. There is a loss of freedom and
meaningful communication and interaction. Colonization can encroach on the
how people live their everyday lives. In an educational context, colonization can
occur when the rules of the how the classroom should be taught and governed
are changed and the change comes from a top-down approach, and not from a
specific classroom.

Habermas (1987) warns that when colonization occurs there is no longer a
two-way form of a communication but a one-sided form of communication. In
the education context, colonization of the education lifeworld can make learning
and education less meaningful, which can allow for learning to strictly be a means
to an end. Additional examples of one-sided communication in an education
setting include: didactic teaching styles and limited decision-making restricted to
a top-down approach, and larger teaching and advising roles that limit personal
interaction. As advisors take on more students, they are reducing intimate forms
of communication in order to see more students. Colonization of the lifeworld
reduces and eventually eliminates the possibility for an ideal speech situation

to occur and for individuals' hermeneutic horizon to be expanded. Essentially, I argue that little critical thinking is occurring when colonization is occurring, which can work to keep already marginalized and oppressed groups in positions of being powerless and subdued.

For-Profit Sector: Background and Context

Although only 10 percent of college students attend proprietary institutions, these institutions are the driving forces around many postsecondary education policies and practices such as: finance, instruction methods, accountability, and accreditation (Bennett *et al.*, 2010). Even with heavy criticisms and a negative reputation (Illoh, 2016) proprietary institutions are still allowed to function and, in some cases, thrive. My research helps the field of postsecondary education to more holistically understand how proprietary institutions function in the postsecondary education field, and how they are impacted and impact the field.

This chapter focuses on the messages for-profit institutions relay via television commercials, as a way to understand how the hegemonic powers impact education and society. In the field of postsecondary education, public non-profit institutions are the dominant structure (NCES, 2015). For-profit institutions serve a different set of students altogether who have been traditionally neglected, discriminated against, and deemed less deserving of a postsecondary degree (Chung, 2008; Illoh, 2016). Ironically, given their demographics, for-profit institutions are often run by wealthy White businessmen. It is important to understand how proprietary institutions function and how they are operating under this power structure, and what messages they are sending out about their form of education. Analyzing television commercials is a unique way to begin to uncover the many messages. For-profit colleges and universities spend the same amount of money on marketing as they do on instruction; sometimes the marketing costs exceeds the cost of instruction (Senate HELP Committee, 2012). This powerful message must be analyzed. A critical perspective and inquiry is needed and calls for higher levels of accountability in the for-profit sector, as I will describe below.

Application of Theory with Data Analysis

Using Habermas' theory of colonization of the lifeworld is a way to understand how communication is used in society between the system and the lifeworld. Television commercials have become so commonplace that their influence can be overlooked and underestimated. This form of one-sided communication is a very powerful mechanism for communication and must be explored with a critical lens to uncover how capitalistic, hegemonic, and other forms of oppression can be observed, internalized, and normalized. Habermasian theory provides the ability to shift the focus from the dominant voice and perspectives to marginalized and implicit messages.

I apply this notion of the colonization of the lifeworld (Habermas, 1987) and Habermas' discussion of hermeneutics, or understanding, to the for-profit sector of postsecondary education. Specifically, I argue that the economic focus of for-profit institutions could be an example of lifeworld colonization. As for-profit institutions create advertisements to encourage participation, their potentially vulnerable or disadvantaged populations (e.g., students of color, women, veterans, adults with children, and/or first-generation college students), the system-level economic influences may make it such that: 1) the lifeworld concepts of cultural norms, values and beliefs are taken over by economic imperatives (e.g., get a degree to make more money); and 2) the advertisements may lead to communication misunderstandings where students misunderstand what the for-profit institutions may actually provide. While I apply these ideas to an example of media related to for-profit postsecondary institutions, the analytic ideas could be relevant to other studies that emphasize ways in which social systems influence individual actions.

For-profit institutions use television commercials as one mechanism to communicate with students, policy makers, and other stakeholders. Using a Habermasian critical theoretical framework, I assert that these commercials could be a mechanism to colonize the lifeworld of its students. This is important to understand because the for-profit sector spends more on marketing than instruction (Bennett *et al.*, 2010; Breneman, Pusser, & Turner, 2006) sending very powerful messages about its priorities as an institutional sector. The advertisements are examples of colonization of the lifeworld because the lifeworld is being told how it is to function. The lifeworld communication is becoming streamlined and isolated in the name of efficiency.

Secondly, the advertisements may betray the possibility for hermeneutic understanding for prospective students. By presenting a particular notion of the role of for-profit institutions as a place to finally get a chance or to finally become upwardly mobile in order to help one's family, for example, these commercials may misrepresent the real possibilities of education and education at for-profit institutions. Data shows that students are not employed at higher rates and they are not employed in the fields and careers advertised by the institutions (Floyd, 2007; Senate HELP Committee, 2012).

I offer a way to analyze data using Habermasian concepts through the example from a television commercial from the University of Phoenix entitled, *More Than Brains – University of Phoenix Commercial: 30 v5, (More than Brains v5)* (University of Phoenix, 2016). The television commercial is treated as one unit of analysis, to explore how colonization of the lifeworld is depicted. Television commercials are a popular of example of "mass media" that Habermas (1987) discusses in volume two of his book, *Theory of Communicative Action*. I use Carspecken's (1996) *Critical Ethnography in Educational Research* to show how television commercials are not only examples of mass media, but are also a way to better understand system-level analysis. I expand Carspecken's system-level analysis conversation by providing my own coding technique.

Carspecken uses Habermasian ideas to provide a rigorous way to analyze qualitative data. The first step is to apply low-level codes to the text; the television commercials. In this step, I summarize key parts of the commercial, developing short codes (two to five words) that are similar to the words used in the commercial. Next, I construct a meaning field, a technique that was developed by Carspecken (1996), which can be used to expand knowledge of range of possible meanings in an excerpt of text. In meaning field analysis, the initial statement of the text is analyzed with subsequent statements of what the text might mean by offering ideas of possible meaning separated by "and," "or," or "and/or." For instance, if one said, "The sky is blue" the meaning field might be as follows such that the range of possible meanings might be teased out:

> *Meaning field: The sky is blue AND It is a clear day outside AND There are not many clouds in the sky AND It is not likely to rain AND/OR I feel happy AND/OR I am sad and "blue" even if I look happy AND/OR One should notice the sky AND/OR One should be able to differentiate one sky from another*

Following that step, I created a reconstructive horizon analysis, also developed by Carspecken (1996) to understand the embedded meanings in a statement. Carspecken (1996) used Habermas' theorizing of validity claims: Objective (that which is accessible to all, referring to an environment or space that is shared), Subjective (that which is accessible to the individual, in one's mind, the location of feelings or opinions), and Normative (that which is ethical or moral within a statement). In reconstructive horizon analysis, the researcher takes portions of text and teases out the objective, subjective, and normative analysis of meanings (Carspecken, 1996).

Marketing Positionality Coding

Expanding upon Carspecken's (1996) data analysis technique that he rooted in Habermasian theory, I will be adding a coding technique entitled: Marketing Positionality Coding. This is the last step in the coding and analysis process after low-level coding, meaning field analysis, and reconstructive analysis. The marketing positionality code was chosen because television commercials are often ways that for-profit colleges and universities market themselves to viewers. Marketing positionality allows for economic system structures to be more evident. Not only do commercials market themselves to viewers; they are also communicating and sending very powerful messages to consumers. The viewers of these commercials are not just prospective students, but they are also likely sending messages to: other institutional competitors, policy makers, financial investors, and a host of other stakeholders. I developed a high-level, high-inference coding scheme that could address the many messages, both visual and auditory, that commercials can give.

The marketing positionality code allows a researcher to ask the following of the data:

1. Who is the statement targeting?
2. What messages are being sent as they relate to the economic system?
3. Why are these messages potentially being sent and how does this relate to system-level forces?

Applied specifically to my project on commercials for for-profit postsecondary institutions, I ask:

1. Who are the institutions targeting with this commercial?
2. What messages are they sending to prospective for-profit students?
3. Why are for-profit institutions sending these messages and how might this relate to system-level forces?

The marketing positionality code is a way to analyze the objective, subjective, and normative claims that commercials make simultaneously, to understand how economic system-level forces might be embedded in text – in the case of proprietary institutions, how they market their services to students and capture the desires, needs, and goals of their targeted audiences. Below is an example of how I might analyze text using the marketing positionality technique, coupled with Carspecken's (1996) meaning field and reconstructive horizon analysis to point out system-level constructs.

Example from the University of Phoenix *More than Brains* v5 commercial.

Song Lyrics of *More Than Brains* v5 Commercial:

> So my kids don't have to forage
> Got two jobs to pay a mortgage
> And I've also got a brain
> Life's short, talk is cheap
> I'll be workin' while you sleep
> Still don't think I've got a brain?
> I took two bullets in the chest
> Got three kids, I never rest
> So yeah, I've got a brain
> A degree is a degree
> You're gonna want someone like me
> But only if you have a brain

Images of the *More than Brains v5 Commercial with the Song Lyrics*

1. 0:00–0:004:
    a. Image
        i. A White mother nursing and caring for her small infant child in a working-class restaurant while also studying on a laptop at the table in the morning
    b. Lyrics:
        i. So my kids don't have to forage
        ii. Got two jobs to pay a mortgage
2. 0:05–0:07:
    a. Image:
        i. A White man on the bus on some sort of vehicle studying, reading a textbook. The book has different colourful taps on the pages
    b. Lyrics
        i. And I've also got a brain
        ii. Life's short, talk is cheap
3. 0:07–0:08
    a. Image:
        i. Older Black professional male, in his office, holds a book in his hands and closes the door
        ii. Lyrics:
            1. Life's short, talk is cheap
4. 0:09–0:11
    a. Image:
        i. Older White male, at the crack of dawn, on his tractor in the field reading a book
    b. Lyrics:
        i. I'll be working while you sleep
5. 0:12–0:13
    a. Image:
        i. White woman with a nametag on a white blouse looks up at the camera
    b. Lyrics:
        i. Still don't think that I've got a brain
6. 0:14–0:17
    a. Image:
        i. Old White man, shirtless, boxing with a large cut/scar down the center of his chest
    b. Lyrics:
        i. I took two bullets in the chest
        ii. Got three kids

7. 0:18–0:22
   a. Image
      i. Black woman on a crowded bus standing and reading a book
   b. Lyrics:
      i. Got three kids, I never rest
      ii. So yeah, I've got a brain
8. 0:22–0:26
   a. Image:
      i. White woman studying in the library, she is highlighting until it closes, the lights in the library are turning off, and the woman dismisses the Black security guard and he is coming to tell her that the library is closing/closed to finish studying
   b. Lyrics
      i. A degree is a degree
9. 0:26–0:27
   a. Image:
      i. Black screen with the words: WE RISE
   b. Lyrics:
      i. You're gonna want someone like me
10. 0:29–0:30
    a. Image:
       i. Black background: With the words: University of Phoenix and their contact information and log
    b. Lyrics:
       i. But only if you've got a brain

Coding Scheme

Low-level Codes

Lyrics: I work while you sleep, I've got a brain, A degree is a degree, I have two jobs, I took two bullets to the chest, I never rest.

Images: People from different backgrounds are working and studying by themselves in public spaces.

Meaning Fields

Students who want to go to Phoenix will work **AND** go to school **AND** will work all the time **AND** will make sacrifices **AND** will come from different backgrounds **AND** the institution can **AND** will accommodate a wide variety of students **AND** students will work hard **AND** students will sacrifice to be a student at Phoenix **OR** they will not be desirable students because students are expected to be focused on school all the time.

Reconstructive Horizon Analysis

Foregrounded (More Obvious)

Objective: Students work constantly and find time to go to school.
Subjective: Students want to work and go to school.
Normative: Students should want to work constantly and go to school, it's normal and common.

Foregrounded

Objective: Phoenix is a place where students can work and go to school.
Subjective: Students who need to work and go to school want to come to Phoenix.
Normative: Phoenix should be a place where students want to come to get a degree and still be able to work.

Backgrounded (Less Obvious, Higher Inference)

Objective: Students must sacrifice as much of their personal time to study when not working or even when working.
Subjective: Students who are a good fit for Phoenix want to sacrifice their time and do not complain and are willing to do whatever it takes.
Normative: Students at Phoenix should and are required to give more of themselves to earn a degree from Phoenix.

Highly Backgrounded

Objective: Students at Phoenix are often studying alone, or by themselves with no other students or faculty around.
Subjective: Students are individually motivated to attend school.
Normative: Students should be willing to keep persevering at Phoenix, no matter what obstacles come their way.

High-level Code – Marketing Positionality

1. Who are the institutions targeting with this commercial? Students, institutional competitors, policy makers.
2. What messages are they sending? The institution helps students do multiple things at once in order to earn a degree.
3. Why are for-profit institutions sending these messages and how might this relate to system-level forces? The degree can help graduates earn more money, or even earn money while getting a degree.

Marketing Positionality Summary

Working-class and middle-class students of all backgrounds can work and go to school at Phoenix because this institution is accommodating and flexible. Students at Phoenix sacrifice their personal time to earn a degree that is worth the same at any other institution. Phoenix helps students learn to multitask and give up other things to be better off later. Additionally, students from Phoenix are competition to the non-profit sector because they possess the same characteristics of hard work.

Further Analysis Using the Marketing Positionality Technique

From this commercial, the University of Phoenix is talking to three main audiences: prospective students, institutional competitors, and policy makers. I explain this in a narrative format below to offer an example of how this data analysis technique might be applied in other studies. In particular, I provide narrative about each audience in the marketing positionality.

Prospective Students

The prospective students are shown what it is like to attend the University of Phoenix, who their peers are, and what some common experiences are like. On the surface level, the institution is saying that they can accommodate a wide variety of students from different backgrounds. All students are welcomed to attend an institution that fits into their busy lifestyles; the University of Phoenix is accommodating. Most importantly, the University of Phoenix is portraying itself as a viable option for employment and financial stability, linking the commercial messaging to system-level economic forces. The candidates that leave the University of Phoenix are now desirable to employers and society.

Through a Habermasian lens, I noticed that the students were mostly working-class students who were working and studying in isolation; they were not in dialogue with other people about the material they were reading or in dialogue with the text. In the commercial, the waitress and the mother were studying in isolation. The mother was nursing her child and studying by herself. The farmer/tractor worker and people on the bus were reading in a crowed location. This is an example of one-sided dialogue that Habermas (1987) discusses. The students are there to absorb the material that is being learned and not to challenge it, discuss it, or critique it. Their understanding was not being expanded in a critical or meaningful way.

Moreover, the students in the commercial were constantly working, which reflects the capitalism that Habermas discusses. The businessman was at work while studying and the farmer/tractor worker was reading on an operating tractor machine early in the morning. The students were often reading in public places such as on crowded public transportation that was busy; this is restricting some of the intimate lifeworld communication. Dialectical conversation has almost vanished because information is just being absorbed with little reflection.

Self-motivation, sacrifice, and constant working are characteristics that the University of Phoenix wants of its students. A clip of the older man boxing with the large scar down his chest shows that despite having heart troubles he is continuing to move on and rise up – this is represented economically, at least, which reinforces system-level economic forces.

A deeper analysis shows that the working-class students are somehow inadequate before they enroll at the University of Phoenix. The working-class students are portrayed and defined as not having a brain, but needing to acquire one, as if their financial status is associated with their intellect, which draws on an economic/system-level idea of the economic structure as the most important to structure other social forces. Phoenix students are conforming to an outside notion of what it means to be an educated working-class adult student. The students in the commercial are sacrificing their time to gain access to a different social class. After going through this education process the working-class students will be desirable and smart because they will have a "brain." The value of the working-class student is tied to their ability to sacrifice all for a degree. The University of Phoenix is sending a message about the type of students they have and the type of students they want to have enrolled at their institutions.

Utilizing a critical Habermasian lens, I explored how the communication in the lifeworld has been made informal, less meaningful in this commercial. Communication is a means to an end to finish the course, complete the degree, and get a job. Students who are hardworking and possess grit and determination will be successful. However, success is only a job where they are working for others. "You're going to want someone like me" is a line in the commercial. The students want to be employed and work for others; they are not becoming business owners or entrepreneurs. The students at Phoenix are not taught to think critically for themselves, but to instead adopt a set of external norms imposed on them and their lifeworld, which the students willingly accept without question.

Overall, this commercial begins to capture how the lifeworld is colonized. Students, especially those from working-class backgrounds, are having their lifeworlds being dictated by external forms of communication; they are not in positions of power to determine what their education experiences will be. Hegemonic powers (power and influence of a dominant group) are dictating what their school life is like, and the students are accepting of this and embracing this. The burden is placed on the students to work all the time. Faculty, administrators, other peers in the same program or class are not referenced at all, making the learning isolating, not individualized.

Institutional Competitors and Policy Makers

While much of the commercial is targeted to students, there are some underlying messages to institutional competitors and policy makers. The University of Phoenix is also talking to other competitors and policy makers when the song lyrics say, "A degree is a degree". This is saying that they are competitive with almost any other institution for-profit and non-profit, and that there is no significant difference between institutional certificates and degrees. Phoenix is also saying their students are competitive in the job market because their students also possess the hard work, sacrifice, grit, and determination to succeed.

By using Habermas' ideas about the importance of understanding, I have shown how the messages in this television commercial are problematic, because the ideal speech situation is not occurring. Communication is happening in one direction. The University of Phoenix is not trying to engage others in dialogue. The for-profit sector of higher education is encroaching on the lifeworld of the students; it is aligning itself with the current economic structure that is in place and giving the rationale for the importance of a degree as linked to that economic structure. The students are not questioning this process but taking it as a given, that this is somehow normal because they want to be successful and earn a degree no matter what.

The University of Phoenix is attempting to elevate the institution to the status of other institutions both for-profit and non-profit. It is using their platform and its voice to silence the instructors and people that do not believe in what they do. Using the marketing positionality as a coding technique, I can understand how the University of Phoenix defines its form of education. Education is a means to an end to get a job, which aligns with an economic imperative to fulfill market needs (demand and supply for jobs and skilled employees in those jobs). Students go through this process to be employable for someone else. They are not trained to think critically or think for themselves. The University of Phoenix is training and credentialing students. As referenced earlier, this credentialing may not lead to employment. The importance is not on learning, but working to get a degree to signal to the market this student can enter the workforce. Moreover, the University of Phoenix is filling a demand for the market by providing trained working-class students to work for others. They lack a "brain" until they have a degree. From a Habermasian perspective, the working-class students are being marginalized and market forces subsume their individuality. These students are seen and utilized as tools for others.

Conclusion: Where to Go from Here

The marketing positionality coding that I have developed, as an extension of Carspecken's (1996) Habermasian analysis techniques, is useful when looking at mass media and advertising. It may not be applicable to all forms of data and data analysis. My data analysis technique allows for the exploration of mass media and marketing to be explored on a system level. Mass media are quick, yet influential and powerful ways to communicate. In this case, for-profit colleges and universities spend a significant portion of their budget (Senate HELP Committee, 2012) to tug at the heartstrings of the working-class citizens who want to better their life outcomes and their families. Working-class students being targeted by this particular commercial are in a vulnerable place; and without being fully knowledgeable they can be taken advantage of.

The reason I chose the University of Phoenix is because of the high-quality commercials, where there are many underlying and complex meanings. The commercials send so many complex and competing messages that it becomes essential to view them from a critical perspective to connect those messages back to larger social systems. Without this critical perspective, these covert and implicit messages can become internalized and normalized without question. Questioning what is being communicated and why can put those being marginalized in positions of power to ensure their lifeworlds are being protected.

By bringing critical theory directly into the data analysis technique, I was able to demonstrate how media can relate to system-level economic structures. This is an example of how critical theory can inform data analysis such that a researcher can be better able to demonstrate how text, or statements by participants, might actually be evidence of large social structural issues.

References

Apling, R. N. (1993). Proprietary Schools and Their Students. *The Journal of Higher Education,* 64(4), 379–416.

Bennett, D. L., Lucchesi, A. R., & Vedder, R. K. (2010). *For-Profit Higher Education Growth, Innovation and Regulation.* Washington, DC: Center for College Affordability and Productivity.

Breneman, D. W., Pusser, B., & Turner, S. E. (2006). *For-Profit Colleges in the Context of the Market for Higher Education.* Albany, NY: State University of New York Press.

Canella, G. S., Pérez, M. S., & Pasque, P. A. (2015). *Critical Qualitative Inquiry: Foundations and Future.* Walnut Creek, CA: Left Coast Press.

Carspecken, P. F. (1996). *Critical Ethnography in Educational Research.* New York: Routledge.

Chung, A. S. (2008). *The Choice of For-Profit College.* Ann Arbor, MI: Munich Personal RePEc Archive MPRA.

Floyd, C. E. (2007). Know Your Competitor: Impact of For-Profit Colleges on the Higher Education Landscape. *New Directions for Higher Education,* 140(27), 121–129.

For Profit U. (2015). *Fact Sheet.* Retrieved from For Profit U: http://forprofitu.org/fact-sheet/#_ftn4

Habermas, J. (1984). *The theory of communicative action: Reason and the rationalisation of society,* Volume 1 (Trans: T. McCarthy). Boston, MA: Beacon Press.

Habermas, J. (1987). *The Theory of Coummunicative Action.* Boston, MA: Beacon Press.

Illoh, C. (2016). Exploring the For-Profit Experience: An Ethnography of a For-Profit College. *American Educational Research Journal,* 53(3), 427–455.

Jones, J. (1985). *Labor of Love, Labor of Sorrow: Black Women, Work, and the Family from Slavery to the Present.* New York: Basic Books.

NCES, N. (2015, March). Table 303.10: Total fall enrollment in degree-granting post-secondary institutions, by attendance status, sex of student, and control of institution: Selected years, 1947 through 2024. Retrieved from *Digest of Education Statistics*: http://nces.ed.gov/programs/digest/d14/tables/dt14_303.10.asp?current=yes

Pasque, P. A., Carducci, R., Kuntz, A. M., & Gildersleeve, R. E. (2012). *Qualitative Inquiry for Equity in Higher Education: Methodological Innovations, Implications, and Interventions.* San Francisco, CA: Wiley.

Senate HELP Committee. (2012). *For Profit Higher Education: The Failure to Safeguard the Federal Investment and Ensure Student Success.* Washington, DC: United States Senate Health, Education, Labor, and Pensions Committee.

University of Phoenix. (2016, April 7). *More than Brains – University of Phoenix Commercial: 30 v5.* Retrieved from YouTube: University of Phoenix: https://www.youtube.com/watch?v=8QfB1QQ_oBM

14

USING SOCIAL MEDIA TO (RE)CENTER BLACK WOMEN'S VOICES IN EDUCATIONAL RESEARCH

Jamila Lee-Johnson and Lora Henderson

Theory: Du Bois's Double Consciousness
Type of qualitative data: Twitter
New data analysis technique: Double Consciousness coding
Substantive topic in education: Black women's voices and experiences being silenced in the workplace

---

Racism and sexism have often been evident in online social media discourse (Nakamura, 2007; Clark, 2014). We employ critical discourse analysis (Fairclough, 2013) and double consciousness (Du Bois, 1903) to analyze Twitter data. Recently, social media, specifically "Black Twitter," has been used as a platform for Black women to express their work experiences when, historically, they have not always had a voice or a space for self-expression in the workforce. We use data from the Twitter hashtag, #Blackwomenatwork, to demonstrate how critical qualitative research can be used to analyze social media data and how social media is used as a space for Black women to have a voice, when often times they feel silenced.

This chapter focuses on the experiences of Black[1] women at work who must balance work expectations, microaggressions,[2] and being a Black woman in America. While this chapter is not specifically grounded in Black women's educational experiences, rather in the workplace, we argue that many tweets from the Black women's work experiences are comparable to Black women/ girls' experiences in educational spaces. In so doing, we offer an example of how researchers may apply Du Bois' (1903) idea of double consciousness to examine how Black women have to operate within White communities and their own Black communities in work and educational settings.

Black Women, Workplace Discrimination, and the Media

Though the media often describes Black women as a monolith plagued by poverty, laziness, and incompetence who do not receive the best form of education, many African American women are excelling academically and professionally, and more African American women than ever are attending college (Shorter-Gooden, 2004). For instance, enrollment and graduation rates for Black women have doubled since the 1980s (Patton & Croom, 2017; Winkle-Wagner, 2015). Black women's contributions to the workforce are immeasurable, however, their experiences often signal to them that they are not seen or valued wholly (Jones & Shorter-Gooden, 2009). Furthermore, job opportunities for Black women are greater than ever. They are a consistent and stable part of the workforce in the United States, but still only make 64 cents to every dollar that White men earn (National Partnership.org, 2017; Patten, 2016). Black women's work lives are impacted by systemic inequalities, racism, discrimination, and other lingering effects of slavery (Jones & Shorter-Gooden, 2009).

For Black women in the United States, negative experiences and discrimination in the workplace and in the media are nothing new. For centuries, Black women have been pressured to present themselves in ways that are deemed acceptable to the world. For example, Black women's experiences are often "swept under the rug" and ignored instead of being handled in affirming and validating manners (Gasman, 2007; Winkle-Wagner, Luedke, & McCallum, 2017, p. 44). In addition to political and societal challenges, African American women also have to deal with the stressors of operating within the culture of the dominant (White) society and that of their own racial/cultural group as they traverse through the K-12 educational system, undergraduate and graduate academic pursuits, and ultimately professional careers (Winkle-Wagner, 2009).

The negative treatment of Black women in the workplace also extends into how highly-educated Black women are profiled and treated by the media. In 2017 during a live television interview, former Fox News commentator Bill O'Reilly (a White man) insulted African American United States Congresswoman Maxine Waters[3] by saying, "I didn't hear a word she said. I was looking at the James Brown wig. Do we have a picture of James Brown? It's the same wig," (Wang, 2017). O'Reilly stated these comments in response to Congresswoman Waters after she made remarks about the 45th president of the United States, Donald Trump. One of the cohosts laughed while O'Reilly made the comments. O'Reilly's comments came just hours after former White House Press Secretary Sean Spicer ordered Black journalist, April D. Ryan, to stop shaking her head as they engaged in a heated question and answer dialogue on the presidential administration. Spicer's words suggested that Black women should control their attitudes and that when their attitudes manifest, verbally or physically, they must be controlled. In other words, Black women need to respect authority (i.e., White men). In what is a true sign of the times, both Congresswoman Waters and Ryan took to social media, specifically Twitter, to respond to the racist and sexist treatment that they had received from White men in positions of power. Congresswoman Waters tweeted, "I'm a strong Black woman and I cannot be intimidated. I cannot be undermined. I cannot be thought to be afraid of Bill O'Reilly or anybody" (Hill, 2017; Wang, 2017). Ryan simply tweeted, "Lawd!!!!" After witnessing these attacks that were publicized in the media and discussed on social media, activist Brittany Packnett took to "Black Twitter" and started the #Blackwomenatwork hashtag in response to the attacks on Waters and Ryan.

Twitter as Data

Twitter is an online social network used by over 60 million people (Greenwood, Perrin, & Duggan, 2016). The interface allows users to post short messages (up to 140 characters) that can be read by any other Twitter user. Users declare the people they are interested in following and get notified when those people create new posts. Twitter is a public sphere that encourages discourse and debate by allowing strangers to engage in conversations as well as contribute to live Twitter debates (Cormorde & Krishnamurthy, 2008; Donath & Boyd, 2004; Marwick, 2013, Westling, 2007).

Black Twitter

A 2013 study by the Pew Research Centers showed that African Americans use Twitter at higher rates than other ethnic groups (Smith, 2014). The study found that more than a quarter of Black Twitter users are college-educated and between the ages of 18 and 45 (Brenner & Smith, 2013; Smith, 2014). Generally, tweets are a novel source of primary data that can be collected and analyzed quickly in order to examine a social phenomenon and this may be particularly true for "Black Twitter." Journalist Soraya Nadia McDonald describes "Black Twitter" as "part cultural force, cudgel, entertainment and refuge. It is its own society within Twitter, replete with inside jokes, slang and rules, centered on the interests of young Blacks online" (McDonald, 2014, p. 1). Black Twitter may receive negative feedback for often dragging[4] and calling out others on controversial topics, but Black Twitter more importantly serves as a platform for activism. For example, Black Twitter has brought awareness to millions about Black and Brown women who have been killed by police violence (Freelon, McIlwain, & Clark, 2016). Black Twitter users often communicate using "Blacktags" or hashtags related to the experiences of Black people (Sharma, 2013). Sharma (2013) refers to Blacktags as "racialized digital objects in relation to the techno cultural assemblages they are produced in" (p. 48). In other words, Black people come together to create their own racialized community by using Twitter as their platform. This segregation of Black users creates a ripe space for interrogation into the lived and virtual experiences of Black women at work.

#BlackWomenAtWork

The #BlackWomenAtWork hashtag is just one example of how Black Twitter operates. Once social media activist Brittany Packnett started the hashtag; the responses demonstrated the collective power that groups of people can have on social media. Black women used the hashtag to share their experiences of discrimination, racism, and sometimes annoyance with situations that they had encountered in the workplace. Thousands of women engaged through liking posts, retweeting (sharing someone else's tweet), or writing their own tweets (140 characters or less describing their own experiences). Some tweeted using text, while others also used memes[5] (i.e., a humorous image, gif or short animation), or pictures to emphasize their points.

We selected examples of tweets to demonstrate how double consciousness and critical discourse can be used to understand #BlackWomenAtWork who choose to voice and express themselves through Twitter as a way to demonstrate a new data analysis technique that is rooted in Du Bois' (1903) double consciousness.

Double Consciousness

W.E.B. Du Bois introduced double consciousness in his 1903 book, *The Souls of Black Folk*, which highlighted ongoing racial disparities. Du Bois' ideas represent a critical theory that is, unfortunately, still relevant in the United States over 100 years later. Du Bois described double consciousness as a way in which Black people have to operate as both American and Black. He posited that a symbolic "veil"[6] makes it difficult for White individuals to view African Americans as truly American and it leads to African Americans feeling the need to assimilate to meet the expectations of the dominant, White culture. Du Bois believed that Black people were only viewed through a one-sided veil (a lens only centered around Whiteness), resulting in their isolation, alienation, and marginalization. Additionally, the theory suggests that Black people also see themselves through the lens making it difficult for them to be fully self-aware and engage in behaviors that may be deemed as inappropriate by White America. The veil ultimately focuses on what White people think of Black people and could lead to the onset of self-sabotage if Black people were to view themselves in the ways that White people stereotype them. Double consciousness and the veil create discomfort for Black people who constantly feel at the juncture of American and African American cultures. There is great tension and discomfort from being "othered" as the world "looks on in amused contempt and pity" (Du Bois, 1903, p. 9). Thus emerged what Du Bois coined as double consciousness, described as follows:

> It is a peculiar sensation, this double-consciousness, this sense of always looking at one's self through the eyes of others, of measuring one's soul by the tape of a world that looks on in amused contempt and pity. One ever feels his two-ness, an American, a Negro; two souls, two thoughts, two unreconciled strivings; two warring ideals in one dark body, whose dogged strength alone keeps it from being torn asunder. The history of the American Negro is the history of this strife, this longing to attain self-conscious manhood, to merge his double self into a better and truer self. In this merging he wishes neither of the older selves to be lost. He does not wish to Africanize America, for America has too much to teach the world and Africa. He wouldn't bleach his Negro blood in a flood of White Americanism, for he knows that Negro blood has a message for the world. He simply wishes to make it possible for a man to be both a Negro and an American without being cursed and spit upon by his fellows, without having the doors of opportunity closed roughly in his face,
>
> *(pp. 2–3)*

Du Bois spoke to the strength of the "Negro" and how that alone is what allows Black people to continue to reconcile their own racial and cultural experiences with that of White America. This perceived strength, likely rooted in slavery, has been and is still used against Black women as they are often labeled "the strong Black woman" or the "angry Black woman" without regard to the burden that these "Eurocentric" labels have placed upon them. Though the initial focus of Du Bois' work was men, both men and women experience "two-ness" or double consciousness. However, African American women face unique layered challenges being double minorities, at the intersection of gender and race, in their educational and occupational pursuits (Winkle-Wagner, 2009). Additionally, depending on which career a woman chooses to pursue, she may add an additional minority label. For example, Black women in the fields of science, technology, engineering, and math (STEM) would be operating within their own culture(s), that of the dominant society, and that of the historically White and/or Asian male-driven STEM fields (Winkle-Wagner, 2010).

Throughout their academic and career endeavors, African American women are often not treated as equals to their White counterparts and have to operate within a double consciousness framework (Jones & Shorter-Goodwin, 2009). Bell (1990) described some of the same challenges as Du Bois did in 1903 as she discussed the experiences of career-oriented African American women in the 1980s: "Beyond the pressures to conform to professional standards and dominant culture values found in organizations, Black professional women must also manage expectations, values, and roles in relation to the Black community—a community with its own norms regarding the status of women" (p. 460). Furthermore, another example of double consciousness in Black women was in Melissa Harris-Perry's book, *Sister Citizen* (2011), where she illustrated the dual problem of "hypervisibility and invisibility" of Black women during Hurricane Katrina. Harris-Perry (2011) articulated the story of how Black women's voices were unheard during the storm. However, during Katrina the media often would show pictures of them stealing or looting. Harris-Perry addressed how Black women's race and gender have affected how the American media tried to shame these women during Hurricane Katrina (Harris-Perry, 2011). She compared the women's experiences from Hurricane Katrina to Zora Neale Hurston's (1937) *Their Eyes Were Watching God* in how the politics of race and gender often intersect and influence the challenges of self-perception of Black women (Harris-Perry, 2011 p. 1). In both of these examples, Black women were protecting and supporting their families, and still were being unfairly disgraced by the media. These women experienced double consciousness by the media portraying them as one way and not being that way or perceived negatively by their families or own cultural group.

Du Bois' description of double consciousness also inherently acknowledges the strengths of the African American people despite their history of oppression in the United States. Du Bois explained how African Americans have much to teach Americans while also learning from them. Interestingly enough, he argued that African Americans do not wish to "Africanize" America.

In Winkle-Wagner's (2009) book, *The Unchosen Me*, she explored the experiences of Black women and how they navigate being on a predominantly White campus and being a Black woman in a White world. Winkle-Wagner (2009) used double consciousness to show that while Black women have many challenges on predominantly White campuses, they also bring knowledge to these spaces.

In spite of the many stereotypes and labels given to African Americans and specifically Black women, Du Bois' narrative of double consciousness gives a poignant voice to those who are often marginalized. Double consciousness recognizes Black women's rights to, desire to, and/or need to express themselves differently dependent upon the setting, including their workplaces. This narrative goes against much of the research about African Americans that comes from a deficit perspective and describes how they reject the dominant culture and resist the White norms of the United States (Bell, 1990; Parker, 2001). Instead, Du Bois illustrated an internal struggle of simultaneously being a part of two distinct worlds that had not converged in 1903 and, for many African Americans, still have not converged in 2018. In general, power and privilege explain why narratives developed by White people that pathologize African American people have been more heavily adopted than Du Bois' explanation of a psychological and internal challenge that African Americans face in the United States. Given the history of silencing the already oppressed, qualitative methods will give voice to those who experience double consciousness in their professional pursuits. In the case of this chapter, Du Bois' ideas give voice to Black women.

Critical Discourse Analysis and Double Consciousness

Qualitative research methods are often used to provide in-depth insight into human experiences beyond what quantitative measures can explain (Creswell, 2013). As such, qualitative methods connect well to critical research, which strives to recognize power in research, and to research individuals who have traditionally been marginalized or underrepresented (Carspecken, 1996). Critical Discourse Analysis (CDA) uses the critical tradition of social analysis in language studies and contributes to critical social structures. It also sees both "concrete social events and abstract social structures as part of social reality" (Fairclough, 2013, p. 75). CDA allows for scholars to unpack how language is used and perceived in society. Additionally, CDA can be understood as a normative and explanatory critique (Everett & Croom, 2017, p. 80; Fairclough, 2013, p. 76). It is a normative critique in that it does not simply describe existing realities but also evaluates them (Everett & Croom, 2017, p. 80). Everett and Croom (2017) state, "CDA aims to name the unarticulated understandings in text, and constructs to the larger context in the society in which they exist" (p. 80). Fairclough (2013) asserted, "social structures and social events of critical discourse are interceded by social practices, that control the selective actualization of potentials" (p. 74). Social texts are shaped by social practices and social structures, and by social agents (Fairclough, 2013). For example, the women whose tweets were analyzed in our chapter used 140 words or less on Twitter to express themselves as a result of highly political events where Black women might have historically been silenced. By using Twitter and the hashtag #Blackwomenatwork, we demonstrate how some Black women use social media as a way to both express themselves and to connect with other Black women who may have had similar experiences.

Data Analysis

In academia, analysis of Twitter is often done quantitatively (e.g., measuring the number of users who engage with a tweet or retweet it) or temporally (e.g., assessing engagement with a topic or hashtag over a period of time; Bruns & Stieglitz, 2013). However, we use the #BlackWomenAtWork hashtag to demonstrate how Twitter can be used in qualitative research data analysis. Given that Twitter is a social media platform and communication tool that allows users to contribute their individual voices to the Twitter community, analysis of tweets beyond quantification is necessary.

We are proposing a novel coding process using in vivo coding (i.e., using participants' own language to create codes; Saldaña, 2015) to allow researchers to interpret 140 character "tweets" posted by Twitter users. We explicitly looked for instances in which Twitter users described "two-ness," or hiding behind the veil, and without carefully analyzing the data as a whole, traditional in vivo coding could potentially miss examples of double consciousness or "two-ness." Double consciousness coding involves the careful comparison of real-life/world experiences, in order to identify instances in which the individual may be operating differently in White or American culture (e.g., at work) and within their own African American culture (e.g., at home or in the community). This type of coding is especially relevant for large datasets of social network data given the diversity of consumers and the "snapshots" that tweets or other posts give into the lived experiences of the consumers. Specifically, double consciousness coding can help researchers, especially those who study Black women, understand the experiences of a large subset of individuals such as Black women who use Twitter.

CDA analyzes discourse or communication between people and includes identifying words or phrases that display social roles and gender norms. (Bloor & Bloor, 2013). For instance, when using CDA, we are looking for Black women who use words to signify how their gender, race, or the intersectionality of their identities present themselves as problems in their White-dominated workplaces. Furthermore, applying CDA allowed for us to analyze how Black women participated in a speech community (Bloor & Bloor, 2013) using the hashtag #BlackWomenAtWork.

Double Consciousness Coding Examples

In this section, we present three tweets using the #BlackWomenatWork hashtag and demonstrate how CDA can be used to unpack the experiences of double consciousness and two-ness that Black women experience in the workplace.

Double Consciousness Coding Example 1

Tweet: "At my last job, I was pulled into daily 'meetings' where I was told to smile and laugh because they couldn't 'read' me. **#BlackWomenAtWork"**

CDA: In examining the writer's word choice, it is notable that she included actions such as "pulled" and "told to," demonstrating that she did not have the autonomy to decide whether or not she wanted to smile, laugh, or attend the meetings. In addition, her description of "daily meetings" implies that the woman's lack of smiles and laughter were significant issues to others with whom she worked. Lastly, the notion that her co-workers could not "read" her, suggests that her demeanor concerned her co-workers simply because she was not an open book as if that were an expectation to fulfill the requirements for her job.

Double consciousness: This tweet is an example of double consciousness and the enforcement of the veil as the writer is being told how to present herself to others. By telling her how to look and behave in meetings, the writer's co-workers are forcing stereotypical gender and racial roles on her instead of allowing her to behave in a way that she deems acceptable. This woman was told by others how she should act, thus representing a departure from the authentic self if she were to conform to the expectations of others.

Analysis: The writer's use of the word "they" implies that someone who is different from her (likely of a different race or gender) was criticizing her and initiating the meetings in which her demeanor was frequently discussed. This tweet demonstrates how this particular woman operated within a double consciousness framework as she was expected by others to behave differently at work.

Double Consciousness Coding Example 2

Tweet: "I've had so many ideas and initiatives taken with no credit given to me it's an injustice. People want your anointing but not your pain. #BlackWomenatWork"

CDA: The writer uses words and phrases that demonstrate the negative experiences she has had at work as her ideas have been "taken" with "no credit given." The magnitude of these situations is demonstrated by her description of "injustice." The phrase, "People want your anointing but not your pain," explains her perception that others want the accolades that come with her new ideas and initiatives without actually working for them.

Double consciousness: The way in which this woman presents her ideas, but then is made "invisible" as her ideas are "taken" from her demonstrates the two-ness that she experiences as a competent professional who is not acknowledged for her contributions.

Analysis: This tweet is consistent with literature describing how women are often overlooked in the workplace and their ideas are not always taken seriously. Further, her experiences are common for women, but may be exacerbated by her double-minority status of being a Black woman.

Double Consciousness Coding Example 3

Tweet: "#BlackWomenAtWork ★Pulls me to the side★ . . . You are very smart & great at your job but you would get so much further if you change your hair."

CDA: The writer's use of the phrase, "pulls me to the side," suggests that she is being chastised or singled out. The writer proceeds to use positive adjectives such as "smart" and "great" to describe others' appraisals of her ability to do her job. Despite being told that she performs well, the writer is asked to "change" an aspect of her identity to make others feel more comfortable or value her more.

Double consciousness: The writer wears hairstyles that are likely consistent with her own racial or cultural background with which she is comfortable. However, the norms of the dominant society place more value on certain hairstyles (usually straightened hair). This Black woman is forced to operate within two different "worlds" at home and at work.

Analysis: This tweet provides an example of how Black women's physical features may impact other's perceptions of them in the workplace. Even when Black women such as the one who wrote this tweet are effective in their roles, other extraneous factors may hinder their ability to successfully compete for promotions and other acknowledgements. While most Black women do not have to worry about how their hairstyle will be accepted by others from their racial or cultural group, it can be a great concern at work.

In summary, for researchers who want to use the double consciousness analysis technique, the following general steps are necessary:

1. **CDA coding**: During this phase of analysis, a researcher considers the larger social structural meanings that might be embedded in some of the chosen words in the data. The words are chosen because they appear to have deeper meaning or possible double meanings. For example, we identified words where the author demonstrated she had no power or control of the situation, when being accused or asked to do something.

2. **Double consciousness coding**: For this analysis, a researcher searches the data to find evidence that a person's actions, thoughts, or responses might present differently in their own cultural group and in the dominant society. In other words, double consciousness coding should be used when an individual is clearly articulating that they have to change something about themselves or hide behind the veil. For example, we coded for double consciousness based on what society has identified for being its "norm" in society, which in turn allowed us to interpret many things that often cause Black women to hide behind the veil or not want to fully expose who they are in the workplace.

3. **Analysis**: At the end, all of the coding is synthesized and a brief memo is written to offer insight into what this means for the larger project. Some of these memos may be used in the findings section of an article/chapter/book.

Discussion: Double Consciousness Coding – How did we do this? And why?

As critical Black women scholars who are analyzing the experiences of Black women via social media, we were able to speak to the data based on sharing some of the same common experiences that these women chose to share via Twitter. It is also important as critical Black women scholars to acknowledge that while Du Bois was an advocate for Black women he also had some gendered views regarding Black women (Griffin, 2000; Njoku, Butler, & Beatty, 2017). The key to our analysis was to ensure that each one of the participants' voices was heard, and not taken out of context. This chapter leveraged social media data to give Black women a voice in research. Using tweets provides researchers with a snapshot of the experiences of Black women that may be more "raw" than data garnered from formal surveys and interviews. We analyzed each tweet based on the critical discourse analysis definition of "text" and then we interpreted the tweet in the form of double consciousness and how it was relatable to Black women.

In the future, researchers who are interested in using this coding technique should consider the following:

1. Double consciousness should only be used for African American and other minoritized populations such as Indigenous Peoples and people of Latino/a descent.
2. Coding using this type of data can be for both men and women, television shows, movies, focus groups and data gleaned from other social media platforms such as Facebook.
3. Lastly, one of the first things that stood out to us specifically about this type of coding was that Black women used Twitter as a way to speak out and be heard to affirm their existence in workplaces that are often occupied by White men or women.

The thousands of tweets written by Black women to describe their experiences at work are a clear example of the double consciousness or two-ness that Black women experience as they work in spaces where the dominant cultural capital associated with Whiteness is valued. We have shared a method for qualitative analysis that places Black women's voices at the center of their statements when they are often ignored or devalued in the workplace.

Notes

1 On the U.S. Census, Black is a racial category that includes all people with African ancestry except North Africans. However, Black is often used to refer to African Americans.
2 A microaggression is an indirect, subtle, or unintentional discrimination against members of a marginalized group such as a racial or ethnic minority. For example, a White person stating to a Black woman, "I never see you as a Black woman, just as a woman first."
3 Congresswoman Maxine Waters is currently the U.S. Representative for California's 43rd congressional district. She has served in Congress since 1991. She is the most senior of the 12 Black women currently serving in the United States Congress.
4 We use dragging to deliberately mention an unwelcome or unpleasant fact.

5 A meme is a humorous image, video, or piece of text, etc., that is copied, often with slight variations and spread rapidly by Internet users.
6 The concept of the veil refers to three things: (1) the veil suggests literally the darker skin of Blacks, which is very distinct from whiteness, (2) the veil suggests White people's lack of clarity to see Black people as true Americans, and (3) the veil refers to Black people's lack of clarity regarding seeing themselves how White America views them.

References

Bell, E. L. (1990). The bicultural life experience of career-oriented Black women. *Journal of Organizational Behavior*, 11(6), 459–477.

Bloor, M., & Bloor, T. (2013). *The practice of critical discourse analysis: An introduction.* New York: Routledge.

Brenner, J., & Smith, A. (2013). 72% of online adults are social networking site users. Washington, DC: Pew Internet & American Life Project.

Bruns, A., & Stieglitz, S. (2013). Towards more systematic Twitter analysis: metrics for tweeting activities. *International Journal of Social Research Methodology*, 16(2), 91–108.

Carspecken, P. F. (1996). *Critical ethnography in educational research: A theoretical and practical guide.* New York: Psychology Press.

Clark, M. D. (2014). *To tweet our own cause*: A mixed-methods study of the online phenomenon "Black Twitter" (Order No. 3668450). Available from ProQuest Dissertations & Theses Global. (1648168732). Retrieved from: http://search.proquest.com.ezproxy.library.wisc.edu/docview/1648168732?accountid=465.

Cormode, G., & Krishnamurthy, B. (2008). Key differences between Web 1.0 and Web 2.0. *First Monday*, 13(6).

Creswell, J. W. (2013). *Qualitative inquiry and research design*, 3rd Edition. Thousand Oaks, CA: Sage Publications.

Donath, J., & Boyd, D. (2004). Public displays of connection. *bt technology Journal*, 22(4), 71–82.

Du Bois, W. E. B. (1903). *The Souls of Black Folk.* Edited with an introduction by David W. Blight and Robert Gooding-Williams. Boston, MA: Bedford Books.

Everett, K., & Croom, N. (2017). From Discourse to Practice: Making Discourses about Black Undergraduate Womyn Visible in Higher Education Journals and Student Affairs Practice. In L. D. Patton & N. N. Croom, *Critical perspectives on Black women and college success.* New York: Routledge, 75–87.

Fairclough, N. (2013). *Critical discourse analysis: The critical study of language.* New York: Routledge.

Freelon, D., McIlwain, C. D., & Clark, M. D. (2016). *Beyond the hashtags: #Ferguson, #Blacklivesmatter, and the online struggle for offline justice.* Center for Media & Social Impact, American University. Available at SSRN: https://ssrn.com/abstract=2747066

Gasman, M. (2007). Swept under the rug? A historiography of gender and Black colleges. *American Educational Research Journal*, 44(4), 760–805.

Greenwood, S., Perrin, A., & Duggan, M. (2016). Social media update 2016. Retrieved from http://www.pewinternet.org/2016/11/11/social-media-update-2016/

Griffin, F. J. (2000). Black feminists and Du Bois: Respectability, protection, and beyond. *The ANNALS of the American Academy of Political and Social Science*, 568(1), 28–40.

Harris-Perry, M. V. (2011). *Sister citizen: Shame, stereotypes, and Black women in America.* New Haven, CT: Yale University Press.

Hill, L. (2017). Maxine Waters has some news for Bill O'Reilly: 'I cannot be intimidated. I cannot be undermined'. Latimes.com. Retrieved from http://www.latimes.com/ entertainment/la-et-entertainment-news-updates-march-maxine-waters-has-words-for-bill-1490803685-htmlstory.html

Hurston, Z. (1937). *Their eyes were watching God.* Philadelphia, PA: Lippincott Publishing.

Jones, M. C., & Shorter-Gooden, K. (2009). *Shifting: The double lives of Black women in America.* New York: Harper Collins.

Marwick, A. (2013). Ethnographic and qualitative research on Twitter. In Weller, K., Bruns, A., Puschmann, C., Burgess, J. and Mahrt, M. (Eds.), *Twitter and society.* New York: Peter Lang, 109–122. Retrieved from http://www.tiara.org/blog/wp-content/uploads/2014/03/Marwick_Ethnographic-and-Qualitative-Research-on-Twitter_2013.pdf

McDonald, S.N. (2014). Black Twitter: A virtual community ready to hashtag out a response to cultural issues. Retrieved from: http://www.Washingtonpost.com/lifestyle/style/Black-twitter-a-virtual-community-ready-to-hastag-out-a-response-to-cultural-issues/2014/01.20/41 ddacf6-7ec5-11e3-9556-4a4bf7bcbd84_story.html? utm.term=. ca61ed3ade82

Nakamura, L. (2007). *Digitizing race: Visual cultures of the Internet.* Minneapolis, MN: University of Minnesota Press.

National Partnership.org. (2017). Retrieved December 2, 2017, from http://www.nation alpartnership.org/research-library/workplace-fairness/fair-pay/african-american-women-wage-gap.pdf.

Njoku, N., Butler, M., & Beatty, C. C. (2017). Reimagining the historically Black college and university (HBCU) environment: Exposing race secrets and the binding chains of respectability and othermothering. *International Journal of Qualitative Studies in Education, 30*(8), 783–799.

Parker, P. S. (2001). African American women executives' leadership communication within dominant-culture organizations: (re) conceptualizing notions of collaboration and instrumentality. *Management Communication Quarterly, 15*(1), 42–82.

Patten, E. (2016). Racial, gender wage gaps persist in U.S. despite some progress. Retrieved December 02, 2017, from http://www.pewresearch.org/fact-tank/2016/07/01/racial-gender-wage-gaps-persist-in-u-s-despite-some-progress/

Patton, L. D., & Croom, N. N. (Eds.). (2017). *Critical perspectives on Black women and college success.* New York: Taylor & Francis.

Saldaña, J. (2015). *The coding manual for qualitative researchers.* Thousand Oaks, CA: Sage.

Sharma, S. (2013). Black Twitter?: Racial hashtags, networks and contagion. *New Formations: A Journal of Culture/Theory/Politics, 78*(1), 46–64.

Shorter-Gooden, K. (2004). Multiple resistance strategies: How African American women cope with racism and sexism. *Journal of Black Psychology, 30*(3), 406–425.

Smith, A. (2014). African Americans and technology use: A demographic portrait. Retrieved from: http://www.pewinternet.org/2014/01/06/african-americans-and-and-technology-use/

Wang, A. B. (2017). Maxine Waters swings back at Bill O'Reilly: 'I'm a strong Black woman and I cannot be intimidated'. *The Washington Post,* March 29. Retrieved from: https://www.washingtonpost.com/news/the-fix/wp/2017/03/28/bill-oreilly-compared-a-black-congresswomans-hair-to-a-james-brown-wig/?utm_term=.d31029e05bb2

Westling, M. (2007). Expanding the public sphere: The impact of Facebook on political communication. *The New Vernacular.* Retrieved from: http://bytec.co.uk/wp-content/uploads/bytec/manufacturers/pdfs/2012-08-18_afacebook_and_political_communication.pdf

Winkle-Wagner, R. (2009). The perpetual homelessness of college experiences: Tensions between home and campus for African American women. *The Review of Higher Education, 33*(1), 1–36.

Winkle-Wagner, R. (2010). *The unchosen me: Race, gender, and identity among Black women in college.* New York: Johns Hopkins University Press.

Winkle-Wagner, R. (2015). Having their lives narrowed down? The state of Black women's college success. *Review of Educational Research, 85*(2), 171–204.

Winkle-Wagner, R., Luedke, C. L., & McCallum, C. M. (2017). Black women's advice on the role of confidence in the pursuit of a college degree: Believe you will achieve. In L.D. Patton & N. N. Croom, *Critical perspectives on Black women and college success.* New York: Routledge, 44–56.

AFTERWORD

Jamila Lee-Johnson, Ashley N. Gaskew, and
Rachelle Winkle-Wagner

> We must continue to exhume and elevate the untold stories . . .
> *(Voila Davis, 2017 Oscar acceptance speech)*

Immediately, when we heard this quote from Voila Davis at the 2017 Oscars, we knew we had to incorporate her words into our book. In her acceptance of her Oscar Award for her acting in the film, *Fences,* she honored August Wilson, who wrote the play that became the film. Davis said that Wilson "exhumed and exalted the ordinary people," whose stories she wants to share in her work. As critical scholars this quote is exactly what we do. We are doing the work to tell the stories of those who are often marginalized, ignored, or just simply forgotten. Throughout this book we have centered many voices that are neglected and discarded. We have lifted voices that have been suppressed. Additionally, we hope to have challenged the very structure of academia and research. Lastly, the authors in this book have begun to provide alternative analysis and solutions for doing work with and among marginalized and oppressed groups.

We encourage readers of this book to: be critical of what you are taught, challenge academic, social, and cultural norms, ask questions of yourself and others, and wrestle with the issues we have brought up in this book. For instance, how can one take lessons from everyday life and offer those ideas up as a legitimate educational context? How might the education that we receive from one context, perhaps in a country that is different from our home country, be applied to our daily lives and in our research practices? How might research either serve as a catalyst to dismantling or perpetuating oppression, depending on how that research is crafted, theoretically grounded, or carried out? We further encourage you to dialogue with our book, pose questions, challenge our writing and thoughts, and further expand upon this book and the theories and analysis presented in this book, by the various authors.

When we first began this project we all had to grapple with what it means to be "critical" in our research. For instance, Jamila recalled that she had a hard time understanding why scholars were so keen on using the word "critical." She wondered what was critical about the work she was doing on Black women in higher education. Black women have always been a part of the higher education narrative. However, as she began to read more and then understand how society treats Black women and other marginalized and oppressed populations, she understood that even for scholars who are considered "critical," they might still perpetuate oppression in some ways. She also knew that she wanted to be a critical scholar who was not in a Sunken Place,[1] and who not only wanted to tell the untold stories, but also to be able to provide support and/or resources for these populations. In an interview about the term, Peel commented that the Sunken Place was a metaphor, meaning:

> You know when you're going to sleep and it feels like you're about to fall, so you wake up? What if you never woke up? Where would you fall? And that was kind of the most harrowing idea to me. And as I'm writing it becomes clear that the sunken place is this metaphor for the system that is suppressing the freedom of black people, of many outsiders, many minorities. There's lots of different sunken places.
>
> *(Sharf, 2017)*

"Critical" theory looks deeply at inequities and injustices that exist, moving beyond analyzing the issues. Critical theory requires action to be taken so that marginalized populations can have voices and have equity brought to them. This book has allowed us as well as other authors and contributors the opportunity to take action and become allies for those who are marginalized and oppressed.

This book first began as a series of class projects in a class on critical theory and data analysis at the University of Wisconsin-Madison, and over time, has blossomed into an amazing project. Class discussions, presentations, and long conversations have helped lay the foundation for this book. As previously mentioned, our goal for this book is to provide alternative ways of analyzing data that is deeply related to the critical theory in each chapter. The analytic techniques in our book are not designed to be applied universally to all forms of data without thought and reflection. This book is designed for you to think about how various types of data can be used in critical theory and research, and which theories do and do not relate to particular topics or populations of people. We want to provide ideas for other graduate students, scholars, and researchers to employ when studying with and for marginalized populations. We want our book to lay a foundation for discussion and dialogue that challenges and provides solutions to inherent and systemic structures of oppression that seem normal.

Moving forward, we hope to continue conversations beyond this book. We would like to see these conversations in research, conferences, and most importantly, the communities in which we seek to work and live. This book is meant to be a tool to foster open and difficult conversations and to raise complex questions. As scholars and researchers our epistemological stances are deeply intertwined with the theories we use. This book provides several examples of how closely critical theory can be used to analyze data. More importantly, this book shows the need for theory in driving data analysis and how specific theories shape analysis. Many new analytic tools were also put forth as a way to deeply engage with text and with the communities we study. It is our hope that this book is used in multiple ways that will continue to pursue the tenants of critical theory.

We thank all the authors and contributors for this book. They dedicated long hours, wrestled with complex, challenging, and even contradictory ideas and theories to expand their horizons and those of the readers. Doing critical work is not easy. It can be a very isolating experience, and it can alienate and marginalize the authors in this book in their fields. Challenging societal and academic norms and practices could have negative ramifications for the authors in this book, and we recognize the risk that many scholars took in engaging in the way that they did in these pages. We (Rachelle, Jamila, and Ashley) thank them for using their voices and platforms to speak to and against injustices, and silencing marginalized populations. Our hope is that by coming together in this volume, we may have all helped one another to feel less isolated and that our readers may also experience solidarity and community by engaging with the authors and the book. We stand with the authors in this volume, and the readers too, as we all press back against hegemonic forces that seek to oppress us, and those with whom we stand as allies.

Note

1 Sunken Place comes from the movie *Get Out*, written by comedian Jordan Peele.

Reference

Sharf, Z. (2017). 'Get Out': Jordan Peele reveals the real meaning behind the Sunken Place. Retrieved online from: http://www.indiewire.com/2017/11/get-out-jordan-peele-explains-sunken-place-meaning-1201902567

CONTRIBUTORS

About the Editors

Rachelle Winkle-Wagner is an Associate Professor in the Department of Educational Leadership and Policy Analysis at the University of Wisconsin–Madison. Her research focuses on how students of color survive and thrive in college. She is an author or editor of six books including *The Unchosen Me: Race, Gender, and Identity Among Black Women in College* (Johns Hopkins University Press, 2009) and *Diversity and Inclusion on Campus: Supporting Racially and Ethnically Underrepresented Students* (with Angela Locks, Routledge, 2014). Her work has also been published in journals such as *Review of Educational Research, Review of Higher Education, Journal of College Student Development, Journal of Diversity in Higher Education, Race, Ethnicity & Education,* and *The Journal of Higher Education.*

Jamila Lee-Johnson is a doctoral candidate at the University of Wisconsin–Madison in the Educational Leadership and Policy Analysis program. Her research interest centers on the experiences of Black women in higher education, specifically, exploring the experiences of undergraduate Black women at Historically Black Colleges and Universities (HBCUS) in elected student leadership positions. She is a proud graduate of both Clark Atlanta University and Michigan State University. She is also passionate about helping students of color through the college admission process.

Ashley N. Gaskew is a doctoral student at the University of Wisconsin–Madison where she is pursuing a joint doctoral degree in Curriculum and Instruction and Educational Leadership and Policy Analysis. As a doctoral student, Ashley researches and analyzes the impact of for-profit institutions on the field of postsecondary education. Specifically, she explores the impact of abrupt for-profit institutional closings on students. As a critical scholar, Ashley engages research to be more inclusive of the short-term and long-term impacts of proprietary education and institutions.

About the Authors

Mercy Agyepong is a doctoral candidate in the Educational Policy Studies program at University of Wisconsin–Madison with research interests in race theory and the role of schools in the racialization of immigrant and American-born students of color in city schools. Mercy Agyepong is currently writing her dissertation on how perceptions of Blackness and Africanness influence the school experiences and academic achievement of West African immigrants in NYC public schools. Born in Ghana and raised in the Bronx, NY, Mercy Agyepong received a BA in Sociology from SUNY-Geneseo, an MA in Sociology of Education from New York University Steinhardt, and an MSEd in Education, Culture and Society from University of Pennsylvania GSE.

Nathan Beck holds an MS in Educational Leadership and Policy Analysis from the University of Wisconsin–Madison and has directed nationally awarded programs with and for young people. He is interested in educational equity, racial, economic, and environmental justice, and imagining alternatives.

Reginald A. Blockett is an Assistant Professor of Higher Education at Grand Valley State University. His current research mobilizes intersectionality and queer of color critique to understand the world making practices employed by Black queer graduate and undergraduate men at predominantly White and hetero-cis-normative research universities. His scholarship has been published in several prominent research journals, including *Journal of Student Affairs Research and Practice, International Journal of Qualitative Studies in Education,* and *Western Journal of Black Studies.* Blockett received his PhD from Indiana University.

Phil Francis Carspecken is a Professor of Inquiry Methodology at Indiana University. He teaches and conducts scholarly work in the fields of critical qualitative research methodology, social theory, social philosophy, and philosophical issues in inquiry.

Chelsea A. Blackburn Cohen is currently a Research Scientist/Senior Program Officer, North America, for the Scholars at Risk (SAR) Network at New York University. She is a recent PhD graduate from the University of Wisconsin–Madison. Her research interests center on the effects of globalization on higher education, society, and knowledge production—including the freedom of ideas. Her dissertation examined the displacement of academics worldwide due to the political and/or ideological nature of their work, the experiences of those scholars with hosting academic appointments at universities in the United States, and the contested nature of academic freedom.

Barbara Dennis is an Associate Professor of Inquiry Methodology at Indiana University. She writes on methodological concepts, drawing on feminist and critical theory. She also sews, spends time with family, and engages in peace activism.

Jacqueline M. Forbes is a doctoral student at the University of Wisconsin–Madison studying Educational Leadership and Policy Analysis. Her research agenda examines structural barriers to college admission for Black students. Before coming to UW, Jacquie worked as a high school history teacher in Brooklyn, NY and as a college access program administrator in Atlanta, GA. She earned her BA at Spelman College.

Lora Henderson earned her doctorate in Clinical and School Psychology from the University of Virginia. Her research focuses on cultural differences that exist between home and school for racial/ethnic minority and low-socioeconomic students. She plans to pursue a career as a practicing psychologist while continuing to conduct research on home and school experiences for students from diverse backgrounds. She earned her Bachelor's degree in Psychology from Clark Atlanta University and a Master's in Counseling and Mental Health Services from the University of Pennsylvania.

Dina C. Maramba is an Associate Professor of Higher Education at Claremont Graduate University. She uses equity/social justice lenses to study higher education environments and experiences of underserved students and faculty.

Keon M. McGuire is an Assistant Professor of Higher and Postsecondary Education in the Mary Lou Fulton Teachers College and a Faculty Affiliate with the School of Social Transformation. Dr. McGuire's research agenda focuses on the status and experiences of racially minoritized students across postsecondary educational settings. Drawing from Africana and other interdisciplinary frameworks, Dr. McGuire examines how race, gender, and religion shape racially minoritized college students' identities and their everyday experiences. Additionally, Dr. McGuire investigates the ways interpersonal and institutional racism undermine the experiences of racially minoritized college students as well as they ways students resist and respond to such marginalization. Dr. McGuire holds a joint PhD in Higher Education and Africana Studies from the University of Pennsylvania.

Steve D. Mobley, Jr. is an Assistant Professor of Higher Education in the Department of Educational Leadership, Policy, and Technology Studies at the University of Alabama. His scholarship focuses on the contemporary placement of historically Black colleges and universities (HBCUs). Particularly, Dr. Mobley Jr.'s research underscores and highlights the understudied facets of HBCU communities including issues surrounding race, social class, and student sexuality.

Tangela Blakely Reavis is a Postdoctoral Research Associate for the Milwaukee College Access Project at Tulane University. Her research focuses on college access and success for underrepresented students, especially ways that race, class, families, and high school context impact college choice and completion. She received her Master's and PhD in Educational Leadership and Policy Analysis from the University of Wisconsin–Madison and a Bachelor of Arts in Spanish from Spelman College.

Virginia M. Schwarz is a PhD candidate in Composition and Rhetoric at the University of Wisconsin–Madison. Her interests include equity and access in higher education, writing program administration, and assessment.

V. Thandi Sulé is an Associate Professor of Higher Education at Oakland University. Using critical theory frameworks, her research focuses on how underrepresented students and faculty access, belong, and persist in higher education.

Maisha T. Winn is the Chancellor's Leadership Professor, and Co-Director of Transformative Justice in Education (TJE) at the University of California–Davis. Her research spans a wide variety of understudied settings including her earlier work on the literate practices extant in bookstores and community organizations in the African American community to her most recent work in settings where adolescent girls are incarcerated.

Christina W. Yao is an Assistant Professor of Educational Administration at the University of Nebraska–Lincoln. She is a qualitative researcher who primarily studies student engagement and learning in higher education. She operationalizes her research focus through three connected topical areas: international/comparative education, teaching and learning, and graduate education. Some current projects include a collaborative study on doctoral students' international research development, teaching and learning in Vietnam, and the college transition process for Chinese international students in the United States.

INDEX

Note: italics indicate figures; bold indicates tables; 'n' indicates chapter notes.